LIVING

COM
GERMAN
THE BASICS

REVISED & UPDATED

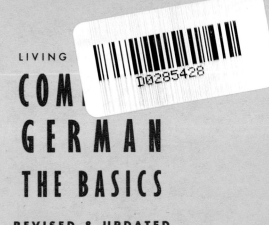

COMPLETE GERMAN

THE BASICS

REVISED & UPDATED

REVISED BY WALTER KLEINMANN

Coordinator of Foreign Languages and

English as a Second Language

Sewanhaka Central High School District

◆

Based on the original by

Genvieve A. Martin

and

Theodor Bertram

LIVING LANGUAGE®
A Random House Company

Copyright © 2005 by Living Language, A Random House Company

Living Language is a member of the Random House Information Group

Living Language and colophon are registered trademarks of Random House, Inc.

Published in the United States by Living Language, A Random House Company

www.livinglanguage.com

Editor: Suzanne McQuade
Production Editor: John Whitman
Production Managers: Helen Kilcullen and Heather Lanigan

ISBN 1-4000-2137-5

Library of Congress Cataloging-in-Publication Data available upon request.

This book is available for special discounts for bulk purchases for sales promotions or premiums. Special editions, including personalized covers, excerpts of existing books, and corporate imprints, can be created in large quantities for special needs. For more information, write to Special Markets/Premium Sales, 1745 Broadway, MD 6-2, New York, New York 10019 or e-mail specialmarkets@randomhouse.com.

PRINTED IN THE UNITED STATES OF AMERICA

10 9 8 7 6 5 4 3 2 1

CONTENTS

INTRODUCTION

Living Language® German makes it easy to learn how to speak, read, and write German. This course is a thoroughly revised and updated version of *Living German The Complete Living Language Course®*. The same highly effective method of language instruction is still used, but the content has been updated to reflect modern usage and the format has been clarified. In this course, the basic elements of the language have been carefully selected and condensed into forty short lessons. If you can study about thirty minutes a day, you can master this course and learn to speak German in a few weeks.

You'll learn German the way you learned English, starting with simple words and progressing to more complex phrases. Just listen and repeat after the native instructors on the recordings. To help you immerse yourself in the language, you'll hear only German spoken. Hear it, say it, absorb it through use and repetition.

This *Living Language® German Coursebook* provides English translations and brief explanations for each lesson. The first five lessons cover pronunciation, laying the foundation for learning the vocabulary, phrases, and grammar which are explained in the later chapters. If you already know a little German, you can use the book as a phrase book and reference. In addition to the forty lessons, there is a Summary of German Grammar, plus verb conjugations, sections on letter writing, email and Internet, and the German Spelling Reform.

Also included in the course package is the *Living Language® German Dictionary*. It contains more than 20,000 entries, with many of the definitions illustrated by phrases and idiomatic expressions. More than 1,000 of the most essential words are capitalized to make them easy to find. You can increase your vocabulary and range of expression just by browsing through the dictionary.

Practice your German as much as possible. Even if you can't manage a trip abroad, watching German movies, reading German magazines, eating at German restaurants, and talking with German-speaking friends are enjoyable ways to help reinforce what you have learned with *Living Language® German*. Now, let's begin.

The following instructions will tell you what to do. *Viel Glück!* Good luck!

COURSE MATERIAL

1. Two 90-minute cassettes or three 60-minute compact discs.
2. *Living Language® German Coursebook.* This book is designed for use with the recorded lessons, but it may also be used alone as a reference. It contains the following sections:

   Basic German in 40 Lessons
   Summary of German Grammar
   Verb Conjugations
   Letter Writing

3. *Living Language® German Dictionary.* The German/English-English/German dictionary contains more than 20,000 entries. Phrases and idiomatic expressions illustrate many of the definitions. More than 1,000 of the most essential words are capitalized.

INSTRUCTIONS

1. Look at page 1. The words in **boldface** type are the ones you will hear on the recording.
2. Now read Lesson 1 all the way through. Note the points to listen for when you play the recording. The first word you will hear is **Albert.**
3. Start the recording, listen carefully, and say the words aloud in the pauses provided. Go through the lesson once and don't worry if you can't pronounce everything correctly the first time around. Try it again and keep repeating the lesson until you are comfortable with it. The more often you listen and repeat, the longer you will remember the material.
4. Now go on to the next lesson. If you take a break between lessons, it's always good to review the previous lesson before starting on a new one.
5. In the manual, there are two kinds of quizzes. With matching quizzes, you must select the English translation of the German sentence. The other type requires you to fill in the blanks with the correct German word chosen from the three given directly below the sentence. If you make any mistakes, reread the section.
6. There are 18 supplemental vocabulary sections throughout the course. Each one focuses on a useful theme that is related to the content of the

course. Practice the lists through repetition, flash cards, or self-quizzes to build a solid foundation in German vocabulary.

7. Even after you have finished the 40 lessons and achieved a perfect score on the Final Quiz, keep practicing your German by listening to the recordings and speaking with German-speaking friends. For further study, try *Complete German: Beyond the Basics, Ultimate German, Ultimate German Advanced,* or *German Without the Fuss,* all from the experts at Living Language. Or go to our website at www.livinglanguage.com for more information.

LIVING LANGUAGE®

COMPLETE
GERMAN
THE BASICS

REVISED & UPDATED

LESSON 1

A. SOUNDS OF THE GERMAN LANGUAGE

Many German sounds are like English sounds. Listen to and repeat the following German names, and notice which sounds are similar and which are different:

Albert	Gustav	Minna
Anton	Hans	Otto
Anna	Heinrich	Paul
Bernhard	Jakob	Paula
Emma	Josef	Richard
Erich	Katharina	Rudolf
Franz	Lotte	Stefan
Friedrich	Ludwig	Thomas
Georg	Martha	Wilhelm

NOTES

1. Each sound is pronounced clearly and distinctly; sounds are not slurred over as they often are in English.
2. Simple words have one stressed syllable, generally the first one.
3. The *Umlaut* (¨) is placed at times on the letters *a, o, u,* and changes their pronunciation. See Lesson 2, "Vowels," for examples.
4. All nouns are capitalized.

B. COGNATES: WORDS SIMILAR IN ENGLISH AND GERMAN

Now listen to and repeat the following words which are similar in English and German. These words are called "cognates" and are descended from the same root. Notice how German spelling and pronunciation differ from English:

Adresse	address
Alkohol	alcohol
Amerikaner	American
Bank	bank
Bad	bath
Bett	bed
Bier	beer
Butter	butter
Charakter	character
Direktor	director
Doktor	doctor
Drama	drama
Ende	end
Export	export
Film	film
Garage	garage
Gas	gas
hier	here
Hotel	hotel
Hunger	hunger
Lampe	lamp
lang	long
Linie	line
Maschine	machine
Nation	nation
national	national
Oper	opera
Operette	operetta
Papier	paper
Person	person
parken	(to) park

Prinz	prince		
Problem	problem		
Publikum	public		
Radio	radio		
Restaurant	restaurant		
Signal	signal		
Station	station		
Telefon	telephone		
Tee	tea		
Theater	theater		
Tempel	temple		
Triumph	triumph		
Tunnel	tunnel		
Wolf	wolf		
Zone	zone		

LESSON 2

A. VOWELS

The following groups of words will give you some additional practice in spelling and pronunciation:

1. The long *a* sound in the English "ah" or "father":

sagen	to say	**Laden**	shop
Datum	date	**Tafel**	board

2. The short *a* sound is similar to the English *o* in "hot":

kann	can	**was?**	what?
Mann	man	**Pfanne**	pan

3. The long *ä* sound is similar to the English *ai* in "fair":

spät	late	**Währung**	currency
Erklärung	explanation	**Ernährung**	nutrition

4. The short *ä* sound is similar to the *e* in "bet":

Männer   men

5a. The long *e* sound is similar to the *ay* in "may":

geben   (to) give   **stehen**   (to) stand

b. The *ee* and *eh* sounds are also long, like the *a* in "care":

mehr   more   **Heer**   army

6. Short *e* is similar to the *e* in "bent":

Adresse	address	**wetten**	to bet
Moment	moment	**rennen**	to run

7. The *e* sound at the end of a word is similar to the *e* in "pocket":

beide	both	**Karte**	card
heute	today	**seine**	his

8. The long *i* sound is pronounced like the *ee* in "see":

Miete	rent	**Liebe**	love
dienen	to serve	**Dieb**	thief

9. The short *i* sound is said like the *i* in "ship":

mit	with	**Witz**	joke
Sitte	custom	**mittags**	at noon

10. The long *o* sound is like the *o* in "lone":

oben	above	**Boden**	floor
Obst	fruit	**holen**	(to) fetch

11. The short *o* sound is similar to the *o* in "off":

oft	often	**Stoff**	material
kommen	(to) come	**Loch**	hole

12. The long *ö* sound is somewhat similar to the German *e* in *geben*, and is pronounced by rounding the lips and saying long *e:*

König	king	**hören**	(to) hear
Löwe	lion	**böse**	angry

13. Short *ö* is said like a short *u* with rounded lips, as in "pup":

können	(to) be able to	**möchte**	would like
Töchter	daughters	**Röcke**	skirts

14. The long *u* sound is like the English *oo* in "noon":

Blume	flower	**Hut**	hat
Huhn	chicken	**gut**	good

15. The short *u* sound is similar to the *u* in "bush":

muss	has to	**bummeln**	(to) stroll
dumm	dumb	**Russland**	Russia

16. Long *ü* is said like the *ee* in "see," but with rounded lips:

über	over	**früher**	sooner
drüben	over there	**Frühstück**	breakfast

17. The short *ü* sound is pronounced by keeping the tongue in the same position as for short *i*, but with rounded lips:

Stück	piece	**dünn**	thin
Brücke	bridge	**müssen**	(to) have to

18. The same sound is used to pronounce *y*:

typisch	typical	**Lyrik**	lyrics

B. DIPHTHONGS

1. The *ai* and *ei* sounds are pronounced almost like the *y* in "by," only with greater emphasis:

Mai	may	**Heimat**	homeland
Ei	egg		

2. The *au* sound is pronounced almost like the *ou* in "house":

Haus	house	**Baum**	tree
Maus	mouse	**Pflaume**	plum

3. The *äu* and *eu* sounds are pronounced somewhat like the English *oy* in "boy":

Häuser	houses	**Leute**	people
träumen	(to) dream	**heute**	today

LESSON 3

A. CONSONANTS

1. *B* is generally pronounced like the English *b:*

Bett	bed	**Gabe**	gift

However, *b* at the end of a word is pronounced like the *p* in the English word "trap."

Grab	tomb	**Trab**	trot

2. *C* before *e, i, ä, ö, y,* is pronounced like *ts;* however, this is a rather rare combination. Generally *z* precedes these letters.

    C before *a, o, u* is pronounced like *k*, but the letter *k* is generally substituted. These two pronunciations of the *c* occur mostly in foreign words:

Cäsar	Caesar	**Cato**	Cato

3. *D* is generally pronounced like the English *d:*

Datum	date	**Norden**	Nord

However, *d* at the end of a word is pronounced like the *t* in the English word "but":

Bad   bath   **Hund**   dog

4. *F* is like the English *f:*

Fliege   fly   **Fluss**   river

5. *G* is generally pronounced like the *g* in the English word "garden"; it is pronounced like the *g* in the English word "general" only in words of foreign origin:

Garten   garden   **Garage**   garage
General   general

6. *H* is pronounced like the English *h* at the beginning of a word, or before an accented syllable:

hundert   hundred   **Geheimnis**   secret
Heimat   native country **behalten**   keep

In other cases, it is not pronounced:

Schuh   shoe   **fröhlich**   merry

7. *J* is pronounced like the English *y* as in "York":

Jahr   year   **jemand**   someone

8. *K* is pronounced like the English *c* before *a, o, u* ("canal," "corn," "cut"):

Katze   cat   **Keller**   cellar
Kind   child   **Kunde**   customer

9. *L* is pronounced like the *l* in the English words "land," or "life":

Land	land	**Leben**	life
Wolf	wolf		

10. *M* and *N* are pronounced as in English:

Meile	mile	**nur**	only
Maler	painter	**Neffe**	nephew

11a. *P* is pronounced like the English *p:*

Preis	price	**Papier**	paper

b. The cluster *pf* is pronounced as one sound and has no English equivalent:

Pfanne	pan	**Pferd**	horse
Pfennig	penny		

12. *Q*, always used in combination with *u*, is similar to the English *q:*

Quelle	spring	**Qualität**	quality

13. *R* is more rolled than in English and always strongly pronounced:

Rede	speech	**reine**	clean

14. *S* before a vowel is pronounced like the English *z* in "zoo":

süß	sweet	**Sahne**	cream

At the end of a word or a syllable, it is pronounced like the *s* in the English word "son":

| **Maus** | mouse | **Eis** | ice |

15. *T* is pronounced as in the English "tea":

| **Tanz** | dance | **Tasse** | cup |

There is no sound equivalent to the English *th*. This combination is simply pronounced like *t:*

| **Theater** | theater | **Thron** | throne |

16. *V* is pronounced, except in a few cases, like the English *f* in "fair":

| **Vogel** | bird | **Vater** | father |

The exceptions are a few Latin roots:

| **Vase** | vase | **Vulkan** | volcano |

17. *W* is pronounced like the English *v* in "vain," never like the English *w* in "want":

| **Wein** | wine | **Waffe** | weapon |

18. *X* is pronounced as in English:

| **Axt** | axe | **Hexe** | witch |

19. *Z* is pronounced like the English combination *ts:*

| **Zahn** | tooth | **Zauber** | magic |

20. *ß* is a special symbol that is pronounced the same as *ss:*

Süß	sweet	**Straße**	street

B. Special German Sounds

Practice the following sounds which have similar sounds in English:

1. The German combination *ch* has three different sounds:

    a. The sound as pronounced in the English "character":

Christ	Christian	**Charakter**	character
Chor	chorus		

When followed by an *s*, this combination generally has the sound of *ks:*

Fuchs	fox	**Wachs**	wax

b. A sound near the English *h* in "hue":

China	China	**mich**	me
Kirche	church	**sicher**	certain

c. A guttural sound which does not exist in English and can be only approximated by the Scotch word "loch":

Ach!	ah!	**Dach**	roof
Bach	brook	**Buch**	book

2. When in final position, the combination -*ig* often approximates the -*ch* sound as in the word *ich:*

ewig	eternal	**männlich**	manly
König	king	**persönlich**	personally

When the -*ig* sound is followed by -*lich* or -*e* it is often pronounced like hard *g* or hard *k:*

wenigstens	at least	(pronounced like *k*)
richtige	correct	(pronounced like *g*)
königlich	royally	(pronounced like *g*)

3. Note the following combinations containing *s:*

   a. sch, equivalent to the English *sh* in "shoe":

Kirsche	cherry	**amerikanisch**	American
Schuh	shoe		

   b. sp or *st* at the beginning of a word, with the *s* sounded like *sh:*

stehen	(to) stand	**Spanien**	Spain
Stahl	steel	**Spiegel**	mirror

4. The combination *ng* is pronounced like the English *ng* in "sing"; the two letters are never pronounced separately:

bringen	(to) bring	**anfangen**	(to) begin

5. The combination *tz* is similar to the English *ts:*

Mütze	cap	**Blitz**	lightning

6. The combination *-er* occurring at the end of a word is similar to the English *a* in "father":

kleiner	smaller	**Vater**	father
schöner	nicer	**Wetter**	weather

LESSON 4

A. THE GERMAN ALPHABET

LETTER	NAME	LETTER	NAME	LETTER	NAME
a	ah	**j**	yot	**s**	ess
b	beh	**k**	kah	**t**	teh
c	tseh	**l**	ell	**u**	oo
d	deh	**m**	em	**v**	fau
e	eh	**n**	en	**w**	veh
f	eff	**o**	oh	**x**	iks
g	geh	**p**	peh	**y**	üpsilonn
h	hah	**q**	ku	**z**	tsett
i	ee	**r**	err		

ä	(ah-Umlaut)
ö	(oh-Umlaut)
ü	(oo-Umlaut)

B. MORE ENGLISH-GERMAN COGNATES

Building up a German vocabulary is a rather easy matter because, as you have already seen, a great number of words are similar in German and English. Many are spelled almost the same, though they may differ considerably in pronunciation.

diagonal	diagonal	**direkt**	direct
Platz	place	**Frucht**	fruit
Land	land	**original**	original
Zentrum	center	**Problem**	problem
Idee	idea	**Norden**	north
Leder	leather	**Westen**	west
Drama	drama	**Polizei**	police
Material	material	**Revolution**	revolution
Süden	south	**Methode**	method
Park	park	**blond**	blonde
Juwelen	jewels	**Minute**	minute
Wolf	wolf	**Konversation**	conversation
Priester	priest	**Instruktion**	instruction
Datum	date	**General**	general
Intelligenz	intelligence	**spezial**	special
Automobil	automobile	**Präsident**	president
Sekunde	second	**Akt**	act
Appetit	appetite	**modern**	modern
Kapitel	chapter	**Klasse**	class
Medizin	medicine		

LESSON 5

A. GENERAL SPELLING EQUIVALENTS

1. German *k*—English *c:*

Kanal	canal	**Respekt**	respect
Kolonie	colony	**Direktor**	director

2. German *-ik*—English *-ic (s):*

Musik	music	**Politik**	politics
Physik	physics	**Lyrik**	lyrics

3. German *-ekt*—English *-ect:*

Effekt	effect	**Objekt**	object
Projekt	project	**Subjekt**	subject

4. German *-heit, -keit, -tät*—English ending *-ty:*

Freiheit	liberty	**Schwierigkeit**	difficulty
Schönheit	beauty	**Notwendigkeit**	necessity
Autorität	authority	**Qualität**	quality

5. German *-enz*—English *-ncy:*

Frequenz	frequency	**Tendenz**	tendency

6. German *-ie*—English *-y:*

Geographie	geography	**Industrie**	industry
Kopie	copy	**Philosophie**	philosophy

7. German *-tie*—English *-cy:*

Demokratie	democracy	**Diplomatie**	diplomacy

8. German *-ist*—English *-ist:*

Journalist	journalist	**Artist**	artist
Pianist	pianist		

9. German *sch*—English *sh:*

Schiff	ship	**Wäsche**	washing
Schuh	shoe	**Schilling**	shilling

10. German *-voll*—English *-ful:*

wundervoll	wonderful	**gedankenvoll**	thoughtful

11. German *-los*—English *-less:*

herzlos	heartless	**geruchlos**	odorless

12. German *-wärts*—English *-ward:*

westwärts	westward	**vorwärts**	forward

LESSON 6

A. Days and Months

Montag	Monday
Dienstag	Tuesday
Mittwoch	Wednesday
Donnerstag	Thursday
Freitag	Friday
Samstag, or **Sonnabend**	Saturday
Sonntag	Sunday
Januar	January
Februar	February
März	March
April	April
Mai	May

Juni	June
Juli	July
August	August
September	September
Oktober	October
November	November
Dezember	December

B. NUMBERS 1–10

eins	one
zwei	two
drei	three
vier	four
fünf	five
sechs	six
sieben	seven
acht	eight
neun	nine
zehn	ten

C. COLORS

blau	blue
rot	red
gelb	yellow
grün	green
weiß	white
schwarz	black
braun	brown
grau	gray
rosa	pink

D. North, South, East, West

Norden   north
Süden   south
Osten   east
Westen   west

QUIZ 1

Try matching the following two columns:

1. *Sonntag*	a. Thursday
2. *August*	b. brown
3. *Mittwoch*	c. ten
4. *grau*	d. Sunday
5. *Donnerstag*	e. red
6. *neun*	f. August
7. *braun*	g. Monday
8. *acht*	h. July
9. *Juli*	i. five
10. *gelb*	j. white
11. *rot*	k. gray
12. *Montag*	l. nine
13. *fünf*	m. Wednesday
14. *weiß*	n. yellow
15. *zehn*	o. eight

ANSWERS

1—d; 2—f; 3—m; 4—k; 5—a; 6—l; 7—b; 8—o;
9—h; 10—n; 11—e; 12—g; 13—i; 14—j; 15—c.

LESSON 7

A. GREETINGS

Guten Morgen!	Hello! Good morning.
Herr	Mr.
Herr Wagner	Mr. Wagner
Guten Morgen, Herr Wagner.	Good morning, Mr. Wagner.
Guten Tag.	Good afternoon (Good day).
Guten Abend.	Good evening.
Frau	Mrs.
Frau Wagner	Mrs. Wagner
Guten Abend, Frau Wagner.	Good evening, Mrs. Wagner.
Gute Nacht.	Good night.
Wie geht es Ihnen?	How are you? How do you do? ("How is it going with you?")
Wie geht's?[1]	How are you?
Wie geht es dir?	How are you? (*fam.*)
Wie geht es Ihnen, Frau Wagner?	How do you do, Mrs. Wagner? (*pol.*)
sehr	very
gut	well
Sehr gut.	Very well.
Danke.	Thank you. Thanks.
Danke schön.	Thank you.
Sehr gut, danke.	Very well, thanks.
Sprechen Sie!	Speak!
langsam	slowly
Sprechen Sie langsam!	Speak slowly!

---

[1] *Geht's* is a contraction of *geht es*.

Sprechen Sie langsam, bitte.	Speak slowly, please.
Wiederholen Sie!	Repeat!
Wiederholen Sie, bitte.	Please repeat.
danke	thanks
vielmals	much, a lot
Danke vielmals.	Thank you very much. Thanks a lot.
Keine Ursache.	Not at all.
Ich danke Ihnen.	Thank you. (*pol.*)
Gern geschehen.	It was a pleasure.
Bis morgen.	Till tomorrow. See you tomorrow.
Bis Samstag.	Till Saturday. See you Saturday.
Bis Montag.	Till Monday. See you Monday.
Bis Donnerstag.	Till Thursday. See you Thursday.
Bis heute Abend.	Till this evening. See you this evening.
Bis morgen Abend.	Till tomorrow evening. See you tomorrow evening.
Bis nächste Woche.	Till next week. See you next week.
Bis später.	See you later.
Bis gleich.	See you in a little while.
Auf Wiedersehen.	Good-bye.

B. How's the Weather?

Wie ist das Wetter heute?	How's the weather today?
Es ist kalt.	It's cold.
Es ist heiß.	It's hot.

Es ist kühl.	It's cool.
Es ist warm.	It's warm.
Es ist windig.	It's windy.
Es ist sonnig.	It's sunny.
Es regnet.	It's raining.
Es schneit.	It's snowing.
Das ist ein Hundewetter!	That's dog's (terrible) weather!
Ein herrlicher Tag, nicht wahr?	A lovely day, isn't it?

QUIZ 2

1. *sehr gut*	a. Speak . . .
2. *Guten Abend.*	b. how . . .
3. *Sprechen Sie . . .*	c. much, a lot
4. *Danke.*	d. See you tomorrow. (Till tomorrow.)
5. *wie . . .*	e. How are you?
6. *bitte*	f. very well
7. *viel*	g. It's raining.
8. *Bis morgen.*	h. Thank you.
9. *Wie geht es Ihnen?*	i. please
10. *Es regnet.*	j. Good evening.

ANSWERS

1—f; 2—j; 3—a; 4—h; 5—b; 6—i; 7—c; 8—d; 9—e; 10—g.

C. WORD STUDY

The Word Studies point out words which are almost similar in German and English.

Form	form	*Liste*	list
Post	mail	*Gruppe*	group
reich	rich	*Sorte*	sort

Suppe	soup	*Kapitän*	captain
Operation	operation	*Admiral*	admiral
Note	note (musical)	*Orange*	orange
Diamant	diamond	*Ratte*	rat
Pilot	pilot	*Kamel*	camel
Pflanze	plant	*Pirat*	pirate
Sport	sport	*November*	November

SUPPLEMENTAL VOCABULARY 1: WEATHER

weather	*das Wetter*
It's raining.	*Es regnet.*
It's snowing.	*Es schneit.*
It's hailing.	*Es hagelt.*
It's windy.	*Es ist windig.*
It's hot.	*Es ist heiß.*
It's cold.	*Es ist kalt.*
It's sunny.	*Es ist sonnig.*
It's cloudy.	*Es ist bewölkt.*
It's beautiful.	*Das Wetter ist schön.*
storm	*der Sturm (die Stürme)*
wind	*der Wind (die Winde)*
sun	*die Sonne (die Sonnen)*
thunder	*der Donner (die Donner)*
lightening	*der Blitz (die Blitze)*
storm	*der Sturm (die Stürme)*
temperature	*die Temperatur (Die Temperaturen)*
degree	*der/das Grad (die Grade)*
rain	*der Regen*
snow	*der Schnee*
cloud	*die Wolke (die Wolken)*
fog	*der Nebel (die Nebel)*
smog	*der Smog*
umbrella	*der Schirm (die Schirme)*

LESSON 8

A. Do You Have . . . ?

Haben Sie . . . ?	Do you have . . . ?
Wasser	water
Zigaretten	some (any) cigarettes
Feuer	a light
Streichhölzer	some matches
Schreibpapier	notepaper
Papier	paper
etwas zu trinken	something to drink
einen Stadtplan	a map of the city
noch Zimmer frei	any vacancies
einen Reiseführer	a guidebook

B. In a Restaurant

das Frühstück	breakfast
das Mittagessen	lunch
das Abendessen	dinner, supper
Was wünschen Sie, mein Herr?	What will you have? ("What do you wish, sir?")
Guten Tag, mein Herr. Was wünschen Sie?	Good afternoon. What would you like? ("Good day, sir. What do you wish?")
Bringen Sie mir . . .	Give me . . .
Bringen Sie mir die Speisekarte, bitte.	Please bring me a menu.
Die Speisekarte, bitte.	The menu, please.
Ich möchte . . .	I'd like . . .
Brot	bread
Butter	butter

Suppe	soup
Fleisch	meat
Rindfleisch	beef
Eier	eggs
Gemüse	vegetables
Kartoffeln	potatoes
Salat	salad
Milch	milk
Wein	wine
Zucker	sugar
Salz	salt
Pfeffer	pepper
Bringen Sie mir . . .	Bring me . . .
einen Löffel	a spoon
einen Teelöffel	a teaspoon
eine Gabel	a fork
ein Messer	a knife
eine Serviette	a napkin
einen Teller	a plate
ein Glas	a glass
Ich möchte . . .	I'd like . . .
ein Glas Wasser	a glass of water
ein (Glas) Bier	a beer
eine Tasse Tee	a cup of tea
eine Tasse Kaffee	a cup of coffee
eine Flasche Wein	a bottle of wine
eine Flasche Mineral- **wasser**	a bottle of mineral water
eine Flasche Weiß- **wein**	a bottle of white wine
eine Flasche Rotwein	a bottle of red wine
noch ein Ei	another egg
ein wenig davon	a little of that

noch ein wenig davon	a little more of that
noch etwas Brot	some more bread
noch ein wenig Brot	a little more bread
noch etwas Fleisch	some more meat
noch ein wenig Fleisch	a little more meat
Die Rechnung, bitte.	The check, please.

QUIZ 3

1.	*Fleisch*	a.	Bring me . . .
2.	*Rotwein*	b.	matches
3.	*Haben Sie . . . ?*	c.	Give me . . .
4.	*Milch*	d.	meat
5.	*Butter*	e.	some water
6.	*Geben Sie mir . . .*	f.	a light
7.	*Streichhölzer*	g.	milk
8.	*noch etwas Brot*	h.	eggs
9.	*Bringen Sie mir . . .*	i.	red wine
10.	*Wasser*	j.	The check, please
11.	*Feuer*	k.	Do you have . . . ?
12.	*einen Reiseführer*	l.	butter
13.	*Eier*	m.	a cup of coffee
14.	*eine Tasse Kaffee*	n.	some more bread
15.	*Die Rechnung, bitte.*	o.	a guidebook

ANSWERS

1—d; 2—i; 3—k; 4—g; 5—l; 6—c; 7—b; 8—n;
9—a; 10—e; 11—f; 12—o; 13—h; 14—m; 15—j.

SUPPLEMENTAL VOCABULARY 2: FOOD

food	*Essen, Speisen*
dinner	*das Abendessen (die Abendessen)*

lunch	*das Mittagessen (die Mittagessen)*
breakfast	*das Frühstück (die Frühstücke)*
meat	*das Fleisch*
chicken	*das Hähnchen (die Hähnchen)*
beef	*das Rindfleisch*
pork	*das Schweinefleisch*
fish	*der Fisch (die Fische)*
shrimp	*die Garnele (die Garnelen)*
lobster	*der Hummer (die Hummer)*
bread	*das Brot (die Brote)*
egg	*das Ei (die Eier)*
cheese	*der Käse (die Käse)*
rice	*der Reis*
vegetable	*das Gemüse (die Gemüse)*
lettuce	*der grüne Salat (die grünen Salate)*
tomato	*die Tomate (die Tomaten)*
carrot	*die Karotte (die Karotten), die Möhre (die Möhren)*
cucumber	*die Salatgurke (die Salatgurken)*
pepper	*die Paprikaschote (die Paprikaschoten)*
fruit	*die Frucht (die Früchte, das Obst)*
apple	*der Apfel (die Äpfel)*
orange	*die Orange (die Orangen), die Apfelsine (die Apfelsinen)*
banana	*die Banane (die Bananen)*
pear	*die Birne (die Birnen)*

grape	*die Weintraube (die Weintrauben)*
drink (alcoholic)	*der Drink (die Drinks)*
water	*das Wasser (die Wasser)*
milk	*die Milch*
juice	*der Saft (die Säfte)*
coffee	*der Kaffee*
tea	*der Tee*
wine	*der Wein (die Weine)*
beer	*das Bier (die Biere)*
soft drink	*das Getränk (die Getränke)*
soda	*der Sprudel (die Sprudel)*
mineral water	*das Mineralwasser (die Mineralwasser)*
salt	*das Salz (die Salze)*
pepper	*der Pfeffer (die Pfeffer)*
sugar	*der Zucker*
honey	*der Honig (die Honige)*
hot/cold	*heiß/kalt*
sweet/sour	*süß/sauer*

LESSON 9

In the present tense in German, there are two kinds of verbs—regular and irregular. Regular verbs take different endings in the different conjugated forms (just like "I learn" but "he learns"). Irregular verbs take the same endings, but they also have a vowel change in the stem. Notice that German infinitives end in *-en*, which is dropped before adding the endings.

A. To Learn: *Lernen* (regular)

1. I learn.

ich lerne	I learn, I do learn, I'm learning
du lernst	you (*fam.*) learn, you do learn, you are learning
er (*sie, es*) **lernt**	he (she, it) learns, he does learn, he is learning
wir lernen	we learn, we do learn, we are learning
ihr lernt	you (*fam. pl.*) learn, you do learn, you are learning
Sie lernen	you (*pol.*) learn, you do learn, you are learning
sie lernen	they learn, they do learn, they are learning

NOTES

a. Notice the verb endings:

ich	-e
du	-st
er (*sie, es*)	-t
wir	-en
ihr	-t
Sie, sie	-en

b. These forms, which make up the present tense, translated into the English "I learn," "I'm learning," and "I do learn."

c. *du lernst* and *ihr lernt*: The singular and the plural of these forms are used when you address one or several close friends. These *du* and *ihr* forms are called *familiar* forms. Notice the capital *S* in *Sie*. It is used to address one or several persons you don't know very well (whom you would not call by first name in English). This *Sie* form, called the *polite* or *formal* form, is used either in direct speech or writing. This distinction is indicated throughout the course by (*pol.*) and (*fam.*).

d. *Er lernt* means "he learns"; *sie lernt* means "she learns"; *es lernt* means "it learns"; *sie lernen* means "they learn," which, just as in English, is used for all genders.

2. Learn!

Lerne!	Learn (the familiar form used to a person you know well; compare *du lernst* above)
Lernt!	Learn (the familiar plural form; compare *ihr lernt* above)
Lernen Sie!	Learn! (the polite form; compare *Sie lernen* above)
Lerne nicht!	Don't learn! (*fam.*)
Lernt nicht!	Don't learn! (*fam. pl.*)
Lernen Sie nicht!	Don't learn! (*pol.*)

This form of the verb, which is used in commands and requests, is called the *imperative*.

B. To Give: *Geben* (irregular)

1. I give.

ich gebe	I give, I do give, I'm giving
du gibst	you (*fam.*) give, you do give, you're giving
er (*sie, es*) **gibt**	he (she, it) gives, he does give, he's giving
wir geben	we give, we do give, we're giving
ihr gebt	you (*fam. pl.*) give, you do give, you're giving
Sie geben	you (*pol.*) give, you do give, you're giving
sie geben	they give, they do give, they're giving

2. Give!

Gib!	Give! (*fam.*)
Gebt!	Give! (*fam. pl.*)
Geben Sie!	Give! (*pol.*)

Notice that in the case of the irregular verb, the endings are the same as those of the regular verb, but the vowel of the stem changes in the second and third person singular. Some common vowel changes are *e* to *i; e* to *ie; a* to *ä.*

C. NEGATION

To negate a statement, add the word *nicht:*

sprechen	to speak (irregular)
ich spreche	I speak, I do speak, I'm speaking
ich spreche nicht	I don't speak, I'm not speaking
du sprichst nicht	you (*fam.*) don't speak, aren't speaking
er (*sie, es*) **spricht nicht**	he (she, it) doesn't speak, isn't speaking
wir sprechen nicht	we do not speak, aren't speaking
ihr sprecht nicht	you (*fam. pl.*) don't speak, are not speaking
Sie sprechen nicht	you (*pol. s.* and *pl.*) aren't speaking, don't speak
sie sprechen nicht	they do not speak, are not speaking

D. ASKING A QUESTION I

1. To ask a question, invert the word order so that the verb comes before the subject pronoun:

Sie lernen.	You learn. You're learning.
Lernen Sie?	Do you learn? Are you learning?
Lerne ich?	Do I learn? Am I learning?
Lernst du?	Do you learn? Are you learning?
Lernt er?	Does he learn? Is he learning?
Lernt sie?	Does she learn? Is she learning?
Lernen wir?	Do we learn? Are we learning?
Lernt ihr?	Do you learn? Are you learning?

Lernen Sie?	Do you learn? Are you learning?
Lernen sie?	Do they learn? Are they learning?

2. To ask a question in the negative form, also reverse the word order and use the negative *nicht*.

Lerne ich nicht?	Don't I learn?
Lernst du nicht?	Don't you learn?
Lernt er nicht?	Doesn't he learn?
Lernt sie nicht?	Doesn't she learn?
Lernen wir nicht?	Don't we learn?
Lernt ihr nicht?	Don't you learn?
Lernen Sie nicht?	Don't you learn?
Lernen sie nicht?	Don't they learn?

REVIEW QUIZ 1
Choose the correct German word equivalent to the English.

1. Five—
   a. *sechs*
   b. *sieben*
   c. *fünf*

2. Eight—
   a. *acht*
   b. *neun*
   c. *vier*

3. Tuesday—
   a. *Mittwoch*
   b. *Dienstag*
   c. *Freitag*

4. Sunday—
   a. *Sonntag*
   b. *Samstag*
   c. *Montag*

5. March—
   a. *März*
   b. *September*
   c. *April*

6. June—
   a. *Juli*
   b. *Juni*
   c. *Mai*

7. Red—
   a. *blau*
   b. *orange*
   c. *rot*

8. Green—
   a. *gelb*
   b. *grün*
   c. *grau*

9. Black—
   a. *schwarz*
   b. *braun*
   c. *weiß*

10. Brown—
    a. *schwarz*
    b. *rot*
    c. *braun*

11. Good morning—
    a. *Guten Morgen*
    b. *Guten Abend*
    c. *Guten Nacht*

12. Very well—
    a. *Danke*
    b. *sehr gut*
    c. *viel*

13. Thank you—
    a. *schon gut*
    b. *Danke*
    c. *sehr schön*

14. Please—
    a. *Sprechen Sie!*
    b. *danke*
    c. *bitte*

15. Good-bye—
    a. *Bis morgen*
    b. *Auf Wiedersehen*
    c. *Guten Tag*

16. He gives—
    a. *er gibt*
    b. *sie gibt*
    c. *sie geben*

17. We are learning—
    a. *wir lernen*
    b. *Sie geben*
    c. *wir geben*

18. I don't speak—
    a. *er spricht nicht*
    b. *ich gebe*
    c. *ich spreche nicht*

19. Do you give?—
    a. *Geben Sie?*
    b. *Gibt er?*
    c. *Gibt sie?*

20. Do I give?—
    a. *Geben Sie?*
    b. *Gebe ich?*
    c. *Gibt er?*

ANSWERS
1—c; 2—a; 3—b; 4—a; 5—a; 6—b; 7—c; 8—b;
9—a; 10—c; 11—a; 12—b; 13—b; 14—c; 15—b;
16—a; 17—a; 18—c; 19—a; 20—b.

E. WORD STUDY

Anekdote	anecdote	*Detektiv*	detective
Patient	patient	*Talent*	talent
Film	film	*Religion*	religion
Patriot	patriot	*Liste*	list
Dialekt	dialect	*Experiment*	experiment

LESSON 10

A. THE GERMAN DECLENSION

In German, articles, nouns, adjectives, and pronouns
undergo some changes in their endings depending on
their use in a sentence. This variation is called *declension*. There are four case declensions: nominative,
genitive, dative, and accusative.

   1. The nominative case is used for the subject.

Das Buch ist hier.   The book is here.

   2. The genitive case is used to denote possession or
      belonging, and after certain prepositions.

der Name des Lehrers   the name of the teacher
  (*masc.*)

die Farbe der Blume   the color of the flower
  (*fem.*)
während des Tages   during the day

3. The dative case is used for the indirect object, after certain prepositions, and with certain verbs.

der Mann mit dem Stock	the man with the stick
Der Fisch springt aus dem Wasser.	The fish jumps out of the water.
Er gibt dem Mädchen eine Puppe.	He gives the girl a doll.
Wir helfen dem Mann.	We help the man.
Er dankt der Frau.	We thank the woman.

The dative case is often associated with location.

Wir sind in der Altstadt.	We're in the Old Town.
Das Buch liegt auf dem Tisch.	The book is lying on the table.

4. The accusative case is used for the direct object and after certain prepositions.

Sie hält die Feder.	She is holding the feather.
Er geht durch den Wald.	He walks (goes) through the forest.

The accusative case is often associated with direction or motion toward.

Wir gehen in die Altstadt.	We're going to the Old Town.
Ich lege das Buch auf den Tisch.	I lay the book on the table.

B. THE ARTICLE

In German there are three genders: masculine, feminine, and neuter. As already mentioned, the articles are declined in the four cases already given.

1. The definite article is declined as follows:

SINGULAR	MASC.	FEM.	NEUTER
Nom.	*der*	*die*	*das*
Gen.	*des*	*der*	*des*
Dat.	*dem*	*der*	*dem*
Acc.	*den*	*die*	*das*

PLURAL	(ALL GENDERS)
Nom.	*die*
Gen.	*der*
Dat.	*den*
Acc.	*die*

2. The indefinite article is declined as follows:

	MASC.	FEM.	NEUTER
Nom.	*ein*	*eine*	*ein*
Gen.	*eines*	*einer*	*eines*
Dat.	*einem*	*einer*	*einem*
Acc.	*einen*	*eine*	*ein*

C. DECLENSION OF NOUNS

1. Note that the endings of nouns in the singular undergo no changes except for the addition of *s* or *es* in the genitive singular of all neuter and most masculine nouns.
2. Nouns that are derived from adjectives are declined just like adjectives (see page 40) and

certain masculine nouns, called "n-nouns," take
-*n* in all cases but the nominative (*der Herr, des
Herrn, dem Herrn, den Herrn*).
3. In the dative plural, an *n* should be added unless
   the nominative plural ends in -*s*.

D. PLURAL OF NOUNS

Although many noun plurals are irregular and must be
learned individually, here are some guidelines for the
formation of plural nouns in German:

1. MASCULINE NOUNS

a. Most nouns of one syllable form their plurals
by adding -*e*. Most masculine and all feminine
plural nouns add an Umlaut on the stem vowel:

der Hut	die Hüte	hat
der Stuhl	die Stühle	chair
der Brief	die Briefe	letter
der Freund	die Freunde	friend
die Frucht	die Früchte	fruit

b. Some masculine nouns form their plurals
with the ending -*er* and may take an Umlaut
on the stem vowel:

der Mann	die Männer	man
der Geist	die Geister	spirit

c. Some masculine nouns with more than one
syllable form their plural by adding -*e:*

der Abend	die Abende	evening
der Sonntag	die Sonntage	Sunday

d. Some masculine nouns (n-nouns) form their plural by adding an -n or -en, just as they do in the genitive, accusative, and dative singular:

der Junge	die Jungen	boy
der Mensch	die Menschen	person
der Diplomat	die Diplomaten	diplomat

e. Masculine nouns ending in -el, -en, -er do not change their endings. Some take an Umlaut:

der Apfel	die Äpfel	apple
der Acker	die Äcker	acre
der Lehrer	die Lehrer	teacher (*masc.*)
der Kuchen	die Kuchen	cake
der Ofen	die Öfen	oven

2. FEMININE NOUNS

a. Most feminine nouns form their plurals by adding -n or -en:

die Tür	die Türen	door
die Frage	die Fragen	question
die Zeitung	die Zeitungen	newspaper

b. Some add an -e or -e and an Umlaut on the last vowel. Feminine nouns ending in -is will double the *s* in the plural:

die Kenntnis	die Kenntnisse	knowledge
die Frucht	die Früchte	fruit

c. Feminine nouns ending in -in form their plurals by adding -innen to the stem:

die Ärztin	die Ärztinnen	doctor
die Schülerin	die Schülerinnen	student

NOTE

Feminine nouns are easily recognizable since they may end in -e, -in, -ung, -heit, -keit, and -is.

die Seite	side/page	**die Sauberkeit**	cleanliness
die Freiheit	freedom	**die Übung**	exercise

3. NEUTER NOUNS

a. Some neuter nouns form their plural by adding -er and may have an Umlaut on the stem vowel:

das Bild	**die Bilder**	picture
das Licht	**die Lichter**	light
das Bad	**die Bäder**	bath
das Dorf	**die Dörfer**	village
das Haus	**die Häuser**	house

b. Some neuter nouns add -e:

das Heft	**die Hefte**	notebook
das Brot	**die Brote**	bread
das Jahr	**die Jahre**	year

c. Some neuter nouns form their plural by adding -n or -en:

das Auge	**die Augen**	eye
das Ohr	**die Ohren**	ear

d. Neuter nouns ending in -el, -er, -en, -chen, -lein remain unchanged in the plural:

das Mädchen	**die Mädchen**	girl
das Büchlein	**die Büchlein**	little book
das Fünftel	**die Fünftel**	one fifth

e. Some nouns have only a plural form:

die Ferien   vacation   **die Leute**   people

4. SOME NOUNS TO LEARN

Singular	Plural	Meaning (sing.)
der Herr	*die Herren*	gentleman, sir
das Datum	*die Daten*	date
das Gebäude	*die Gebäude*	building
die Mutter	*die Mütter*	mother
das Kino	*die Kinos*	movie theater
das Büro	*die Büros*	office
der Bürgersteig	*die Bürgersteige*	sidewalk
die Antwort	*die Antworten*	answer
der Verkäufer	*die Verkäufer*	salesperson
die Stadt	*die Städte*	city
das Hemd	*die Hemden*	shirt
der Anzug	*die Anzüge*	suit
der Fahrstuhl	*die Fahrstühle*	elevator
die Anweisung	*die Anweisungen*	direction
der Verkehr	_____	traffic

E. DECLENSION OF ADJECTIVES

1. *a.* The possessive adjectives and the word *kein*
(not any) are declined like the indefinite article:

das Buch <u>meines Bruders</u>   my brother's book
Er hat <u>keinen Hut</u>.   He has no hat.

b. An adjective used predicatively is not declined:

Das Wasser ist <u>warm</u>.   The water is warm.

2. Adjectives may be declined in three ways:

   a. Without article or pronoun. In this case the adjective takes the same case ending as the definite article, except in the masculine and neuter genitive, where it takes *en* instead of *es:*

	MASC.	FEM.
Nom.	*roter Wein*	*rote Tinte*
Gen.	*roten Weines*	*roter Tinte*
Dat.	*rotem Wein*	*roter Tinte*
Acc.	*roten Wein*	*rote Tinte*

	NEUTER	PLURAL (ALL GENDERS)
Nom.	*rotes Buch*	*rote Weine*
Gen.	*roten Buches*	*roter Weine*
Dat.	*rotem Buch*	*roten Weinen*
Acc.	*rotes Buch*	*rote Weine*

Du darfst nicht mit <u>roter Tinte</u> schreiben.	You aren't allowed to write with red ink.
<u>Roten Wein</u> trinken unsere Gäste nicht.	Our guests don't drink red wine.

   b. With the definite article the adjective takes an *e* in the following five cases:
   Nominative singular: masculine, feminine, and neuter.
   Accusative singular: feminine and neuter.
   en in all other cases.

	MASC.	FEM.
Nom.	*der rote Wein*	*die rote Tinte*
Gen.	*des roten Weines*	*der roten Tinte*
Dat.	*dem roten Wein*	*der roten Tinte*
Acc.	*den roten Wein*	*die rote Tinte*

	NEUTER	PLURAL (ALL GENDERS)
Nom.	*das rote Buch*	*die roten Weine*
Gen.	*des roten Buches*	*der roten Weine*
Dat.	*dem roten Buch*	*den roten Weinen*
Acc.	*das rote Buch*	*die roten Weine*

Ich möchte <u>den roten Wein</u>.

I'd like the red wine.

Er kommt mit <u>dem roten Heft</u> an.

He arrives with the red notebook.

   c. Since the indefinite article has no ending in the masculine and neuter nominative and in the neuter accusative, the adjective takes the ending of the definite article. In the nominative and accusative feminine, it takes an *e;* in all other cases *en.*

	MASC.	FEM.
Nom.	*ein roter Wein*	*seine rote Tinte*
Gen.	*eines roten Weines*	*seiner roten Tinte*
Dat.	*einem roten Wein*	*seiner roten Tinte*
Acc.	*einen roten Wein*	*seine rote Tinte*

	NEUTER	PLURAL (ALL GENDERS)
Nom.	*kein rotes Buch*	*meine roten Weine*
Gen.	*keines roten Buches*	*meiner roten Weine*
Dat.	*keinem roten Buch*	*meinen roten Weinen*
Acc.	*kein rotes Buches*	*meine roten Weine*

<u>Ein roter Wein</u> würde gut schmecken.

A red wine would taste good.

<u>Meine roten Weine</u> sind die feinsten.

My red wines are the finest.

F. Comparative and Superlative

1. The comparative and the superlative of most adjectives and adverbs are formed as in English by adding *er* for the comparative and *st* (or *est*) for the superlative to the adjective. Some short adjectives also take an Umlaut (¨) on their vowel.

schlecht, schlechter, schlechtest	bad, worse, worst
alt, älter, ältest	old, older, oldest

2. "Than" is translated by *als*.
3. Adjective endings are added to the comparative and superlative.
4. There are a few adjectives and adverbs that have an irregular comparative. Here are the most common ones:

gern	*lieber*	*der (die, das) liebste, am liebsten*	gladly, preferably, like the most
gut	*besser*	*der (die, das) beste, am besten*	good, better, best
groß	*größer*	*der (die, das) größte, am größten*	big, bigger, biggest
hoch	*höher*	*der (die, das) höchste, am höchsten*	high, higher, highest
nah	*näher*	*der (die, das) nächste, am nächsten*	close, closer, closest
viel	*mehr*	*der (die, das) meiste, am meisten*	much, more, the most

5. Examples:

Das Mädchen ist kleiner als der Junge.	The girl is smaller than the boy.
London ist die größte Stadt in Europa.	London is the largest city in Europe.

G. Prepositions

1. The following prepositions always take the genitive:

während	during
wegen	because of
statt, anstatt	instead of
trotz	despite

während des Krieges	during the war
wegen der Leute	because of the people
anstatt eines Stiftes	instead of a pen
trotz der Kälte	despite the cold

2. The following always govern the accusative:

durch	through, by
für	for
gegen	against, toward
ohne	without
um	round, about, at (time)

durch die Stadt	through the city
für den Mann	for the man
gegen den Krieg	against the war
ohne einen Lehrer	without a teacher
um den See	around the lake

3. The following always govern the dative:

aus	from, out of
außer	except for
bei	at, by, near
mit	with
nach	after, to (place)
seit	since
von	of, by, from
zu	to, at
aus der Schule	out of, from school
außer den Gästen	except for the guests
bei meinen Eltern	at my parents'
mit gutem Appetit	with a good appetite
nach dem Frühstück	after breakfast
seit einem Jahr	for (since) one year
von dem Hafen	from the port
zu den Freunden	to the friends

4. The following take the accusative if they denote motion toward a place. In this case they are used in reply to the question *Wohin?* (Where to?) But they also can take the dative if they denote rest (or motion) at a place. In this latter case they are used in reply to the question *Wo?* (Where?)

an	at, to
auf	on, upon, in
hinter	behind
in	in, into, at
neben	beside, near
über	over, across
unter	under, among
vor	before, ago
zwischen	between

an die Ecke	to the corner
an der Ecke	at the corner
auf dem Land	in the countryside
hinter dem Hotel	behind the hotel
in dem Wasser	in the water
neben der Kirche	next to the church
über den Wolken	over the clouds
unter dem Dach	under the roof
vor dem Rathaus	before the town hall
zwischen den Schultern	between the shoulders

5. Some of the preceding prepositions may be contracted with the definite article in the following way:

am	for	*an dem*
im	for	*in dem*
beim	for	*bei dem*
vom	for	*von dem*
zum	for	*zu dem*
zur	for	*zu der*
ins	for	*in das*
ans	for	*an das*

Examples:

Wo liegt Rom?	Where does Rome lie?
Rom liegt am Tiber.	Rome lies on the Tiber.
Wohin fahren Sie heute?	Where are you going today?
Ich fahre an den Strand.	I am going to the beach.
Wo steht die Lampe?	Where is the lamp standing?
Auf dem Tisch.	On the table.
Wohin gehen die Touristen?	Where are the tourists going?

Sie gehen auf das Schiff.	They are going to the ship.
Wo liegt der Garten?	Where is the garden located?
Hinter dem Haus.	Behind the house.
Wohin stellen Sie den Schirm?	Where are you putting the umbrella?
Hinter die Tür.	Behind the door.
Wo wohnt Herr Müller?	Where does Mr. Müller live?
Er wohnt in dieser Straße.	He lives on this street.
Wohin gehen die Leute?	Where are the people going?
Sie gehen ins Kino.	They are going to the movies.
Wo fliegt das Flugzeug?	Where is the plane flying?
Es fliegt gerade über den Bergen.	It is now flying over the mountains.
Wohin laufen die Kinder?	Where are the children running?
Sie laufen über die Brücke.	They are running over the bridge.
Wo ist die Katze?	Where is the cat?
Unter dem Bett.	Under the bed.
Wohin legt er das Heft?	Where is he putting the notebook?
Er legt es unter das Lineal.	He is putting it under the ruler.
Wo ist der Brunnen?	Where is the fountain?
Vor dem Schloss.	In front of the castle.
Wohin tragen Sie den Koffer?	Where are you carrying the suitcase?
Vor das Hotel.	In front of the hotel.
Wo liegt Luxemburg?	Where is Luxemburg located?

Es liegt zwischen Deutschland und Frankreich.	It is located between Germany and France.
Wohin legen Sie den Bleistift?	Where are you putting the pencil?
Zwischen die Seiten des Buches.	Between the pages of the book.

SUPPLEMENTAL VOCABULARY 3: PEOPLE

people	*Leute*
person	*die Person (die Personen)*
man	*der Mann (die Männer)*
woman	*die Frau (die Frauen)*
adult	*der/die Erwachsene (die Erwachsenen)*
child	*das Kind (die Kinder)*
boy	*der Junge (die Jungen)*
girl	*das Mädchen (die Mädchen)*
teenager	*der Teenager (die Teenager), der/die Jugendliche (die Jugendlichen)*
tall/short	*groß/klein*
old/young	*alt/jung*
fat/thin	*dick/dünn*
friendly/unfriendly	*freundlich/unfreundlich*
happy/sad	*glücklich/traurig*
beautiful/ugly	*schön/hässlich*
sick/healthy	*klank/gesund*
strong/weak	*stark/schwach*
famous	*berühmt*
intelligent	*intelligent*
talented	*talentiert*

LESSON 11

A. WHERE?

Verzeihung, mein Herr.	Excuse me, sir.
wo	where
ist	is
Wo ist es?	Where is it?
das Hotel	the hotel
Wo ist das Hotel?	Where is the hotel?
Wo ist das Restaurant?	Where is the restaurant?
Wo ist das Telefon?	Where is the telephone?
Könnten Sie mir sagen . . . ?	Could you tell me . . . ?
Können Sie mir sagen . . . ?	Can you tell me . . . ?
Können Sie mir sagen, wo das Telefon ist?	Can you tell me where the telephone is?
Können Sie mir sagen, wo der Bahnhof ist?	Can you tell me where the (railroad) station is?

B. HERE AND THERE

hier	here
dort	there
dort drüben	over there
Welche Richtung ist es?	Which way is it?
hier entlang	this way
dort entlang	that way
hier hinunter	down this way
in die/der Richtung	over that way
dort hinunter	in that direction

Das ist dort entlang.	It's over that way.
Es ist nicht hier.	It's not here.
Es ist nicht dort.	It's not there.
Es ist hier.	It's here.
Es ist dort.	It's there.
Es ist dort drüben.	It's over there.
Es ist dort oben.	It's up there.
Er ist hier.	He's here.
Kommen Sie her!	Come here.
Bleiben Sie hier!	Stay here.
Warten Sie dort.	Wait there.
Gehen Sie hier entlang!	Go this way.
Gehen Sie dort entlang!	Go that way.
Wer ist dort?	Who's there?
Legen Sie es hierhin!	Put it (over) here.
Legen Sie es dorthin!	Put it (over) there.

C. THERE

dort, da	there
Ist er in Paris?	Is he in Paris?
Ja, er ist dort.	Yes, he is (there).
Ist Paul da?	Is Paul there?
Ja, er ist da.	Yes, he's there.
Fährt er nach Frankfurt?	Is he going to Frankfurt?
Ja, er fährt dorthin.	Yes, he's going there.
Ich fahre dorthin.	I'm going there.
Ich will nicht dorthin fahren.	I don't want to go there.
Ich wohne dort.	I live there.

D. TO THE RIGHT, ETC.

rechts	to the right
links	to the left
rechts von Ihnen	to your right

zu Ihrer Linken	to your left
auf der linken Seite	on your left
Das ist rechts.	It's to the right.
Das ist links.	It's to the left.
Biegen Sie rechts ab.	Turn right.
Biegen Sie links ab.	Turn left.
Gehen Sie geradeaus.	Keep straight on.
Das ist geradeaus.	It's straight ahead.
Gehen Sie geradeaus.	Go straight ahead.
Es ist direkt gegenüber.	It's directly opposite.
Es ist weiter oben.	It's farther up.
Es ist weiter unten.	It's below (farther down).
Es ist an der Ecke.	It's on the corner.

E. NEAR AND FAR

nah	near
sehr nahe	very near; quite close
in der Nähe des Denkmals	near the monument
in der Nähe der Hauptstrasse	near the main street
in seiner Nähe	near him
Es ist sehr nah.	It's very near.
Es ist ganz in der Nähe.	It's very near here.
weit	far
Ist es weit bis dorthin?	Is it far to get there?
Es ist weit.	It's far.
Es ist nicht weit.	It's not far.
Das ist weit von hier.	That's far from here.

QUIZ 4

1. *Können Sie mir sagen, wo das Telefon ist?*
a. It's this way.

2. *Wo befindet sich das Hotel?*
b. It's to the right.

3. *Das ist hier entlang.*
c. Turn left!

4. *Das ist geradeaus*
d. That's directly opposite.

5. *Das ist rechts von hier*
e. It's straight ahead.

6. *Er wohnt dort.*
f. Can you tell me where the telephone is?

7. *Warten Sie dort!*
g. Where is the hotel? (Where is the hotel situated?)

8. *Gehen Sie hier entlang!*
h. He lives there.

9. *Biegen Sie links ab!*
i. That's not here.

10. *Das ist direkt gegenüber!*
j. Stay here.

11. *Das ist nicht weit.*
k. Wait there!

12. *Legen Sie es dorthin!*
l. Go this way!

13. *Das ist nicht hier.*
m. Who's there?

14. *Bleiben Sie hier!*
n. Put it there.

15. *Wer ist dort?*
o. It's not far.

ANSWERS
1—f; 2—g; 3—a; 4—e; 5—b; 6—h; 7—k; 8—l;
9—c; 10—d; 11—o; 12—n; 13—i; 14—j; 15—m

SUPPLEMENTAL VOCABULARY 4:
AT HOME

at home	*zu Hause*
house	*das Haus (die Häuser)*
apartment	*die Wohnung (die Wohnungen)*
room	*das Zimmer (die Zimmer)*
living room	*das Wohnzimmer (die Wohnzimmer)*
dining room	*das Esszimmer (die Esszimmer)*
kitchen	*die Küche (die Küchen)*
bedroom	*das Schlafzimmer (die Schlafzimmer)*
bathroom	*das Badezimmer (die Badezimmer)*
hall	*die Diele (die Dielen), die Eingangshalle (die Eingangshallen)*
closet	*der Schrank (die Schränke)*
window	*das Fenster (die Fenster)*
door	*die Tür (die Türen)*
table	*der Tisch (die Tische)*
chair	*der Stuhl (die Stühle)*
sofa/couch	*das Sofa (die Sofas)*
curtain	*der Vorhang (die Vorhänge)*
carpet	*der Teppich (die Teppiche)*
television	*der Fernseher (die Fernseher)*

cd player	*der CD-Spieler (die CD-Spieler)*
lamp	*die Lampe (die Lampen)*
dvd player	*der DVD-Spieler (die DVD-Spieler)*
sound system	*die Lautsprecheranlage (die Lautsprecher-anlagen)*
painting/picture	*das Gemälde/das Bild (die Gemälde/die Bilder)*
shelf	*das Regal (die Regale)*
staircase	*die Treppe (die Treppen)*
stair, step	*die Stufe (die Stufen)*
ceiling	*die Decke (die Decken)*
wall	*die Wand (die Wände)*
floor	*der Boden (die Böden)*
big/small	*groß/klein*
new/old	*neu/alt*
wood/wooden	*das Holz/hölzern*
plastic/made from plastic	*das Plastik/aus Plastik*

LESSON 12

A. TO BE OR NOT TO BE: *SEIN*

1. I am

ich bin	I am
du bist	you are
er ist	he is

sie ist	she is
es ist	it is
wir sind	we are
ihr seid	you are
Sie sind	you are
sie sind	they are

2. I am not

ich bin nicht	I am not
du bist nicht	you are not
er ist nicht	he is not
sie ist nicht	she is not
es ist nicht	it is not
wir sind nicht	we are not
ihr seid nicht	you are not
Sie sind nicht	you are not
sie sind nicht	they are not

3. Be!

| Seien Sie! | Be! |
| Seien Sie ruhig! | Be quiet. Don't worry! |

4. Am I?

Bin ich?	Am I?
Bist du?	Are you?
Ist er?	Is he?
Ist sie?	Is she?
Ist es?	Is it?
Sind wir?	Are we?
Seid ihr?	Are you?
Sind Sie?	Are you?
Sind sie?	Are they?

5. Where am I?

Wo bin ich?	Where am I?
Wo bist du?	Where are you?
Wo ist er?	Where is he?
Wo ist sie?	Where is she?
Wo ist es?	Where is it?
Wo sind wir?	Where are we?
Wo seid ihr?	Where are you?
Wo sind Sie?	Where are you?
Wo sind sie?	Where are they?

6. Study these examples:

Ich bin Amerikaner.	I'm (an) American.
Ich bin im Zimmer.	I'm in the room.
Ich bin im Hotel.	I'm at the hotel.
Er ist hier.	He's here.
Sie sind hier.	They're here.
Sie sind dort drüben.	They're over there.
Ich bin bereit.	I'm ready.
Sie ist bereit.	She's ready.
Sie sind bereit.	They're ready.

Sind Sie sicher, mein Herr?	Are you certain, sir?
Sind Sie sicher, meine Dame?	Are you certain, madam?
Sind Sie sicher, mein Fräulein?	Are you certain, miss/young lady?
Sind Sie sicher, meine Herren?	Are you certain, gentlemen?
Sind Sie sicher, meine Damen?	Are you certain, ladies?

Sind Sie Engländer?	Are you English?
Ja, ich bin Engländer.	Yes, I'm English.

Nein, ich bin nicht Engländer.	No, I'm not English.
Wie spät ist es?	What time is it?
Woher sind Sie?	Where are you from?
Ich bin aus Berlin.	I'm from Berlin.

B. MY, YOUR, HIS, ETC.

The possessive adjectives are declined like the article *ein*. The following are examples of possessive adjectives in the nominative case.

MASCULINE/NEUTER

Wo ist mein Buch?	Where is my book?
Wo ist dein Buch?	Where is your (*fam.*) book?
Wo ist sein Buch?	Where is his book?
Wo ist ihr Buch?	Where is her book?
Wo ist Ihr Buch?	Where is your (*pol.*) book?
Wo ist ihr Buch?	Where is their book?

FEMININE

Wo ist meine Uhr?	Where is my watch?
Wo ist deine Uhr?	Where is your (*fam.*) watch?
Wo ist seine Uhr?	Where is his watch?
Wo ist ihre Uhr?	Where is her watch?
Wo ist Ihre Uhr?	Where is your (*pol.*) watch?
Wo ist unsere Uhr?	Where is our watch?
Wo ist eure Uhr?	Where is your (*fam.*) watch?
Wo ist Ihre Uhr?	Where is your (*pol.*) watch?
Wo ist ihre Uhr?	Where is their watch?

PLURAL

Wo sind meine Bücher?	Where are my books?
Wo sind deine Bücher?	Where are your (*fam.*) books?
Wo sind seine Bücher?	Where are his books?
Wo sind ihre Bücher?	Where are her books?
Wo sind Ihre Bücher?	Where are your (*pol.*) books?
Wo sind unsere Bücher?	Where are our books?
Wo sind eure Bücher?	Where are your (*fam.*) books?
Wo sind Ihre Bücher?	Where are your (*pol.*) books?
Wo sind ihre Bücher?	Where are their books?

Note that plural endings of the personal pronouns remain the same regardless of the gender of the noun.

Wo sind meine Uhren?	Where are my watches?
Wo sind deine Uhren?	Where are your (*fam.*) watches?
Wo sind seine Uhren?	Where are his watches?
Wo sind Ihre Uhren?	Where are your (*pol.*) watches?
Wo sind ihre Uhren?	Where are her watches?
Wo sind unsere Uhren?	Where are our watches?
Wo sind eure Uhren?	Where are your (*fam.*) watches?

Wo sind Ihre Uhren?   Where are your (*pol.*)
                                watches?

Wo sind ihre Uhren?   Where are their
                                watches?

QUIZ 5

1. *Woher sind Sie?*   a. What time is it?
2. *Wie spät ist es?*   b. Where are you from?
3. *Er ist hier.*   c. Where is he?
4. *Ich bin bereit.*   d. Where is her letter?
5. *Sind Sie sicher?*   e. They are ready.
6. *Wo ist er?*   f. Where are their
                                books?
7. *Wo ist ihr Brief?*   g. I'm ready.
8. *Wo sind ihre*   h. I'm at the hotel.
   Bücher?
9. *Sie sind bereit.*   i. Are you certain?
10. *Seien Sie ruhig!*   j. He's here.
11. *Ich bin im Hotel.*   k. I'm (an) American.
12. *Ich bin Amerikaner.*   l. Be quiet.
13. *Ich bin nicht bereit.* m. I'm from Berlin.
14. *Wir sind hier.*   n. I'm not ready.
15. *Ich bin aus Berlin.*   o. We are here.

ANSWERS
1—b; 2—a; 3—j; 4—g; 5—i; 6—c; 7—d; 8—f;
9—e; 10—l; 11—h; 12—k; 13—n; 14—o; 15—m.

C. WORD STUDY: COGNATES

Instruktion (die)   instruction
energisch   energetic
Instrument (das)   instrument
Regiment (das)   regiment
Violine (die)   violin

Palast (der)	palace
Terrasse (die)	terrace
national	national
Sardine (die)	sardine
Skandal (der)	scandal

LESSON 13

A. IT IS, THAT IS

Es ist gut.	It's good.
Das ist gut.	That's good.
Das ist nicht gut.	It's not good.
Das ist in Ordnung.	It's (that's) all right. (It's in order.)
Das ist nicht in Ordnung.	It's not very good (nice). It's not right (fair).
Das ist schlecht.	It's bad.
Das ist nicht schlecht.	It's not bad.
Das ist klein.	It's small.
Das ist groß.	It's big.
Das ist nichts.	It's nothing.
Das ist schwer.	It's hard (difficult).
Das ist leicht.	It's easy.
Das ist sehr leicht.	It's very easy.
Das ist leicht genug.	It's easy enough.
Das ist leichter.	It's easier.
Das ist weniger schwer.	It's less difficult.
Das ist weit.	It's far.
Das ist nicht sehr weit.	It's not very far.

Das ist in der Nähe.	It's near here.
Das ist sehr in der Nähe.	It's very near here.
Das ist wenig.	It's (a) little.
Das ist zu wenig.	It's too little.
Das ist genug.	It's enough.
Das ist viel.	It's a lot.
Das ist dort.	It's there.
Das ist nicht dort.	It's not there.
Das ist hier entlang.	It's this way.
Das ist dort entlang.	It's that way.
Das ist für mich.	It's for me.
Das ist für dich.	It's for you (*fam.*).
Das ist für ihn.	It's for him.
Das ist für sie.	It's for her.
Das ist für Sie.	It's for you (*pol sing. and pl.*).
Das ist für uns.	It's for us.
Das ist für euch.	It's for you (*fam. pl.*).
Das ist für sie.	It's for them.
Das ist nicht für sie.	It's not for them.
Das ist für die Kinder.	It's for the children.
Das ist es.	That's it.

B. ASKING A QUESTION II

1. In German, a question is usually formed by placing the verb before the subject:

STATEMENT:	*Er geht heute ins Kino.*	He's going to the movies today.
QUESTION:	*Geht er heute ins Kino?*	Is he going to the movies today?

2. A question may also be formed by leaving the word order the same as in a statement and adding a question mark. In this case, the intonation of the speaker rises, and the question is intended to show surprise.

Er geht heute ins Kino?	He's going to the movies today?

3. In German statements, the subject comes before the verb. Questions usually have "inverted word order" (the verb comes before the subject), as you learned earlier.

When question words (interrogatives) are used, the verb remains in second position in the sentence and precedes the subject:

Wer kommt um zehn Uhr?	Who's coming at ten o'clock?
Wohin fährst du heute nachmittag?	Where are you traveling to this afternoon?

4. More questions:

Ist es das?	Is it that? Is it this?
Das ist es?	That is it?
Das ist wahr.	It's true.
Das ist wahr?	Is it true?
Wo ist es?	Where is it?
Sind Sie bereit?	Are you ready? (for something)
Sind Sie fertig?	Are you finished?
Sind sie bereit?	Are they ready?

Kommen Sie?	Are you coming?
Haben Sie Zeit?	Do you have time?
Haben Sie die Uhrzeit?	Do you have the time?
Sprechen Sie Englisch?	Do you speak English?
Sprechen Sie Deutsch?	Do you speak German?

C. WORD STUDY

Asien (das)	Asia	*Lektion (die)*	lesson
alt	old	*Nase (die)*	nose
Feld (das)	field	*Bär (der)*	bear
Alpen (die)	Alps	*Tiger (der)*	tiger
August (der)	August	*Elefant (der)*	elephant

LESSON 14

A. TO HAVE AND HAVE NOT: *HABEN*

1. I have

ich habe	I have
du hast	you have
er hat	he has
wir haben	we have
ihr habt	you have
Sie haben	you have
sie haben	they have

2. I don't have

ich habe nicht	I don't have, I haven't
du hast nicht	you don't have, etc.

er hat nicht	he doesn't have
wir haben nicht	we don't have
ihr habt nicht	you don't have
Sie haben nicht	you don't have
sie haben nicht	they don't have

3. Study these phrases:

Ich habe etwas.	I have something. I've got something.
Ich habe nichts.	I have nothing. I don't have anything. There's nothing wrong with me.
Ich habe Geld.	I have money.
Ich habe genug Geld.	I have enough money.
Ich habe kein Geld.	I have no money. I haven't any money.
Ich habe genug Zeit.	I have enough time.
Sie haben keine Zeit.	They don't have any time.
Ich habe Hunger.	I'm hungry.
Er hat Hunger.	He's hungry.
Ich habe Durst.	I'm thirsty.
Er hat Recht.	He's right.
Er hat Unrecht.	He's wrong.
Sie haben Recht.	You're right.
Sie hat Angst.	She's afraid.
Ich habe Zahnschmerzen.	I have a toothache.
Sie hat Kopfschmerzen.	She has a headache.

4. Do I have?

habe ich?	do I have?
hast du?	do you have?

hat er?	does he have?
haben wir?	do we have?
habt ihr?	do you have?
haben Sie?	do you have (*pol.*)?
haben sie?	do they have?

5. Don't I have?

habe ich nicht?	don't I have? haven't I?
hast du nicht?	don't you have?
hat er nicht?	doesn't he have?
haben wir nicht?	don't we have?
habt ihr nicht?	don't you have?
haben Sie nicht?	don't you have?
haben sie nicht?	don't they have?

6. Now study these sentences:

Hat er Geld?	Does he have any money?
Hat sie genug Geld?	Does she have enough money?
Hat er Freunde in Berlin?	Does he have (any) friends in Berlin?
Haben Sie einen Bleistift?	Do you have a pencil?
Haben Sie einen Kugelschreiber?	Do you have a pen?
Haben Sie eine Briefmarke?	Do you have a stamp?
Haben Sie etwas Papier?	Do you have any paper?
Haben Sie ein Zimmer frei?	Do you have a free room?
Haben Sie E-Mail?	Do you have e-mail?
Haben Sie ein Auto?	Do you have a car?

Haben Sie einen Stadtplan?	Do you have a map of the city?
Was haben Sie?	What's the matter with you?
Was hat er?	What's the matter with him?
Haben Sie Zeit, mit mir zu sprechen?	Do you have time to talk to me?

B. THERE IS

Es gibt . . .	There is . . .
Es gibt etwas.	There is something.
Es gibt nichts hier.	There is nothing here.
Es gibt nichts mehr.	There isn't any more.
Es gibt nichts mehr davon.	There isn't any more of that.
Es gibt keine Antwort.	There is no answer.
Es gibt keinen Unterschied.	There's no difference.
Es gibt keine Schwierigkeit.	There's no difficulty.
Niemand ist dort.	No one is there.
Niemand ist hier.	No one is here.
Sind Briefe für mich da?	Are there any letters for me?
Ist Post da?	Is there any mail?
Ist Post für mich da?	Is there any mail for me?
Sind viele Menschen da?	Are there many people?
Gibt es ein Telefon hier?	Is there a telephone here?
Gibt es ein Restaurant in der Nähe?	Is there a restaurant nearby?

**Gibt es eine Apotheke
    hier in der Nähe?**
Is there a pharmacist
    nearby?

**Gibt es ein Cafe in
    der Nähe?**
Is there a cafe nearby?

Hier sind vier Personen.
There are four people
    here.

C. Ago

vor	ago
vor einer Stunde	an hour ago
vor zwei Stunden	two hours ago
vor drei Stunden	three hours ago
vor einem Tag	a day ago
vor zwei Tagen	two days ago
vor drei Wochen	three weeks ago
vor fünf Monaten	five months ago
vor fünf Jahren	five years ago
vor zehn Jahren	ten years ago
vor langer Zeit	a long time ago
vor ziemlich langer Zeit	a pretty long time ago
vor nicht langer Zeit	not so long ago
vor kurzer Zeit	a short time ago

D. Also, Too

auch	also, too
ich auch	I also (too)
du auch	you also (too)
er auch	he also (too)
sie auch	she also (too)
wir auch	we also (too)
ihr auch	you also (too)

Sie auch	you also (too)
sie auch	they also (too)
Er kommt auch.	He's coming, too.
Sie kommen auch.	They're coming, too.
Er tut es auch.	He's doing it, too.
Ich komme auch.	I'm coming, too.
Sie sind so groß wie die andern.	They're as tall as the others.
Sie sind nicht so klein wie die andern.	They're not as small as the others.
Das ist nicht so gut wie das andere.	That's not as good as the other.
Das ist nicht so groß wie das andere.	That's not as large as the other.
Kommen Sie so schnell wie möglich!	Come as quickly as you can.
Tun Sie es so schnell wie möglich!	Do it as soon as possible.
Machen Sie es so gut wie möglich!	Do it as well as possible.

QUIZ 6

1. *Ich habe genug Zeit.*
2. *Er hat Recht.*
3. *Ich brauche das.*
4. *Er hat Unrecht.*
5. *Ihm ist kalt.*

6. *Ich habe Hunger.*
7. *Ich bin zwanzig Jahre alt.*
8. *Ich habe Durst.*

9. *Wie alt sind Sie?*

a. Not at all. Don't mention it.
b. There's no answer.
c. There's no difference.
d. There's no difficulty.
e. Are there any letters for me?
f. There's nobody here.
g. A day ago.

h. Since three weeks ago.
i. A long time ago.

10. *Hat er Geld?*

    j. Come as quickly as you can.

11. *Wie viel haben Sie davon?*

    k. I have nothing. (I don't have anything.) There's nothing wrong with me.

12. *Hat er Freunde in Paris?*

    l. I have enough time.

13. *Ich habe nichts.*

    m. I'm hungry.

14. *Sie haben Recht.*

    n. I'm thirsty.

15. *Was hat er?*

    o. He's cold.

16. *Seit drei Wochen.*

    p. He's right.

17. *Es gibt keinen Unterschied.*

    q. He's wrong.

18. *Es gibt keine Schwierigkeit.*

    r. You're right.

19. *Keine Ursache.*

    s. I need that.

20. *Vor langer Zeit.*

    t. I'm twenty (years old).

21. *Niemand ist hier.*

    u. Does he have (any) money?

22. *Kommen Sie so schnell wie möglich.*

    v. Does he have (any) friends in Paris?

23. *Sind Briefe für mich da?*

    w. What's the matter with him?

24. *Vor einem Tag.*

    x. How old are you?

25. *Keine Antwort.*

    y. How many of them do you have?

ANSWERS

1—l; 2—p; 3—s; 4—q; 5—o; 6—m; 7—t; 8—n; 9—x; 10—u; 11—y; 12—v; 13—k; 14—r; 15—w; 16—h; 17—c; 18—d; 19—a; 20—i; 21—f; 22—j; 23—e; 24—g; 25—b.

SUPPLEMENTAL VOCABULARY 5:
THE HUMAN BODY

the human body	*der menschliche Körper*
head	*der Kopf (die Köpfe)*
face	*das Gesicht (die Gesichter)*
forehead	*die Stirn (die Stirnen)*
eye	*das Auge (die Augen)*
eyebrow	*die Augenbraue (die Augenbrauen)*
eyelash	*die Wimper (die Wimpern)*
ear	*das Ohr (die Ohren)*
nose	*die Nase (die Nasen)*
mouth	*der Mund (die Münder, die Munde)*
tooth	*der Zahn (die Zähne)*
tongue	*die Zunge (die Zungen)*
cheek	*die Wange (die Wangen)*
chin	*das Kinn (die Kinne)*
hair	*das Haar (die Haare)*
neck	*der Nacken (die Nacken), der Hals (die Hälse)*
chest	*der Brustkorb (die Brustkörbe)*
breast	*die Brust (die Brüste)*
shoulder	*die Schulter (die Schultern)*
arm	*der Arm (die Arme)*
elbow	*der Ellbogen (die Ellbogen*
wrist	*das Handgelenk (die Handgelenke)*
hand	*die Hand (die Hände)*
stomach/abdomen	*der Magen (die Mägen)*
penis	*der Penis (die Penisse)*

vagina	*die Vagina (die Vaginen)*
leg	*das Bein (die Beine)*
knee	*das Knie (die Knie)*
ankle	*der Knöchel (die Knöchel)*
foot	*der Fuß (die Füße)*
finger	*der Finger (die Finger)*
toe	*der Zeh, die Zehe (die Zehen)*
skin	*die Haut (die Häute)*
blood	*das Blut*
brain	*das Gehirn (die Gehirne)*
heart	*das Herz (die Herzen)*
lungs	*die Lunge (die Lungen)*
bone	*der Knochen (die Knochen)*
muscle	*der Muskel (die Muskeln)*
tendon	*die Sehne (die Sehnen)*

LESSON 15

A. DO YOU SPEAK GERMAN?

Sprechen Sie Deutsch?	Do you speak German?
Nein, ich spreche nicht Deutsch.	No, I don't speak German.
Ich spreche nicht gut Deutsch.	I don't speak German very well.
schlecht	poorly
sehr schlecht	very poorly
Ich spreche sehr schlecht.	I speak very poorly.
ein wenig	a little

Ja, ich spreche ein wenig.	Yes, I speak a little.
sehr wenig	very little
Ich spreche sehr wenig.	I speak very little.
Ein paar Wörter.	A few words.
Nur ein paar Wörter.	Only a few words.
Verstehen Sie?	Do you understand?
Nein, ich verstehe nicht.	No, I don't understand.
Ich verstehe nicht sehr gut.	I don't understand very well.
Ich verstehe Deutsch nicht sehr gut.	I don't understand German very well.
Ja, ich verstehe.	Yes, I understand.
Ja, ich verstehe ein wenig.	Yes, I understand a little.
Ich lese, aber ich kann nicht sprechen.	I read but I can't speak.
Verstehen Sie?	Do you understand?
Überhaupt nicht.	Not at all.
Schreiben Sie es!	Write it (down).
Wie schreiben Sie es?	How do you write (spell) it?
Ich kenne dieses Wort nicht.	I don't know this word.

B. PLEASE SPEAK MORE SLOWLY

würden Sie	would you . . . ?
sprechen	(to) speak
etwas langsamer	more slowly ("somewhat slower")

Würden Sie etwas langsamer sprechen?	Would you speak more slowly?
Wenn Sie langsam sprechen, kann ich Sie verstehen.	If you speak slowly, I can understand you, *or,* If you speak slowly, I'll be able to understand you.
bitte	please
Würden Sie bitte etwas langsamer sprechen?	Would you mind speaking a little more slowly, please?
ich bitte Sie	please ("I beg you")
Ich bitte Sie, etwas langsamer zu sprechen.	Would you mind speaking a little more slowly, please?
Würden Sie das bitte wiederholen?	Would you please say that again? ("Would you repeat that, please?")
Bitte sprechen Sie langsam!	Please speak slowly!
Bitte sprechen Sie langsamer.	Please speak more slowly.

C. WHAT DID YOU SAY?

Was haben Sie gesagt?	What did you say? You were saying? What was that?
Wiederholen Sie, bitte.	Repeat (it, that), please.
Wie bitte, was haben Sie gesagt?	What did you say? ("How, please, what did you say?")

Wie sagen Sie das auf Deutsch?	How do you say that in German?
Wie sagt man "Thank you" auf Deutsch?	How do you say "Thank you" in German?
Was wollen Sie sagen?	What do you want to say?

D. THANKS

Danke.	Thanks.
Ich danke Ihnen.	Thanks. ("I thank you.")
Ich danke Ihnen vielmals.	Thank you very much.
Keine Ursache.	Don't mention it.
Danke schön.	Thanks.
Bitte schön.	Not at all. You're welcome.
Entschuldigen Sie, bitte.	Excuse me.
Bitte sehr.	Certainly.
Gestatten Sie?	May I? ("You permit me?")
Bitte sehr!	Of course! Please do!
Ich bitte Sie.	Please do! ("I beg you.")
Wie bitte?	Pardon? What did you say?
Verzeihung, was sagen Sie?	Sorry. What are you saying?
Auf Wiedersehen!	Good-bye. See you soon.
Auf baldiges Wiedersehen!	See you soon. See you later.
Bis heute Abend.	See you this evening. ("Until this evening.")

QUIZ 7

1. *Schreiben Sie!*	a. No, I don't speak German.
2. *Nein, ich spreche nicht Deutsch.*	b. A few words.
3. *Ich verstehe Deutsch nicht gut.*	c. Do you understand?
4. *Verstehen Sie?*	d. I don't understand German very well.
5. *Ein paar Wörter.*	e. Write!
6. *Möchten (Könnten) Sie das bitte wiederholen?*	f. How do you write it?
7. *Wie sagt man "Thank you" auf Deutsch?*	g. I don't know that word.
8. *Was wollen Sie sagen?*	h. How do you say "Thank you" in German?
9. *Wie schreiben Sie es?*	i. What do you mean? ("What do you want to say?")
10. *Ich kenne das Wort nicht.*	j. Would (Could) you please repeat that?

ANSWERS
1—e; 2—a; 3—d; 4—c; 5—b; 6—j; 7—h; 8—i;
9—f; 10—g.

E. WORD STUDY

Äquator (der)	equator
backen	(to) bake
Ballon (der)	balloon
Gras (das)	grass

Problem (das)	problem
weise	wise
Arm (der)	arm
Honig (der)	honey
Winter (der)	winter
Sommer (der)	summer

LESSON 16

A. THIS AND THAT

The demonstrative adjectives *dieser, diese, dieses* follow the same declension as *der, die, das:*[1]

dieser Anzug	this or that suit
diese Nacht	this night
dieses Wochenende	this weekend
dieser Mann	this man
diese Frau	this woman
dieses Kind	this child

To express "that one" in contrast with "this," German simply uses *der* (*die, das*) with a special emphasis in the pronunciation.

Dieser Tisch ist breit und der ist schmal.
This table is wide and that one is narrow.

Diese Wand ist dick und die ist dünn.
This wall is thick and that one is thin.

---

[1] See page 322 for more on demonstrative adjectives and pronouns.

Dieses Kleid ist lang und das ist kurz.
This dress is long and that one is short.

Dieser and *der* are interchangeable, so that you could also say:

Der Tisch ist breit und dieser ist schmal.
Dieser Hund ist groß und der ist klein.

Diese Katze ist grau und die ist schwarz.
Das Bild ist gut und dieses ist schlecht.

Note that both *dieser* and *der* can mean either "this" or "that," although the basic meaning of *dieser* is "this."

QUIZ 8

1. *Ich bevorzuge diesen. (Ich ziehe diesen vor.)*
2. *Was bedeutet das?*
3. *Geben Sie mir das!*
4. *Dieses gehört mir und das gehört Ihnen.*
5. *Das hängt davon ab.*
6. *Das ist es nicht.*
7. *Wie gehts?*
8. *Das ist selbstverständlich.*
9. *Das ist mir gleich.*
10. *Dieses gehört mir.*

a. What does this mean?
b. This is mine. (This one belongs to me.)
c. That goes without saying.
d. It's not that.
e. This one belongs to me and that one belongs to you.

f. Give me that.
g. It's all the same to me.
h. That all depends.
i. How are you?
j. I prefer that one (*masc.*).

ANSWERS

1—j; 2—a; 3—f; 4—e; 5—h; 6—d; 7—i; 8—c; 9—g;
10—b.

B. Not, Not Any

Das ist nicht gut.	That's not good.
Es ist nicht schlecht.	It's not bad.
Das ist es nicht.	That's not it.
Es ist nicht hier.	It's not here.
Das ist nicht zuviel.	That's not too much.
Nicht zu schnell.	Not too fast.
Nicht viel.	Not much.
Nicht viele.	Not many.
Nicht genug.	Not enough.
Nicht oft.	Not often.
Noch nicht.	Not yet.
Überhaupt nicht.	Not at all.
Er fährt nicht zu schnell.	He's not driving too fast.
Wir haben nicht viele.	We don't have many.
Das ist nicht genug.	That's not enough.
Ich gehe nicht oft.	I don't go often.
Er ist noch nicht hier.	He's not here yet.
Das ist überhaupt nicht wahr.	That's not true at all.

Ich habe keine Zeit.	I haven't any time. I have no time.
Ich weiß nicht wie.	I don't know how.
Ich weiß nicht wo.	I don't know where.
Ich weiß überhaupt nichts.	I don't know anything. I know nothing at all.
Er hat nichts gesagt.	He didn't say (hasn't said) anything.

C. NOTHING, NEVER, ONLY, ETC.

Nichts.	Nothing.
Ich habe nichts.	I don't have anything.
Niemals, nie.	Never.
Ich sehe ihn nie.	I never see him.
Er kommt nie *(mals)*.	He never comes.
Wer ist gekommen?	Who came?
Niemand.	Nobody.
Ich sehe niemand.	I don't see anyone.
Ich gehe nicht mehr dorthin.	I don't go there anymore.
Er kommt nicht mehr.	He doesn't come anymore.
Ich habe nur Zehn Euro.	I have only ten euros.
Du hast nur eine Stunde.	You have only one hour.
Er hat nur zehn davon.	He has only ten of them.

D. ISN'T IT? AREN'T YOU? ETC.

Nicht wahr?	Isn't that so?
Das ist schön, nicht wahr?	It's nice, isn't it?

Sie kommen, nicht wahr?	You're coming, aren't you (right)?
Sie haben genug davon, nicht wahr?	You have enough of it, don't you?
Sie haben keine, nicht wahr?	You don't have any, do you?
Sie sind damit einverstanden, nicht wahr?	You agree, don't you?

QUIZ 9

1. *Das ist es nicht.*
2. *Ich weiß nicht wann.*
3. *Ich habe keine Zeit.*
4. *Er sieht nichts.*
5. *Sie kommen, nicht wahr?*
6. *Sie haben nur eine Stunde.*
7. *Ich sehe niemand.*
8. *Ich habe nur hundert Euro.*
9. *Sie haben keine davon, nicht wahr?*
10. *Er hat nichts gesagt.*

a. I don't see anyone.
b. I have only a hundred euros.
c. You have only one hour.
d. You're coming, aren't you?
e. You don't have any of it, do you?
f. That's not it.
g. I don't have any time. I have no time.
h. I don't know when.
i. He didn't say (hasn't said) anything.
j. He sees nothing/ doesn't see anything.

ANSWERS
1—f; 2—h; 3—g; 4—j; 5—d; 6—c; 7—a; 8—b; 9—e; 10—i.

E. WORD STUDY

Sympathie (die)	sympathy
illustrieren	illustrate
Gymnastik (die)	gymnastics
Kristall (das)	crystal
frieren	(to) freeze
packen	(to) pack
Gott (der)	God
Brust (die)	breast
Lokomotive (die)	locomotive

LESSON 17

A. IT'S I (ME), YOU, ETC. (SUBJECT PRONOUNS)

Ich bin es.	It's I (me).
Du bist es.	It's you (*fam.*).
Er ist es.	It's him (he).
Sie ist es.	It's her (she).
Wir sind es.	It's us (we).
Ihr seid es.	It's you (*fam.*).
Sie sind es.	It's you (*pol.*).
Sie sind es.	It's them (they).

B. IT'S MINE, YOURS, ETC. (POSSESSIVE PRONOUNS)

Es ist meiner (*meine, meines*).	It's mine.
Es ist deiner (*-e, -es*).	It's yours (*fam.*).
Es ist seiner (*-e, es*).	It's his.

Es ist ihr (-er, -e, es).	It's hers.
Es ist unser (-er, -e, -es).	It's ours.
Es ist euer (eure, eures)	It's yours (fam. pl.).
Es ist Ihr (-er, -e, -es).	It's yours (pol.).
Es ist ihr (-er, -e, es).	It's theirs.

C. HE SPEAKS TO ME, YOU, ETC.

1. Declension of the personal pronoun.

SINGULAR

Nom:	ich	du	er	sie	es
Dat:	mir	dir	ihm	ihr	ihm
Acc:	mich	dich	ihn	sie	sie

PLURAL

Nom:	wir	ihr	Sie (pol.)	sie
Dat:	uns	euch	Ihnen (pol.)	ihnen
Acc:	uns	euch	Sie (pol.)	sie

Note that the polite forms are always the same as the third person plural (they) forms, but they're written with a capital letter.

Examples:

Ich gebe dir ein Buch.	I give you a book.
Er spricht mit mir.	He is speaking to me.
Sie liebt mich.	She loves me.
Du sprichst mit ihm.	You are speaking with him.
Er hat dich gern.	He likes you.
Wir geben ihr Blumen.	We are giving her flowers.

Wir haben mit ihr gesprochen.	We have spoken to her.
Ihr habt es ihm gegeben.	You have given it to him.
Er gibt Ihnen einen Stift.	He is giving you (*pol.*) a pen.
Sie haben ihnen Geld gegeben.	They have given them money.
Ich habe euch etwas gegeben.	I have given you (*fam. pl.*) something.
Er hat uns nicht sprechen lassen.	He did not let us speak.

2. Study these phrases:

Er spricht mit mir.	He speaks to me.
Er spricht mit dir.	He speaks to you (*fam. sing.*).
Er spricht mit ihm.	He speaks to him.
Er spricht mit uns.	He speaks to us.
Er spricht mit euch.	He speaks to you (*fam.*).
Er spricht mit Ihnen.	He speaks to you (*pol.*).
Er spricht mit ihnen.	He speaks to them.

D. I'M TALKING ABOUT YOU, ETC.

Ich spreche über dich.	I am talking about you (*fam.*).
Ich spreche von dir!	I mean you! It's you I'm talking about.
Du sprichst über mich.	You are talking about me.
Er spricht über ihn.	He is talking about him.

Sie spricht über euch.	She is talking about you (*fam. pl.*).
Man spricht über sie.	People are/one is talking about her.
Wir sprechen über Sie.	We are talking about you (*pol.*).
Ihr sprecht über sie.	You are talking about them.
Sie sprechen über uns.	You (they) are talking about us.

E. I'M THINKING OF YOU, ETC.

Ich denke an dich.	I think of you.
Ich denke an ihn.	I think of him.
Du denkst an sie.	You're thinking of her.
Er denkt an uns.	He is thinking of us.
Wir denken an Sie.	We're thinking of you (*pol.*).

F. HE GIVES IT TO ME, YOU, ETC.

Er gibt es mir.	He gives it to me.
Er gibt es dir.	He gives it to you (*fam.*).
Er gibt es ihm.	He gives it to him.
Er gibt es uns.	He gives it to us.
Er gibt es Ihnen.	He gives it to you (*pol.*).
Er gibt es ihnen.	He gives it to them.

Note that the word order is different if only one pronoun is used. The direct object is second unless replaced by a pronoun.

Sie gibt ihm das Buch.	She is giving the book to him.
Sie gibt Michael das Buch.	She is giving the book to Michael.
Sie gibt es Michael.	She is giving it to Michael.

G. GIVE IT TO ME, ETC.

Geben Sie es mir!	Give it to me.
Geben Sie es ihm!	Give it to him.
Geben Sie es uns!	Give it to us.
Geben Sie es ihnen!	Give it to them.
Geben Sie mir das!	Give it to me.
Geben Sie ihm das!	Give it to him.
Geben Sie uns das!	Give it to us.
Geben Sie ihnen das!	Give it to them.

H. MYSELF, YOURSELF, ETC. (REFLEXIVE PRONOUNS)

Ich wasche mich.	I wash myself.
Du wäschst dich.	You wash yourself.
Er wäscht sich.	He washes himself.
Sie wäscht sich.	She washes herself.
Wir waschen uns.	We wash ourselves.
Ihr wascht euch.	You wash yourselves.
Sie waschen sich.	You wash yourselves.
Sie waschen sich.	They wash themselves.

Notice that myself, yourself, etc., is *mich, dich,* etc. Verbs that take *mich, dich,* etc., are called *reflexive* verbs. A number of verbs that do not take myself, yourself, etc., in English, do so in German:

Ich setze mich.	I sit down.
Ich unterhalte mich.	I'm having a conversation.
Ich erinnere mich.	I remember.
Ich freue mich.	I rejoice/I'm glad.
Ich irre mich.	I am mistaken.
Ich langweile mich.	I'm bored.
Ich amüsiere mich.	I'm having a good time/fun.
Ich rasiere mich.	I'm shaving (myself).
Ich ziehe mich an.	I'm getting dressed.

If the pronoun is not the direct object, the dative reflexive has to be used. Dative and accusative reflexive pronouns are identical except in the first and second person singular.

Ich wasche mich.	I wash myself.
Ich wasche mir die Hände.	I wash my (myself the) hands.
Du kämmst dich.	You comb yourself.
Du kämmst dir die Haare.	You comb your (yourself the) hair.

QUIZ 10

1. *Geben Sie ihr das!*   a. I'm glad to see you again.

2. *Er spricht von ihm.*   b. I bought myself a hat.

3. *Sie sprechen von ihnen.* c. My friends and your friends are having fun.

4. *Er gibt es ihnen.*   d. He washes himself.

5. *Meine Freunde und Ihre Freunde amüsieren sich.*   e. I remember her.

6. *Ich unterhalte mich.*

f. He gives it to them.

7. *Ich erinnere mich an sie.*

g. I'm having a conversation.

8. *Ich habe mir einen Hut gekauft.*

h. He's talking about him.

9. *Er wäscht sich.*

i. Give it to her.

10. *Ich freue mich, Sie wiederzusehen.*

j. They're talking about them.

ANSWERS

1—i; 2—h; 3—j; 4—f; 5—c; 6—g; 7—e; 8—b; 9—d; 10—a.

LESSON 18

A. HELLO, HOW ARE YOU?

Guten Tag.
Hello. Good day.

Guten Morgen.
Good morning.

Guten Tag, Herr Müller.
Hello, Mr. Müller. Good day, Mr. Müller.

Wie geht es Ihnen?
How are you? How do you do? ("How is it going with you?")

Danke, gut. Danke, sehr gut.
Very well, thanks.

Nicht besonders.
So, so.

Und Ihnen? (Und wie geht es Ihnen?)
And you? ("And how are you?")

Nicht schlecht.
Not bad.

Nicht schlecht, danke.
Not bad, thanks.

Danke, es geht.
All right, thank you. Fine. ("Thanks, it goes.")

Danke, es geht mir gut.
I am doing fine, thank you. ("Thanks, it goes well with me.")

B. I'D LIKE YOU TO MEET . . .

Ich möchte Sie Frau Müller vorstellen.
I'd like to introduce you to Mrs. Müller.

Gestatten Sie, dass ich Ihnen Frau Müller vorstelle.
Allow me to introduce ("to you") Mrs. Müller.

Gestatten Sie, dass ich Ihnen Herrn Müller vorstelle.
Allow me to introduce ("to you") Mr. Müller.

Sehr erfreut.
Glad to know you. Glad to meet you. ("Very pleased.")

Es freut mich.
Glad to meet you.

Sehr erfreut, Sie kennenzulernen.
Glad to meet you ("to make your acquaintance").

Das ist Herr Müller.
This is Mr. Müller.

Sehr angenehm, Herr Müller.
Glad to know you, Mr. Müller. ("Very pleasant, Mr. Müller.")

Gleichfalls.
Same here. (I'm also glad to meet you.)

C. HOW ARE THINGS?

Guten Tag.	Hello!
Wie geht's?	How are you? How are things? ("How goes it.")
Es geht gut, danke.	Fine, thanks.
Was gibt es Neues?	What's new?
Nicht viel.	Nothing much.
Rufen Sie mich an!	Phone me!
Vergessen Sie es nicht!	Don't forget.
Sicher?	You're sure? ("Surely?")
Sicherlich!	Certainly!
Ganz bestimmt.	Sure! ("Quite certain.")
Bis später.	See you later.
Bis zum nächsten Mal.	Till next time.

Bis gleich.	See you in a moment. See you in a little while.
Bis Montag.	Till Monday. See you Monday.
Bis morgen.	Till tomorrow. See you tomorrow.
Ich sehe Sie in einer Woche.	I'll see you in a week.
Ich sehe Sie in zwei Wochen.	I'll see you in two weeks.
Ich sehe Sie Freitag Abend.	I'll see you Friday evening.
Ich sehe Sie nächsten Donnerstag.	I'll see you next Thursday.
Ich sehe Sie nächsten Donnerstag um acht Uhr abends.	I'll see you next Thursday at eight o'clock (in the evening).
Wir sehen uns heute Abend.	We'll see each other this evening (tonight).
Wir treffen uns heute Abend.	We'll see each other tonight.

QUIZ 11

1. *Wie geht's?*   a. How are you? How do you do?
2. *Bis morgen.*   b. Very well, thanks.
3. *Sehr erfreut.*   c. Not too bad. ("Not bad.")
4. *Was gibt es Neues?*   d. How are you?
5. *Nun, was gibt es Neues?*   e. Until tomorrow.
6. *Es geht mir gut, danke.*   f. I'm happy to know you.
7. *Nichts Neues.*   g. What's new?

8. *Guten Tag.*	h. Well, what's new?
9. *Nicht schlecht.*	i. Good day. Hello.
10. *Wie geht es Ihnen?*	j. Nothing much. ("Nothing new.")
11. *Bis gleich.*	k. Allow me . . .
12. *Rufen Sie mich an!*	l. Phone me!
13. *Bis zum nächsten Mal.*	m. See you Monday. ("Until Monday.")
14. *Gestatten Sie . . .*	n. Until the next time.
15. *Bis Montag.*	o. See you soon. See you in a little while.

ANSWERS

1—a; 2—e; 3—f; 4—g; 5—h; 6—b; 7—j; 8—i;
9—c; 10—d; 11—o; 12—1; 13—n; 14—k; 15—m.

D. WORD STUDY

Maus (die)	mouse	*Freund (der)*	friend
Garten (der)	garden	*Busch (der)*	bush
Mann (der)	man	*Fuchs (der)*	fox
Sohn (der)	son	*Fisch (der)*	fish
jung	young	*bringen*	bring

LESSON 19

A. HAVE YOU TWO MET?

Er ist ein Freund von mir.	He's my friend/a friend of mine.
Sie ist eine Freundin von mir.	She's my friend/a friend of mine.
Kennen Sie meinen Freund?	Do you know my boyfriend?

Kennen Sie meine Freundin?	Do you know my girlfriend?
Nein, ich glaube nicht.	No, I don't think (believe) so.
Ich glaube, Sie kennen sich schon?	I believe you already know each other.
Ja, wir haben uns schon kennengelernt.	Yes, we've already met.
Nein, ich glaube nicht, dass wir uns schon kennen.	No, I don't believe we've met before.
Ich hatte bereits das Vergnügen.	I've already had the pleasure (of meeting him).

B. GLAD TO HAVE MET YOU

Ich freue mich, Ihre Bekanntschaft gemacht zu haben.
Glad to have met you.

Ich hoffe, Sie bald wiederzusehen.
Hope to see you soon.

Ganz meinerseits.
The same here.

Treffen wir uns doch bald wieder.
Let's get together again one of these days!

Abgemacht!
Fine. ("Agreed.")

Haben Sie meine Adresse und Telefonnummer?
Do you have my address and telephone number?

Nein, geben Sie sie mir!
No, let me have them. ("Give them to me.")

Meine Adresse ist Große Friedrichstraße Nr. 21 (einundzwanzig).
My address is 21 Grosse Friedrichstrasse.

Meine Telefonnummer ist sieben acht eins eins zwei.
My telephone number is 78112.

Geben Sie mir bitte auch Ihre Geschäftsadresse!
Give me your business address, too, please.

Ich schreibe es Ihnen auf. Das ist Kurfürstendamm einhundertzwei.
I'll write it for you. It's 102 Kurfürstendamm.

Sie können mich zu Hause vor neun Uhr morgens erreichen.
You can get me at home before nine in the morning.

Andernfalls im Büro ab zehn Uhr.
Otherwise ("in the other case") at the office after 10.00 A.M.

Gut, ich werde es nicht versäumen.
Good, I'll do that. ("Good, I won't fail to do so.")

Auf Wiedersehen und vergessen Sie nicht anzurufen!
Good-bye, and don't forget to call me.

Nein, ich werde es nicht vergessen. Auf baldiges Wiedersehen!

No, I won't forget. I hope to see you soon!

Auf bald.

See you soon.

QUIZ 12

1. *Nein, ich glaube nicht.*
2. *Ja, wir haben uns schon kennengelernt.*
3. *Nein, geben Sie sie mir!*
4. *Geben Sie mir auch ihre Geschäftsadresse!*
5. *Auf bald.*
6. *Gut, ich werde es nicht versäumen.*
7. *Haben Sie meine Adresse und meine Telefonnummer?*
8. *Ich werde es nicht versäumen.*
9. *Ich hoffe, Sie bald wiederzusehen.*
10. *Ich freue mich, Ihre Bekanntschaft gemacht zu haben.*

a. Yes, we've already met.
b. I won't fail to do it.
c. No, I don't think (believe) so.
d. Glad to have met you.
e. I hope to see you soon.
f. Give me your business address too.
g. No, let me have them. ("Give them to me.")
h. Do you have my address and telephone number?
i. Good, I'll do that. ("Good, I won't fail to do so.")
j. See you soon.

ANSWERS
1—c; 2—a; 3—g; 4—f; 5—j; 6—i; 7—h; 8—b; 9—e; 10—d.

REVIEW QUIZ 2

1. *Würden Sie bitte etwas langsamer* _____
   (speak).
       a. *sagen*
       b. *sprechen*
       c. *wiederholen*

2. *Sprechen Sie bitte* _____(slowly).
       a. *schnell*
       b. *weniger*
       c. *langsam*

3. *Ich gebe dem Kind* _____ (the) *Buch.*
       a. *ein*
       b. *das*
       c. *die*

4. *Er gibt seiner Frau* _____ (a) *Brief.*
       a. *einen*
       b. *die*
       c. *der*

5. *Das ist nicht sehr* _____ (far).
       a. *weit*
       b. *hier*
       c. *dort*

6. *Er gibt* _____ (to the) *Kindern Spielzeug* (toys).
       a. *die*
       b. *den*
       c. *ich*

7. *Ich* _____ (am) *in dem Zimmer.*
       a. *bist*
       b. *bin*
       c. *nicht*

8. *Er kommt nicht* _____ (late).
   a. *bin*
   b. *bald*
   c. *spät*

9. *Wo* _____ (are) *Ihre Bücher?*
   a. *seine*
   b. *sind*
   c. *ist*

10. _____ (Bring) *Sie mir ein Glas!*
   a. *Möchte*
   b. *Geben*
   c. *Bringen*

11. *Das ist* _____ (less) *schwer.*
   a. *weniger*
   b. *mehr*
   c. *nichts*

12. *Das ist* _____ (for) *die Kinder.*
   a. *ihr*
   b. *für*
   c. *durch*

13. *Ich* _____ (have) *kein Geld.*
   a. *habe*
   b. *haben*
   c. *nichts*

14. _____ (Have) *Sie Zeit?*
   a. *Hat*
   b. *Hast*
   c. *Haben*

15. *Ich* _____ (understand) *nicht gut Deutsch.*
    a. *verstehe*
    b. *spreche*
    c. *bitte*

16. *Ich* _____ (thank) *Ihnen vielmals.*
    a. *langsam*
    b. *danke*
    c. *verstehe*

17. *Ist er* _____ (here)?
    a. *wo*
    b. *dass*
    c. *hier*

18. *Sind sie* _____ (ready)?
    a. *wahr*
    b. *bereit*
    c. *spät*

19. *Ist das* _____ (true)?
    a. *langsam*
    b. *wahr*
    c. *dort*

20. *Ich verstehe ein* _____ (little).
    a. *nur*
    b. *sehr*
    c. *wenig*

ANSWERS
1—b; 2—c; 3—b; 4—a; 5—a; 6—b; 7—b; 8—c;
9—b; 10—c; 11—a; 12—b; 13—a; 14—c; 15—a;
16—b; 17—c; 18—b; 19—b; 20—c.

C. WORD STUDY

Mond (der)	moon	*Wetter (das)*	weather
Punkt (der)	point	*Erde (die)*	earth
Onkel (der)	uncle	*Familie (die)*	family
Afrika (das)	Africa	*Kohle (die)*	coal
Ball (der)	ball		

SUPPLEMENTAL VOCABULARY 6: TRAVEL AND TOURISM

travel and tourism	*Reise und Tourismus*
tourist	*der Tourist (die Touristen)*
hotel	*das Hotel (die Hotels)*
youth hostel	*die Jugendherberge (die Jugendherbergen)*
reception desk	*die Hotelrezeption (die Hotelrezeptionen)*
to check in	*sich anmelden*
to check out	*sich abmelden*
reservation	*die Reservierung (die Reservierungen)*
passport	*der Pass (die Pässe)*
tour bus	*der Reisebus (die Reisebusse)*
guided tour	*die Führung (die Führungen)*
camera	*der Fotoapparat (die Fotoapparate), die Kamera (die Kameras)*
information center	*die Touristeninformation*
map	*der Stadtplan (die Stadtpläne)*
brochure	*die Broschüre (die Broschüren)*

monument	*das Monument (die Monumente)*
to go sightseeing	*Sehenswürdigkeiten besichtigen*
to take a picture	*ein Foto machen*
Can you take our picture?	*Könnten Sie ein Foto von uns machen?*

LESSON 20

A. NUMBERS[1]

1. One, Two, Three, etc.

eins	one
zwei	two
drei	three
vier	four
fünf	five
sechs	six
sieben	seven
acht	eight
neun	nine
zehn	ten
elf	eleven
zwölf	twelve
dreizehn	thirteen

[1] In Germany, as elsewhere in Europe, numerical punctuation is different from English punctuation. The use of commas and decimal points is reversed, so that 1,000 English style becomes 1.000, and 6.5 is written 6,5 *(sechs* comma *fünf)* in German.

vierzehn	fourteen
fünfzehn	fifteen
sechzehn	sixteen
siebzehn	seventeen
achtzehn	eighteen
neunzehn	nineteen
zwanzig	twenty
einundzwanzig	twenty-one
zweiundzwanzig	twenty-two
dreiundzwanzig	twenty-three
dreißig	thirty
einunddreißig	thirty-one
zweiunddreißig	thirty-two
dreiunddreißig	thirty-three
vierzig	forty
einundvierzig	forty-one
zweiundvierzig	forty-two
dreiundvierzig	forty-three
fünfzig	fifty
einundfünfzig	fifty-one
zweiundfünfzig	fifty-two
dreiundfünfzig	fifty-three
sechzig	sixty
einundsechzig	sixty-one
zweiundsechzig	sixty-two
dreiundsechzig	sixty-three
siebzig	seventy
einundsiebzig	seventy-one
zweiundsiebzig	seventy-two
dreiundsiebzig	seventy-three
achtzig	eighty
einundachtzig	eighty-one

zweiundachtzig	eighty-two
dreiundachtzig	eighty-three
neunzig	ninety
einundneunzig	ninety-one
zweiundneunzig	ninety-two
dreiundneunzig	ninety-three

2. One Hundred, One Thousand, etc.

hundert	one hundred
hunderteins	one hundred (and) one
hundertzwei	one hundred (and) two
hundertdrci	one hundred (and) three
hundertzwanzig	one hundred (and) twenty
hundert-zweiundzwanzig	one hundred (and) twenty-two
hundertdreißig	one hundred (and) thirty
hundertvierzig	one hundred (and) forty
hundertfünfzig	one hundred (and) fifty
hunderteinundsiebzig	one hundred (and) seventy-one
hundertachtundsiebzig	one hundred (and) seventy-eight
hundertachtundneunzig	one hundred (and) ninety-eight
hundertneunund-neunzig	one hundred (and) ninety-nine
zweihundert	two hundred
dreihundert-vierundzwanzig	three hundred (and) twenty-four
achthundertfünfund-siebzig	eight hundred (and) seventy-five
tausend	one thousand
tausendeins	one thousand (and) one
tausendzwei	one thousand (and) two
tausenddrei	one thousand (and) three

zehntausenddreihundert- **fünfundsiebzig**	ten thousand three hundred (and) seventy-five
eine Million	one million
eine Milliarde	one billion
eine Billion	one trillion

B. MORE NUMBERS

The ordinal numbers are declined as adjectives. The endings depend on the case they govern, the number, and the gender. For example:

Ich sehe den dritten Bus. (acc., masc., sing.)	I see the third bus.
Er kauft sich ein drittes Hemd. (acc., neut., sing.)	He buys himself a third shirt.

1.	**erster, erste, erstes**	first
• 2.	**zweiter** (-e, -es)	second
3.	**dritter** (-e, -es)	third
4.	**vierter** (-e, -es)	fourth
5.	**fünfter** (-e, -es)	fifth
6.	**sechster** (-e, -es)	sixth
7.	**siebter** (-e, -es)	seventh
8.	**achter** (-e, -es)	eighth
9.	**neunter** (-e, -es)	ninth
10.	**zehnter** (-e, -es)	tenth

das erste Buch	the first book
die erste Sache	the first thing
der zweite Akt	the second act
die dritte Klasse	the third class
die vierte Etage	the fourth floor

der fünfte Mann	the fifth man
der sechste Tag	the sixth day
die siebte Woche	the seventh week
der achte Monat	the eighth month
das neunte Jahr	the ninth year
der zehnte Brief	the tenth letter
die elfte Person	the eleventh person
das zwölfte Kapitel	the twelfth chapter
der dreizehnte Gast	the thirteenth guest
das vierzehnte Paket	the fourteenth package
die fünfzehnte Tür	the fifteenth door
das sechzehnte Schiff	the sixteenth boat
die siebzehnte Strasse	the seventeenth street
die achtzehnte Ausgabe	the eighteenth edition
das neunzehnte Auto	the nineteenth car
das zwanzigste Haus	the twentieth house
der einundzwanzigste Januar	the twenty-first of January

QUIZ 13

1.	*sechs Kilometer*	a.	third class
2.	*zwei junge Mädchen*	b.	the eighth month
3.	*zwanzig Minuten*	c.	the ninth year
4.	*dritte Klasse*	d.	six kilometers
5.	*der neunzehnter Tag*	e.	two young girls
6.	*die elfte Person*	f.	twenty minutes
7.	*siebzehnter Stock*	g.	the eleventh person
8.	*der achte Monat*	h.	thirteenth of August
9.	*dreizehnter August*	i.	seventeenth floor
10.	*das neunte Jahr*	j.	the nineteenth day

ANSWERS
1—d; 2—e; 3—f; 4—a; 5—j; 6—g; 7—i; 8—b;
9—h; 10—c.

C. ADDITION, SUBTRACTION, MULTIPLICATION, DIVISION

1. Addition

Zwei und eins macht drei.
Two and one are ("makes") three.

Oder or

Zwei und eins sind drei.
Two and one are three.

Zwei und zwei macht vier.
Two and two are ("makes") four.

Oder or

Zwei und zwei sind vier.
Two and two are four.

Vier und drei macht sieben.
Four and three are ("makes") seven.

2. Subtraction

Dreißig weniger achtzehn sind zwölf.
Thirty minus eighteen is twelve.

Hundert weniger vierundzwanzig sind sechsund-siebzig.
One hundred minus twenty-four is seventy-six.

3. Multiplication

Drei mal fünf ist fünfzehn.
Three times five is fifteen.

Vier mal siebzehn ist achtundsechzig.
Four times seventeen is sixty-eight.

4. Division

Zwanzig durch fünf ist vier.
Twenty divided by five is four.

Achtundneunzig durch zwei ist neunundvierzig.
Ninety-eight divided by two is forty-nine.

LESSON 21

A. IT COSTS . . .

Das kostet . . .
This costs . . .

Das kostet fünf Euro.
This costs five euros.

Dieses Buch kostet zehn Euro fünfzig.
This book costs ten and a half euros.

Dieser Hut hat mich vierunddreißig Euro gekostet.
This hat cost me thirty-four euros.

Ich habe hundert Euro für dieses Kleid bezahlt.
I paid a hundred euros for this dress.

Ich habe diesen Wagen für fünfzehntausend Euro gekauft.
I bought this car for fifteen thousand euros.

Das ist drei Euro der Meter.
It's three euros a meter.

Der Preis ist elfhundert Euro.
The price is eleven hundred euros.

Sie kosten fünfundzwanzig Cent.
They cost twenty-five cents.

B. THE TELEPHONE NUMBER IS . . .

Meine Telefonnummer ist 5 43 13 (fünf vier drei eins drei).
My telephone number is 5 43 13.

Versuchen Sie die Nummer 2 21 12 (zwei zwei eins eins zwei).
Try number 2 21 12.

Meine Telefonnummer hat sich geändert: sie ist jetzt 5 33 89 (fünf drei drei acht neun).
My telephone number has been changed: It's now 5 33 89.

Ihre Telefonnummer ist 4 60 91 (vier sechs null neun eins).
Their telephone number is 4 60 91.

C. MY ADDRESS IS . . .

Ich wohne Leipziger Straße Nummer siebzehn.
I live at 17 Leipziger Street.

Er wohnt Schillerstraße 4.
He lives at 4 Schiller Street.

Unsere Adresse ist Breite Straße elf.
Our address is 11 Breite Straße.

Wir wohnen in der Kaiserstraße Nummer zwei-hundertdreiundsechzig.
We live at 263 Kaiserstraße.

Meine Zimmernummer ist zweiundvierzig.
My room number is 42.

D. SOME DATES

Er schrieb das Buch achtzehnhunderteinundneun-zig.
He wrote the book in 1891.

Die Berliner Mauer fiel neunzehnhundertneunund-achtzig.
The Berlin Wall fell in 1989.

Ich war neunzehnhundertneunzig in Frankfurt.
I was in Frankfurt in 1990.

Ich bin 1980 (neunzehnhundertachtzig) geboren.
I was born in 1980.

All das geschah (im Jahre) 2003 (zweitausenddrei)
All this happened in 2003.

Die Olympischen Spiele waren 2004 (zweitausend-vier) in Griechenland.
The Olympics were in Greece in 2004.

Sie sind 1998 (neunzehnhundertachtundneunzig) nach Hamburg gezogen.
They moved to Hamburg in 1998.

QUIZ 14

1. *Das kostet fünf Euro.*
2. *Ihre Telefonnummer ist drei zwei eins eins vier.*
3. *Ich habe diesen gebrauchten Wagen für sechstausend Euro gekauft.*
4. *Ich war neunzehnhunderteinundfünfzig in Berlin.*
5. *Sie kosten fünfzig Cent das Stück.*

a. That costs five euros.
b. I bought this used car for six thousand euros.
c. Their phone number is 3 21 14.
d. They cost fifty cents each (a piece).
e. I was in Berlin in 1951.

ANSWERS
1—a; 2—c; 3—b; 4—e; 5—d.

E. WORD STUDY

mild	mild	*tausend*	thousand
Korn (das)	grain	*hundert*	hundred
reich	rich	*Hitze (die)*	heat
Weg (der)	way	*heiß*	hot
Million (die)	million	*Konzert (das)*	concert

LESSON 22

A. WHAT TIME IS IT?

When you want to specify "seven A.M." or "seven P.M." you say *sieben Uhr morgens* (seven o'clock in the morning) or *sieben Uhr abends* (seven o'clock in the evening).

Official time (formal announcements of meetings,

timetables, etc.) is on a twenty-four hour basis, like our Army time. Thus, in a formal announcement you may see *siebzehn Uhr dreißig* for 5:30 P.M. Ordinarily, however, you say *fünf Uhr dreißig* or *halb sechs nachmittags*—that is, instead of our A.M. and P.M., you add, as necessary, *morgens, nachmittags,* or *abends.*

Wie spät ist es?
What time is it?/How late is it?

Wie viel Uhr ist es, bitte?
What time is it, please?

Es ist ein Uhr.
It's one o'clock.

Es ist zwei Uhr.
It's two o'clock.

Es ist drei Uhr.
It's three o'clock.

Es ist vier Uhr.
It's four o'clock.

Es ist fünf Uhr.
It's five o'clock.

Es ist sechs Uhr.
It's six o'clock.

Es ist sieben Uhr.
It's seven o'clock.

Es ist acht Uhr.
It's eight o'clock.

Es ist neun Uhr.
It's nine o'clock.

Es ist zehn Uhr.
It's ten o'clock.

Es ist elf Uhr.
It's eleven o'clock.

Es ist zwölf Uhr.
It's twelve o'clock.

Es ist Mittag.
It's noon.

Es ist dreizehn Uhr.
It's one P.M. ("thirteen o'clock").

Es ist vierzehn Uhr.
It's two P.M. ("fourteen o'clock").

Es ist fünfzehn Uhr.
It's three P.M. ("fifteen o'clock").

Es ist sechzehn Uhr.
It's four P.M. ("sixteen o'clock").

Es ist siebzehn Uhr.
It's five P.M. ("seventeen o'clock").

Es ist achtzehn Uhr.
It's six P.M. ("eighteen o'clock").

Es ist neunzehn Uhr.
It's seven P.M. ("nineteen o'clock").

Es ist zwanzig Uhr.
It's eight P.M. ("twenty o'clock").

Es ist einundzwanzig Uhr.
It's nine P.M. ("twenty-one o'clock").

Es ist zweiundzwanzig Uhr.
It's ten P.M. ("twenty-two o'clock").

Es ist dreiundzwanzig Uhr.
It's eleven P.M. ("twenty-three o'clock").

Es ist vierundzwanzig Uhr.
It's twelve P.M. ("twenty-four o'clock").

Es ist Mitternacht.
It's midnight.

B. TIME PAST THE HOUR

Die Sekunde   second
Die Minute   minute
Die Stunde   hour

Es ist Viertel nach zwei.
It's a quarter after two.

Es ist zwei Uhr fünfzehn.
It's two-fifteen.

Es ist Viertel vor vier.
It's a quarter to four.

Es ist Viertel nach drei.
It's a quarter after three.

Es ist drei Uhr fünfundvierzig.
It's three forty-five.

Es ist halb drei.
It's half past two.

Es ist zwei Uhr dreißig.
It's two-thirty.

Es ist zwanzig vor fünf.
It's twenty to five.

Es ist neun Uhr fünfunddreißig.
It's nine thirty-five.

Es ist fünf vor zwölf.
It's five to twelve.

Es ist fünf nach zwölf.
It's five past twelve.

Es ist ein Uhr morgens.
It's one o'clock in the morning.

Es ist ungefähr fünf Uhr.
It's about five.

Es ist fast elf Uhr.
It's almost eleven.

Es ist genau acht Uhr.
It's exactly eight o'clock.

Es ist erst halb sieben.
It's only half past six.

Es ist schon nach fünf.
It's already after five.

Er kommt gegen sieben *(Uhr).*
He's coming around seven (o'clock).

C.   WHEN CAN YOU COME, ETC.?

Wann kommen Sie?
When will you come?

Um wie viel Uhr kommen Sie?
What time will you come?

Ich werde um drei Uhr dort sein.
I'll be there (at) three o'clock.

Sie ist um zwanzig vor drei gekommen.
She came at twenty to three.

Er wird um zwei Uhr nachmittags kommen.
He'll come at two P.M.

Wir werden gegen neun Uhr fünfundzwanzig dort sein
We'll be there about nine twenty-five.

Er wird um zehn Uhr dreißig heute Abend zurückkommen.
He'll be back at ten-thirty tonight.

Ich werde Sie dort gegen Viertel nach acht sehen.
I'll see you there about ("toward") eight-fifteen.

Wir treffen uns um sechs.
We'll meet at six.

Ich gehe um vier Uhr aus.
I'm going out at four o'clock.

Kommen Sie zwischen sieben und acht!
Come between seven and eight.

Kommen Sie um zehn Uhr heute Abend!
Come at ten o'clock tonight.

Der Zug fährt um neun Uhr vierzig ab.
The train leaves at nine-forty.

D. IT'S TIME

Es ist Zeit.
It's time.

Es ist Zeit zu gehen.
It's time to leave.

Es ist Zeit, nach Hause zu gehen.
It's time to go home.

Ich habe Zeit.
I have time.

Ich habe genug Zeit.
I have enough time.

Ich habe keine Zeit.
I don't have any time.

Wie lange beabsichtigen Sie, hier zu bleiben?
How long do you intend to stay here?

Seit wann sind Sie hier?
How long have you been here?

Er verliert keine Zeit.
He's wasting no time.

Es wird Zeit.
It's about time.

Geben Sie ihm Zeit dafür.
Give him time for it!

Gib mir Zeit, mich anzuziehen!
Just give me enough time to get dressed!

Er kommt von Zeit zu Zeit.
He comes from time to time.

QUIZ 15

1. *Es ist halb drei.*
2. *Es ist Viertel nach zwei.*
3. *Es ist neun Uhr fünfunddreißig.*
4. *Kommen Sie zwischen sieben und acht!*
5. *Ich werde Sie dort gegen Viertel nach acht sehen.*
6. *Der Zug kommt um sieben Uhr dreiundzwanzig an.*
7. *Kommen Sie heute Abend gegen zehn Uhr!*
8. *Es ist ein Uhr morgens.*
9. *Wir werden gegen neun Uhr fünfundzwanzig dort sein.*
10. *Es ist Zeit zu gehen.*

a. I'll see you there about eight-fifteen.
b. The train arrives at seven twenty-three.
c. Come between seven and eight.
d. Come around ten o'clock tonight.
e. It's one o'clock in the morning.
f. It's time to leave.
g. We'll be there about nine twenty-five.
h. It's two-fifteen. (It's a quarter after two.)
i. It's half past two. (It's two-thirty.)
j. It's nine thirty-five.

ANSWERS
1—i; 2—h; 3—j; 4—c; 5—a; 6—b; 7—d; 8—e;
9—g; 10—f.

E. WORD STUDY

hoffen	(to) hope	*Krone (die)*	crown
Distanz (die)	distance	*Pflanze (die)*	plant
Seite (die)	side	*Kredit (der)*	credit
Welt (die)	world	*wandern*	(to) wander,
Jahr (das)	year		hike

SUPPLEMENTAL VOCABULARY 7: IN THE OFFICE

in the office	*im Büro*
office	*das Büro (die Büros)*
desk	*der Schreibtisch (die Schreibtische)*
computer	*der Computer (die Computer)*
telephone	*das Telefon (die Telefone)*
fax machine	*die Faxmaschine (die Faxmaschinen)*

book shelf	*das Bücherregal (die Bücherregale)*
file cabinet	*der Aktenschrank (die Aktenschränke)*
file	*die Akte (die Akten)*
boss	*der Chef (die Chefs)*
colleague	*der Kollege (die Kollegen)*
employee	*der/die Angestellte (die Angestellten)*
staff	*die Belegschaft (-)*
company	*die Firma (die Firmen)*
business	*das Geschäft (die Geschäfte)*
factory	*die Fabrik (die Fabriken), das Werk (die Werke)*
meeting room	*das Konferenzzimmer (die Konferenzzimmer)*
meeting	*das Meeting (die Meetings), die Sitzung (die Sitzungen)*
appointment	*der Termin (die Termine)*
salary	*das Gehalt (die Gehälter)*
job	*der Arbeitsplatz (die Arbeitsplätze)*
busy	*beschäftigt*
to work	*arbeiten*
to earn	*verdienen*

LESSON 23

A. Morning, Noon, and Night

der Morgen	morning
der Mittag	noon

der Nachmittag	afternoon
der Abend	evening
die Nacht	night

der Tag	the day
die Woche	the week
vierzehn Tage	two weeks ("fourteen days")
der Monat	the month
das Jahr	the year
gestern	yesterday
heute	today
morgen	tomorrow

vorgestern	the day before yesterday
übermorgen	the day after tomorrow
vor Langem	a long time ago
vor Kurzem	a while ago
jetzt	now
einen Augenblick, bitte	in a moment, please
lange her	a long time ago
heute Morgen	this morning
gestern Morgen	yesterday morning
morgen früh	tomorrow morning
heute Nachmittag	this afternoon
gestern Nachmittag	yesterday afternoon
morgen Nachmittag	tomorrow afternoon

heute Abend	this evening
gestern Abend	last evening
morgen Abend	tomorrow evening

heute Nacht	tonight
gestern Nacht	last night
morgen Nacht	tomorrow night

B. THIS WEEK, NEXT MONTH, ONE OF THESE DAYS

diese Woche
this week

{ **letzte Woche**
{ **vorige Woche**
  last week

nächste Woche
next week

in zwei Wochen
in two weeks

vor zwei Wochen
two weeks ago

dieser Monat
this month

der vorige Monat
last month

der nächste Monat
next month

in zwei Monaten
in two months

vor zwei Monaten
two months ago

dieses Jahr
this year

voriges Jahr
last year

nächstes Jahr
next year

in zwei Jahren
in two years

vor zwei Jahren
two years ago

am Morgen
in the morning

am Abend
in the evening

gegen Mittag
toward noon

nach dem Abendessen
after dinner

am Ende der Woche
at the end of the week

vor einer Stunde
an hour ago

in einer Viertelstunde
in a quarter of an hour

eines Tages
one of these days

alle Tage
every day

den ganzen Tag
all day (long)

die ganze Nacht
all night (long)

Er arbeitet von morgens bis abends.
He works from morning to night.

Der Wievielte ist heute?
What's today's date?

C. EXPRESSIONS OF PAST, PRESENT, AND FUTURE

Vergangenheit	*Gegenwart*	*Zukunft*
Past	Present	Future
Vor einem Augenblick	*In diesem Augenblick*	*im nächsten Augenblick*
a moment ago	now	in a moment
gestern Morgen	*heute Morgen*	*morgen früh*
yesterday morning	this morning	tomorrow morning
gestern Nachmittag	*heute Nachmittag*	*morgen Nachmittag*
yesterday afternoon	this afternoon	tomorrow afternoon
gestern Abend	*heute Abend*	*morgen Abend*
last evening, last night	this evening, tonight	tomorrow evening, tomorrow night
vorige Woche	*diese Woche*	*nächste Woche*
last week	this week	next week

vorigen[1] Monat	diesen Monat	nächsten Monat
last month	this month	next month
voriges[1] Jahr	dieses Jahr	nächstes Jahr
last year	this year	next year
		nächstes Wochenende
		next weekend

LESSON 24

A. Days of the Week

Montag	Monday
Dienstag	Tuesday
Mittwoch	Wednesday
Donnerstag	Thursday
Freitag	Friday
Samstag or Sonnabend	Saturday
Sonntag	Sunday

B. What Day Is Today?

The following expressions are all used for "What's the date today?"

Der Wievielte ist heute?
What is today's date?
"The how many is it?"

---

[1] *Letze, letzter, letztes* also may be used to say "last."

Welches Datum ist heute?
"What date is today?"

Den Wievielten haben wir heute?
"The how many do we have today?"

Der Wievielte ist Sonntag?
What's the date Sunday?

Heute ist der Zehnte.
Today's the tenth.

Heute haben wir den Zwanzigsten.
Today is ("we have") the twentieth.

Welchen Tag haben wir heute?
What day is it today?

Ist heute Dienstag oder Mittwoch?
Is today Tuesday or Wednesday?

Heute ist Mittwoch.
Today is Wednesday.

Kommen Sie nächsten Samstag zurück!
Come back next Saturday.

Er fährt nächsten Sonntag fort.
He's leaving next Sunday.

Er ist letzten Montag angekommen.
He arrived last Monday.

Er kommt nächsten Donnerstag an.
He's arriving next Thursday.

QUIZ 16

1. *vorgestern*	a. afternoon
2. *heute*	b. day before yesterday
3. *Nachmittag*	c. today
4. *vor Kurzem*	d. day after tomorrow
5. *morgen Nachmittag*	e. a while ago
6. *heute Nachmittag*	f. tomorrow afternoon
7. *übermorgen*	g. this evening
8. *Er verliert Zeit.*	h. He's wasting time.
9. *heute Nacht*	i. this afternoon
10. *Seit wann sind Sie hier?*	j. How long have you been here?
11. *nächste Woche*	k. in two months, the month after next
12. *vorige Woche*	l. two weeks ago, the week before last
13. *vor zwei Wochen*	m. next week
14. *in zwei Monaten*	n. two years ago, the year before last
15. *vor zwei Jahren*	o. last week
16. *Es ist Zeit.*	p. It's time to go home.
17. *Ich habe Zeit.*	q. tomorrow night
18. *Es ist Zeit, nach Hause zu gehen.*	r. tonight
19. *morgen Abend*	s. It's time.
20. *heute Abend*	t. I have time.

ANSWERS

1—b; 2—c; 3—a; 4—e; 5—f; 6—i; 7—d; 8—h; 9—r; 10—j; 11—m; 12—o; 13—l; 14—k; 15—n; 16—s; 17—t; 18—p; 19—q; 20—g.

C. Months and Dates

Januar	January
Februar	February
März	March
April	April
Mai	May
Juni	June
Juli	July
August	August
September	September
Oktober	October
November	November
Dezember	December

Heute ist der erste Juni.
Today is the first of June.

Ich wurde am zwölften April geboren.
I was born (on) April 12.

Mein Geburtstag ist am zweiten Februar.
My birthday is (on) February 2.

Ich komme am vierzehnten Juli.
I'll come (on) the fourteenth of July.

Die Schule beginnt am zwanzigsten September.
School begins (on) the twentieth of September.

Ich bin am zweiundzwanzigsten März zurück.
I'll be back (on) March 22.

Der erste Januar ist ein Feiertag.
January 1 is a holiday.

Er fährt am sechsten Juli ab.
He's leaving (on) July 6.

Der Brief ist vom neunten Juni.
The letter is dated June 9.

Wir besuchen Sie am elften Mai.
We'll come to see you (on) May 11.

D. SEASONS

der Frühling	spring
der Sommer	summer
der Herbst	autumn
der Winter	winter

im Winter	in winter
im Sommer	in summer
im Herbst	in autumn, in the fall
im Frühling	in spring

Ich liebe den Sommer.
I love summer.

Ich ziehe den Frühling vor.
I prefer the spring.

QUIZ 17

1. *Welches Datum ist heute?*
2. *Eines Tages werden wir zusammenkommen.*
3. *Den ganzen Tag muss ich arbeiten.*
4. *Im Sommer gehen wir schwimmen.*

5. *In einer Viertelstunde.*
6. *Er kommt nächsten Montag an.*
7. *Heute ist Montag.*
8. *Kommen Sie nächsten Samstag!*
9. *Der Winter ist schon hier.*
10. *Sonntage sind immer schön.*
11. *Wir haben heute den Zwanzigsten.*
12. *Der Wievielte ist Dienstag?*
13. *Ich komme am vierzehnten Juli.*
14. *Heute ist der erste Juni.*
15. *Der Brief ist vom sechsten Juni.*

a. Sundays arc always nice.
b. in a quarter of an hour
c. One day we'll get together.
d. I have to work all day.
e. What's today's date?
f. In the summer we go swimming.
g. Winter is already here.
h. What's the date Tuesday?
i. Today's the twentieth.
j. Today's Monday.
k. Come next Saturday.
l. He'll arrive next Monday.
m. The letter is dated June 6.
n. I'll come (on) the fourteenth of July.
o. Today is the first of June.

ANSWERS
1—e; 2—c; 3—d; 4—f; 5—b; 6—l; 7—j; 8—k;
9—g; 10—a; 11—i; 12—h; 13—n; 14—o; 15—m.

E. AM ZEITUNGSSTAND[1]
(AT THE NEWSSTAND)

1. *Kunde: Guten Morgen! Geben Sie mir bitte* Die
Welt *und auch die Illustrierte* Der Stern. *Könnten
Sie mir einen Hunderteuroschein wechseln? Ich
habe leider kein Kleingeld dabei.*
Customer: Good morning. Please give me *Die
Welt* and also the magazine *Der Stern*. Could
you change a hundred-euro bill? I'm sorry, I
have no change on me.

2. *Verkäuferin: Ich kenne Sie doch, Herr Mergl.
Die drei Euro fünfzig bleiben Sie mir schuldig.
Sie können morgen zahlen.*
Saleslady: I know you, Mr. Mergl. You'll owe
me the three and a half euros. You can pay
tomorrow.

3. *Kunde: Ich danke Ihnen recht schön. Übrigens, gehen die Busse heute oder muss ich
wieder mit der U-bahn fahren?*
Customer: Thank you very much. By the way,
are the busses running today or do I have to take
the subway again?

4. *Verkäuferin: Während der letzten Viertelstunde
sind schon drei Busse vorbeigefahren. Sie waren
voll. Heute wäre es besser mit der Untergrundbahn zu fahren.*
Saleslady: During the last fifteen minutes three
busses went by. They were full. It would be better to go by subway today.

5. *Kunde: Also, dann muss ich mich beeilen. Es
ist schon Viertel nach acht, und ich muss Punkt
neun Uhr im Büro sein. Auf Wiedersehen, bis
morgen!*

---

[1] Another word for "newsstand" is *Zeitungskiosk*.

Customer: Well, then, I really have to hurry up. It's already a quarter past eight, and I have to be at the office at nine on the dot. So long, see you tomorrow. (Until tomorrow.)

6. *Verkäuferin: Auf Wiedersehen, Herr Mergl!*
   Saleslady: Good-bye, Mr. Mergl.

NOTES

1. *der Kunde*—the customer
2. *die Verkäuferin*—the saleslady
3. *die Illustrierte*—the magazine
4. *Könnten Sie . . . ?*—Could you . . . ? Would you be able to . . . ?
5. *wechseln*—to (ex)change
6. *schuldig sein*—to owe (from *schulden,* dative verb, "to owe"): *Er schuldet mir, ihm (ihr, uns, ihnen) zwanzig Euro.* He owes me (him, her, us, them) twenty euros.
7. *apropos*—by the way
8. *die U-Bahn* (Untergrundbahn)—the subway
9. *vorbeifahren*—to drive by: *Der Bus ist einfach vorbeigefahren, ohne anzuhalten.* The bus simply drove past without stopping.
10. *sich beeilen*—to hurry: *ich beeile mich, du beeilst dich, er, sie, es beeilt sich, wir beeilen uns, ihr beeilt euch, sie (Sie) beeilen sich*
11. *also*—well then
12. *das Büro*—the office
13. *Es wäre* (subjunctive form of *sein*)—it would be
14. *Er geht ins Büro*—He's going to the office (acc.).
15. *Er arbeitet im Büro.*—He's working in the office (dat.).

LESSON 25

A. To Go, to Walk: *Gehen*

1. I go

ich gehe	I go, I'm going
du gehst	you go
er geht (*sie, es*)	he goes
wir gehen	we go
ihr geht	you go
Sie gehen	you go
sie gehen	they go

2. I don't go

ich gehe nicht	I don't go; I'm not going
du gehst nicht	you don't go
er geht nicht	he doesn't go
wir gehen nicht	we don't go
ihr geht nicht	you don't go
Sie gehen nicht	you don't go
sie gehen nicht	they don't go

3. Some common expressions with *gehen:*

Geh!
Go (*fam.*)!

Gehen Sie!
Go!

Gehen Sie langsam!
Go slowly.

Gehen Sie weiter!
Go on! Keep going!

Gehen Sie es suchen!
Go look for it! Go get it!

Wo gehen Sie hin?
Where are you going?

Gehen Sie nicht dorthin!
Don't go there.

Gehen Sie nicht dort hinüber!
Don't go over there.

Wir müssen dorthin gehen.
We have to go there. (We must go there.)

Ich gehe zum Bannhof.
I'm going to the station.

Ich gehe zur Bank.
I'm going to the bank.

Ich gehe ins Theater.
I'm going to the theater.

Er geht aufs Land.
He's going to the countryside.

Ich gehe Hans besuchen.
I'm going to Hans's place (home). ("I'm going to visit Hans.")

Sie geht nachmittags einkaufen.
She is going shopping in the afternoon.

Wie geht es Ihnen?
How are you? ("How goes it with you?")

Es geht mir gut.
Well, thanks. Fine, thanks.

Wie geht's?
How are you? How are things?

Gut. Danke.
Fine. All right. O.K.

B. To Go, to Ride, to Drive: *Fahren*

When speaking of a trip, you may also use the verb
fahren.

1. I go

ich fahre	I go
du fährst	you go
er fährt	he goes
wir fahren	we go
ihr fahrt	you go
Sie fahren	you go
sie fahren	they go

2. Study these examples:

Wo fahren wir hin?
Where are we going?

Wohin fährst du?
Where are you going?

Wohin fährt er?
Where is he going?

Sie fährt nach Berlin.
She is going to Berlin.

Wohin fahren wir?
Where are we going?

Wohin fahren Sie?
Where are you going?

Fahrt ihr nach Berlin?
Are you going to Berlin?

Nein, wir fahren nach Frankfurt.
No, we are going to Frankfurt.

Wohin fahren sie?
Where are they going?

Wie fährst du in die Stadt?
How are you (going) getting to the city?

Ich fahre mit der Bahn.
I'm going by train.

C. A Few Action Phrases

Achtung!
Watch out! Pay
   attention!

Langsamer fahren!
Drive more slowly!

Vorsicht!
Be careful! Watch out!

Früher.
Sooner.

Schnell.
Fast.

Später.
Later.

Schneller.
Faster.

Ich komme.
I'm coming.

Sprechen Sie nicht so schnell!
Don't speak so fast!

Bis später.
See you later.

Nicht zu schnell.
Not too fast.

Beeilen Sie sich!
Hurry up!

Langsamer.
More slowly.

Beeilen Sie sich nicht!
Don't hurry up.

Ich habe es eilig.
I'm in a hurry.

Ich rufe ihn sofort an.
I'll phone/call him right away.

Ich habe es nicht eilig.
I'm not in a hurry

Bald.
Soon.

Lassen Sie sich Zeit.
Take your time.

Es wird bald regnen.
It's going to rain soon.

Einen Moment!
Just a minute!

Ich komme sofort.
I'm coming right away.

Sofort.
Right away.

D. WORD STUDY

Feuer (das)   fire
Grammatik (die)   grammar
Suppe (die)   soup

füllen	(to) fill
Argument (das)	argument
Monument (das)	monument
flach	flat
dick	thick
Stein (der)	stone

Supplemental Vocabulary 8: At School

at school	*in der Schule*
school	*die Schule (die Schulen)*
university	*die Universität (die Universitäten)*
classroom	*das Klassenzimmer (die Klassenzimmer)*
course	*der Kurs (die Kurse)*
teacher (male)	*der Lehrer (die Lehrer)*
teacher (female)	*die Lehrerin (die Lehrerinnen)*
professor (male)	*der Professor (die Professoren)*
professor (female)	*die Professorin (die Professorinnen)*
(school) student (male)	*der Schüler (die Schüler)*
(school) student (female)	*die Schülerin (die Schülerinnen)*
(college) student (male)	*der Student (die Studenten)*
(college) student (female)	*die Studentin (die Studentinnen)*
subject	*das Fach (die Fächer)*
notebook	*das Schulheft (die Schulhefte) das Heft (die Hefte)*

textbook	*das Fachbuch (die Fachbücher)*
math	*die Mathematik*
history	*die Geschichte*
chemistry	*die Chemie*
biology	*die Biologie*
literature	*die Literatur*
language	*die Sprache (die Sprachen), die Sprachwissenschaft (-en)*
art	*die Kunst*
music	*die Musik*
gym	*der Sport*
recess (from school)	*die Ferien*
break, recess (from college)	*die Semesterferien*
test	*die Klassenarbeit*
test, exam (in college)	*die Klausur*
grade	*die Zensur (die Zensuren)*
report card	*das Zeugnis (die Zeugnisse)*
diploma	*das Diplom (die Diplome)*
degree	*der Abschluss (die Abschlüsse)*
difficult/easy	*schwierig/leicht*
to study	*studieren*
to learn	*lernen*
to pass	*bestehen*
to fail	*nicht bestehen*

LESSON 26

A. ONE, THEY, PEOPLE

man
one; they; people; we

Man sagt, dass . . .
They say that . . . It's said that . . . People say that . . .

Man hat mir gesagt, dass . . .
I've been told that . . .

Man sagt es.
They say it.

Man sagt, dass es wahr ist.
They say it's true.

Man hat es mir gesagt.
I've been told that.

Man weiß es nicht.
Nobody knows.

Man spricht hier Deutsch.
German is spoken here.

Hier spricht man Englisch.
English is spoken here.

Man spricht hier Spanisch.
We speak Spanish here.

Spricht man Englisch hier?
Do they speak English here?

Wie sagt man das auf Deutsch?
How do you say that in German?

Wie sagt man "Good morning" auf Deutsch?
How do you say "Good morning" in German?

Wie schreibt man dieses Wort auf Deutsch?
How is this word written (spelled) in German?

Man schließt um acht.
They're closing at eight.

Was spielt man heute Abend im Theater?
What's playing at the theater tonight?

Notice that *man* can often be translated by the English passive:

Man sagt, dass . . .
It's said that . . .

Man hat mir gesagt, dass . . .
I've been told that . . .

Wie schreibt man dieses Wort?
How is this word written?
(How does one write this word?)

QUIZ 18

1. *Ich habe es eilig.*   a. Right away.
2. *Ich komme sofort.*   b. In a minute.
3. *Einen Moment.*   c. I'm in a hurry.
4. *Sofort.*   d. I'm coming right away.

5. *Lassen Sie sich Zeit.*   e. Take your time.
6. *Man hat mir gesagt.*   f. Nobody knows.
7. *Man weiß es nicht.*   g. I've been told.
8. *Hier spricht man Englisch.*   h. How do you say that in German?
9. *Wie sagt man das auf Deutsch?*   i. English spoken here.

ANSWERS
1—c; 2—d; 3—b; 4—a; 5—e; 6—g; 7—f; 8—i; 9—h.

B. WORD STUDY

Logik (die)	logic	*Szene (die)*	scene
tanzen	(to) dance	*frei*	free
privat	private	*modern*	modern
Preis (der)	price	*Name (der)*	name

C. A LITTLE AND A LOT

wenig
a little

viel oder wenig
a lot or a little

ein wenig
a little

sehr wenig
very little

ein klein wenig
a very little

ein ganz klein wenig
a very little bit

allmählich
little by little

Das ist zu wenig.
It's not enough.

noch ein wenig
a little bit more

Er spricht wenig.
He doesn't talk much.

Wollen Sie viel oder wenig davon?
Do you want a lot of it or a little?

Bleiben wir noch ein wenig hier!
Let's stay here a little longer.

Geben Sie mir ein wenig davon!
Give me a little of it.

Geben Sie mir ein wenig Wasser!
Give me a little water.

Ich spreche sehr wenig Deutsch.
I speak very little German.

viel
much, a lot, very

Ich habe nicht viel Geld.
I haven't much money.

Ich habe nicht viel Zeit.
I haven't much time.

Ich mag ihn sehr.
I like him a lot.

Ich habe viel zu tun.
I have a lot to do.

D. TOO MUCH

zu viel
too, too much

Das ist zu viel.
It's too much.

Das ist nicht zu viel.
That is not too much.

zu wenig
too little

zu heiß
too hot

zu kalt
too cold

zu viel Wasser
too much water

E. MORE OR LESS

mehr oder weniger
more or less

höchstens
at the most

wenigstens
at the least

immer mehr
more and more

immer weniger
less and less

sechs mal mehr
six times more

Es gibt nichts mehr davon.
There's no more of it.

Es ist mehr als das.
It's more than that.

Das ist das am meisten gelesene Buch, das ich kenne.
This is the most popular book I know.
("This is the most read book I know.")

F. ENOUGH AND SOME MORE

genug
enough

Ist es genug?
Is it enough?

Das ist genug.
It's enough.

Das ist nicht genug.
That is not enough.

Das ist mehr als genug.
It's more than enough.

Das ist groß genug.
That's large enough.
That's rather large.

gut genug
fairly well, rather well

Haben Sie genug Geld?
Do you have enough money?

Sagen Sie es noch einmal!
Say it again!

Wiederholen Sie, bitte.
Please repeat it.

noch
some more

Noch mehr? Noch etwas?
Some more?

noch ein wenig
a little more, another little bit

noch mehr Brot
some more bread

noch ein Glas Wasser
another glass of water

noch etwas Fleisch
some more meat

noch viel mehr
much more, lots more

Kommen Sie wieder.
Come again.

LESSON 27

A. GOOD

Gut!
Good!

Das ist gut.
That's good.

Das ist sehr gut.
That's very good. It's very good.

Das ist nicht gut.
That's not good. It's not good.

Das ist nett.
That's nice. That's lovely.

Das ist großartig!
That's great! That's neat!

Das ist fantastisch!
That's fantastic!

Das ist ausgezeichnet.
That's excellent.

Das ist hervorragend!
That's outstanding!

Das ist bewundernswert.
That's admirable. It's wonderful.

Das ist wunderbar. Das ist wundervoll.
That's wonderful.

Das ist perfekt.
That's perfect.

Der Wein ist gut.
This wine is good.

Das Fleisch ist gut.
This meat is good.

Sie sind gut.
They're good.

Guten Tag!
Hello! Good afternoon. Good day.

Guten Abend!
Good evening!

Gute Nacht!
Good night!

B. GOOD, WELL

gut
good, well

nicht so gut
not too good

Sehr gut, mein Herr.
Very well, sir.

Ist es gut?
Is it good?

Du hast das gut gemacht.
You did that well.

Alles geht gut.
Everything's going well. Everything's all right.

Es geht viel besser.
It's going much better.

Ich fühle mich nicht wohl.
I don't feel well.

Gute Besserung!
Get well soon!

Es passt sehr gut.
It fits well.

Das passt mir gut.
That suits me fine.

C. BEAUTIFUL, NICE, FINE

schön
beautiful

Es ist sehr schön.
It's very beautiful.

Das ist schön.
That's beautiful.

nicht sehr schön
not very beautiful (nice)

schönes Wetter
nice weather

ein schönes Land
a beautiful country

ein schöner Tag
a nice day

Es ist schön draußen.
It's nice out.

die schönen Künste
the fine arts

schön und gut
well and good

QUIZ 19

1. *Alles geht gut.*
2. *Das ist sehr gut.*
3. *Ist es gut?*
4. *Es ist sehr schön.*
5. *Haben Sie genug davon?*
6. *Sagen Sie es noch einmal.*
7. *Wiederholen Sie, bitte!*

8. *Kommen Sie wieder!*
9. *Das ist großartig!*
10. *schön und gut*

a. That's very good.
b. Do you have enough of it?
c. Say it again.
d. well and good
e. That's great!
f. It's very beautiful.
g. Everything is going well. Everything's all right.
h. Is it good?
i. Please repeat it.
j. Come again.

ANSWERS
1—g; 2—a; 3—h; 4—f; 5—b; 6—c; 7—i; 8—j;
9—e; 10—d.

D. WORD STUDY

nervös	nervous
Episode (die)	episode
Summe (die)	sum
meinen	(to) mean, think (believe)
natürlich	natural
Nagel (der)	nail
elektrisch	electrical
Braut (die)	bride
Zeremonie (die)	ceremony

SUPPLEMENTAL VOCABULARY 9:
SPORTS AND RECREATION

sports and recreation	*Sport und Erholung*
soccer	*der Fußball*

basketball	*der Basketball*
baseball	*der Baseball*
American football	*der amerikanische*
	Fußball
hockey	*das Hockey*
tennis	*das Tennis*
skiing	*das Skifahren*
cross country skiing	*das Skilaufen*
mountain climbing	*das Bergsteigen*
game	*das Spiel (die Spiele)*
team	*die Mannschaft (die*
	Mannschaften)
stadium	*das Stadion (die Stadien)*
coach	*der Trainer (die Trainer)*
player	*der Spieler (die Spieler)*
champion	*der Champion (die*
	Champions)
ball	*der Ball (die Bälle)*
(to go) hiking	*wandern*
(to go) camping	*zelten (gehen)*
to play (a sport)	*Sport treiben*
to play (a game)	*ein Spiel austragen*
to win	*gewinnen*
to lose	*verlieren*
to draw/tie	*unentschieden spielen*
cards	*die Karten*
pool/billiards	*das Billiard*

LESSON 28

A. LIKE, AS

wie
like, as

wie ich
like me

wie das
like this (that)

wie die anderen
like the others

wie dieses
like this

nicht so wie das
not like this (that)

wie Sie wünschen
as you wish

Wie früh es ist!
It's so early.

Wie spät es ist!
It's so late.

Wie teuer das ist!
This is so expensive!

B. ALL, EACH, EVERY, ETC.

all, alle, alles
all

jeder, jede, jedes
every, each

jeder Mensch
every human being

jeder Mann
every man, each man

jede Frau
every woman, each woman

jedes Kind
every child, each child

alle Menschen
all human beings

alle Männer
all men

alle Frauen
all women

jeder, jederman
everybody, everyone

jeden Tag
every day

Alles ist hier.
Everything's here.

den ganzen Tag
all day long ("the whole day")

Alles ist fertig.
Everything's ready/done.

Alle sind fertig.
All are ready.

Nehmen Sie sie alle!
Take all of them!

Wir sind alle da.
We're all here.

Das ist alles.
That's all. That's the whole lot. That'll do.

Ist das alles?
Is that all? Is that everything? Is that the whole lot?

alle
everybody (all of them)

Jeder weiß es.
Everybody knows it.

ganz
entire, entirely; complete, completely; whole, wholly

Er hat die ganze Torte aufgegessen.
He ate (up) the whole cake.

ganz schlecht
completely bad, very bad

Ganz und gar nicht.
Not at all.

Überhaupt nicht.
Not at all.

C. SOME, ANY, NOTHING, ETC.
   (COMBINATIONS WITH *DA*—)

1. *Da*- is often combined with a preposition to form
   the following expressions:

davon:	of it, of that
darin:	in it, in them
daran:	at it, at them
darüber:	about/over it, about/over them
darunter:	among/under it, among/under them
dadurch:	through it, through them
dazu:	to it, to them
dafür:	for it, for them
daraus:	from/out of it, from/out of them

**Hier ist die Tafel Schokolade. Geben Sie jedem
Kind ein Stück davon.**
Here is the chocolate bar. Give each child a piece of it.

Sie gab mir eine Pfeife. Was soll ich damit tun?
She gave me a pipe. What should I do with it?

**Bitte nehmen Sie dieses Buch! Wir haben schon
darüber gesprochen.**
Please take this book. We have already spoken about it.

Ich habe genug davon.
I have enough of it. (That's sufficient.)

Geben Sie uns etwas davon!
Give us some of it!

Geben Sie ihnen nichts mehr davon.
Don't give them any more of it.

Ich habe mit ihr darüber gesprochen.
I spoke to her about it.

Ich habe mit ihr über Politik und Sport gesprochen.
I spoke with her about politics and sports.

Kommt er aus Deutschland?
Does he come from Germany?
Is he from Germany?

Was halten Sie davon?
What do you think of (about) it?

Was halten Sie von ihm (*ihr*)**?**
What do you think of him (her)?

2. *etwas*
some, any

Hat er (etwas) Geld?
Does he have any money?

Ja, er hat etwas.
Yes, he has some.

Haben Sie (etwas) Geld?
Do you have any money?

Nein, ich habe keins.
No, I don't have any.

Ist noch etwas von dem guten Wein übrig?
Is there (still) anything left of the good wine?

Nein, es ist nichts mehr davon übrig.
No, there is nothing (no more) left of it.

Hier ist etwas Geld.
Here's some money.

Geben Sie Hans etwas davon!
Give some of it to Hans.

Geben Sie mir etwas!
Give me something!

Geben Sie ihm etwas!
Give him something!

Ich habe ihm etwas davon gegeben.
I gave him some of it.

Geben Sie ihr nichts!
Don't give her anything! (Give her nothing!)

Es gibt etwas.
There is something.

Gibt es noch etwas davon?
Is (are) there any more of it?

D. PREPOSITIONAL COMPOUNDS REFERRING TO PEOPLE

When the prepositional phrase refers to a person, the *da*-compounds are not used. Instead, the preposition and a pronoun are used. The preposition governs the case.

EXAMPLES

Er hält nicht viel von meinem Bruder.
He doesn't think much of my brother.

Er hält nicht viel von ihm.
He doesn't think much of him.

NOTE

Halten von is an expression meaning "to consider someone to be." The preposition *von* governs the dative case.

Er denkt immer an seinen Vater.
He always thinks of his father.

Er denkt immer an ihn.
He always thinks of him.

NOTE

The preposition *an* is a two-way preposition governing the accusative or dative case. Here it is used in the accusative case because the expression *denken an* governs the accusative case.

E. IDIOMATIC EXPRESSIONS WITH PREPOSITIONS

Below is a list of useful idiomatic expressions. The case each governs is in parentheses:

AN
sich erinnern an (acc.)　　to remember
glauben an (acc.)　　to believe in
leiden an (dat.)　　to suffer from

schreiben an (acc.)	to write to
sich wenden an (acc.)	to turn to
teilnehmen an (dat.)	to take part in

AUF

achten auf (acc.)	to pay attention to
bestehen auf (acc.)	to insist on
böse sein auf (acc.)	to be angry with
sich freuen auf (acc.)	to look forward to
hoffen auf (acc.)	to hope for
stolz sein auf (acc.)	to be proud of
sich verlassen auf (acc.)	to rely on
warten auf (acc.)	to wait for

ÜBER

denken über (acc.)	to think about
sich freuen über (acc.)	to be happy about
sich beschweren über (acc.)	to complain about
lachen über (acc.)	to laugh about
sich unterhalten über (acc.)	to converse about (something)

OTHER EXPRESSIONS

bitten um (acc.)	to ask for
sich bewerben um (acc.)	to apply for
sich kümmern um (acc.)	to take care of
sich interessieren für (acc.)	to be interested in
Angst haben vor (dat.)	to be afraid of
warnen vor (dat.)	to warn against
gehen in (acc.)	to go (in)to
bleiben in (dat.)	to remain

QUIZ 20

1. *Gibt es noch etwas davon?*

    a. It's very beautiful.

2. *Es gibt etwas.*   b. Nice weather today.

3. *Haben Sie etwas Geld?*   c. A nice day is finally here.

4. *Haben Sie etwas davon?* d. It's nice out. The weather's nice.

5. *Geben Sie ihm etwas mehr davon!* e. America is a beautiful country.

6. *Geben Sie mir etwas!*   f. I gave him something.

7. *Nein, sie haben nichts.* g. It's good.

8. *Was halten Sie davon?* h. Do you have any?

9. *Ich habe ihm etwas gegeben.* i. Do you have any money?

10. *Das ist gut.*   j. Give me something.

11. *Ein schönes Land ist Amerika.* k. Give him some more of it.

12. *Wir haben heute schönes Wetter.* l. There is something.

13. *Das ist sehr schön.*   m. Is (are) there more of it?

14. *Das Wetter ist schön.* n. No, they haven't any.

15. *Ein schöner Tag ist endlich hier.* o. What do you think of it?

ANSWERS

1—m; 2—l; 3—i; 4—h; 5—k; 6—j; 7—n; 8—o; 9—f; 10—g; 11—e; 12—b; 13—a; 14—d; 15—c.

LESSON 29

A. OF COURSE, I SUPPOSE SO, ETC.

Aber sicher!
Of course! Certainly!

Natürlich!
Of course! Naturally!

Einverstanden!
Agreed!

In Ordnung.
Agreed! That's okay.

Ich bin damit einverstanden.
I agree with that (to it).

Das versteht sich.
Of course. Naturally. Certainly.

Tatsächlich?
Indeed? In fact? Really?

Wirklich?
Really?

Um so schlimmer.
So much the worse.

Um so besser.
So much the better.

Ich denke ja!
I think so.

Ich nehme es an.
I suppose so.

Ich nehme es nicht an.
I suppose not.

{ **Ich hoffe.**
{ **Hoffentlich.**
  I hope so.

{ **Ich hoffe nicht.**
{ **Hoffentlich nicht.**
  I hope not.

Vielleicht doch.
Perhaps so.

Das hängt davon ab.
That all depends.

Sicher, Sicherlich.
Certainly.

Sicher nicht.
Certainly not.

B. IT'S A PITY, IT DOESN'T MATTER, ETC.

Das ist schade!
It's a pity! It's a shame! Too bad!

Schade!
Too bad!

Das macht nichts.
That's not important. That doesn't matter.

Das macht gar nichts.
That doesn't matter at all.

Das macht mir nichts aus.
It doesn't matter to me. I don't mind.

Wenn es Ihnen nichts ausmacht,
If you have no objection;
If it doesn't inconvenience you,

Das ist mir völlig gleich.
I don't care. It's all the same to me.

{**Ich mache mir nicht das Geringste daraus.**
{**Das ist mir total egal!**
 Es ist mir Wurst (*coll.*).[1]
 I couldn't care less.

C. HE'S A GREAT GUY,
   SHE'S A GREAT GAL

Er ist ein großartiger Kerl.
He's a great guy.

Er ist Klasse (*coll.*).
He's a great guy.

Er ist sehr nett.
He's very nice.

Sie ist eine fabelhafte Frau.
She's a fabulous woman.

---

[1] *Coll.* stands for "colloquial." Literally, "It's a sausage (to me)."
Note that this expression is *highly* colloquial.

Sie ist Klasse (*coll.*).
She's great.

Sie ist sehr liebenswürdig.
She's very kind (amiable).

Sie sind sehr liebenswürdig.
You're very kind. That's very kind of you.

QUIZ 21

1. *Das ist schade!*	a. of course, certainly!
2. *Das macht nichts.*	b. I agree to it.
3. *Das macht mir nichts aus.*	c. Agreed!
4. *Das hängt davon ab.*	d. He's a great guy.
5. *Einverstanden!*	e. I suppose so.
6. *Ich bin damit einverstanden.*	f. I hope so.
7. *Ich hoffe.*	g. It's a pity (shame). Too bad!
8. *Aber sicher!*	h. That all depends.
9. *Er ist ein grossartiger Kerl.*	i. That's nothing. That's not important. That doesn't matter.
10. *Ich nehme es an.*	j. I don't care. It doesn't matter to me.

ANSWERS
1—g; 2—i; 3—j; 4—h; 5—c; 6—b; 7—f; 8—a;
9—d; 10—e.

D. THE SAME, MYSELF

dasselbe (*derselbe, dieselbe*)
the same

Das ist dasselbe.
That's the same thing.

Das sind nicht dieselben.
These aren't the same.

zur selben Zeit
at the same time

im (*in dem*) selben Augenblick
at the same moment

in derselben Stadt
in the same town

selbst/selber
myself, yourself, etc.

{**Ich mache es selbst.**
{**Ich mache es selber.**
I'm doing it myself.

{**Du machst es selbst.**
{*Du machst es selber.*
You're doing it yourself.

{**Er macht es selbst.**
{*Er macht es selber.*
He's doing it himself.

{**Wir machen es selbst.**
{*Wir machen es selber.*
We're doing it ourselves.

{**Ihr macht es selbst.**
{*Ihr macht es selber.*
You're doing it yourselves.

Sie machen es selbst.
You're doing it yourself.

Sie machen es selbst.
They are doing it themselves.

E. ALREADY

schon
already

Er ist schon da.
He's already here.

Er ist noch nicht da.
He is not here yet.

Er hat es schon getan.
He's already done that.

Ist er schon fort?
Has he left already?

Nein, er ist noch da (hier).
No, he is still here.

Er ist noch nicht fort.
He hasn't left yet.

Sind Sie schon fertig?
Have you finished already?

F. WORD STUDY

Milch (die)	milk	*Öl (das)*	oil
Stahl (der)	steel	*Sand (der)*	sand

Zinn (das)	tin	*Eis (das)*	ice
Sturm (der)	storm	*Amerika (das)*	America
Wolle (die)	wool	*Finger (der)*	finger

LESSON 30

A. I LIKE IT, IT'S GOOD

Mir gefällt es.[1]
I like it. (It's pleasing to me.)

Das gefällt mir.
I like (the looks of) that.

Das habe ich gern.
I like that.

Ich mag es.
I like it.

Das ist gut.
It's good.

Das ist toll!
That's great!

Ich mag es.
I like it (food).

---

[1] Note that the verb *gefallen* usually refers to liking the looks of something or someone. It would not, then, normally be used with food.

Das ist sehr gut.
It's very good.

Das gefällt mir sehr.
I like that very much.

Es gefällt mir großartig.
It's grand. I like it a lot.

Ich bin begeistert davon.
I'm enthusiastic about it.

Magst du es gern?
Do you like it?

Er gefällt ihr.
She likes him.

Sie gefällt ihm.
He likes her.

Amerikaner gefallen ihr.
She likes (the look of) Americans.

Sie mag Amerikaner.
She likes Americans.

B. I Don't Like It, It's Bad

Ich mag es nicht.
I don't like it.

Das gefällt mir nicht.
I don't like that. ("It doesn't please me.")

Ich mag ihn nicht.
I don't like him.

Ich mag sie nicht.
I don't like her.

Das ist nicht gut.
That's not good.

Das ist schlecht.
It's bad. That's bad.

Es ist nicht schön.
It's not nice (beautiful).

Das ist nicht schön von Ihnen.
That's not nice of you.

Das ist wertlos.
It's worthless.

Das ist komisch.
That's strange, odd.

Es ist langweilig.
It's boring.

Es ist blöd!
It's stupid!

Es ist nervtötend (*coll.*).
It's boring! It's a drag!

QUIZ 22

1. *Ich mag es nicht.*   a. It's strange.
2. *Das ist wertlos.*   b. It's boring.
3. *Das ist schön.*   c. Do you like it?
4. *Es ist langweilig.*   d. She likes him.

5. *Magst du es gern?*   e. I like it.
6. *Er gefällt ihr.*   f. That's bad.
7. *Das gefällt mir nicht.*   g. That's beautiful.
8. *Das ist schlecht.*   h. I don't like that.
9. *Mir gefällt es.*   i. I don't like it.
10. *Das ist komisch.*   j. It's worthless.

ANSWERS
1—i; 2—j; 3—g; 4—b; 5—c; 6—d; 7—h; 8—f;
9—e; 10—a.

C. EIN WITZ

Zwei Freunde gehen in ein Restaurant und jeder bestellt ein Beefsteak. Ein paar Minuten später kommt der Kellner zurück und bringt ein großes und ein kleines Stück Fleisch. Der eine Freund nimmt sich sofort das große Stück. Der andere wird wütend und sagt zu ihm:

„Was für schlechte Manieren du hast! Weißt du nicht, dass du als erster das kleinere Stück hättest nehmen sollen?"

Der andere Freund antwortet:
„Welches Stück hättest du denn genommen, wenn du an meiner Stelle gewesen wärest?"

„Das kleinere, natürlich," sagt der eine.

„Nun gut," antwortet der andere, „Worüber beschwerst du dich denn? Du hast es doch, nicht wahr?"

A JOKE

Two friends go to a restaurant and each orders a steak. A few minutes later the waiter comes back with a large piece of meat and a small one. One of the two friends immediately takes the larger piece. The other is furious and says to him:

"What bad manners you have! Don't you know that, since you were the first to help yourself, you should have taken the smaller piece?"

The other answers:
"If you had been in my place, which piece would you have taken?"
"The smaller one, of course," says the first one.

"Well, then," the other answers, "what are you complaining about? You have it, don't you?"

NOTES

1. *ein paar*—a few.
   ein Paar—a pair.
2. *Später kommt der Kellner zurück:* example of inverted word order (verb-subject).
3. *Werden* here is not used as an auxiliary but as the equivalent of "to become" in English.
4. *Ich hätte nehmen sollen:* pluperfect subjunctive. There is no *zu* before *nehmen,* because the modal *sollen* rules the phrase.
5. *Du hättest genommen:* pluperfect subjunctive of *nehmen.*
   wärest: Pluperfect of *sein* ("to be"). Note the use of the pluperfect subjunctive in the contrary-to-fact statement referring to past tense.

If the contrary-to-fact statement were in reference to present time, it would read:

Welches Stück nähmest du (or: *würdest du nehmen*), *wenn du an meiner Stelle wärest?* Which piece would you take, if you were in my place?

6. *Worüber: über was.*

REVIEW QUIZ 3

1. *Er hat es _____ (in) seine Tasche gesteckt.*
   a. *auf*
   b. *in*
   c. *im*

2. *Es ist _____ (under) dem Stuhl.*
   a. *darin*
   b. *unter*
   c. *unten*

3. *Sie können es _____ (without) Schwierigkeit tun.*
   a. *ohne*
   b. *durch*
   c. *mit*

4. *Ich habe es _____ (under) einem Haufen Papier gefunden.*
   a. *über*
   b. *unter*
   c. *oben*

5. *Man sagt, es sei _____ (true).*
   a. *spricht*
   b. *wahr*
   c. *das*

6. *Ich* _____ (am going) *zur Bank.*
   a. *gehen*
   b. *geht*
   c. *gehe*

7. *Er* _____ (is going) *aufs Land.*
   a. *geht*
   b. *muss*
   c. *gehen*

8. *Geben Sie mir ein* _____ (little) *Wasser!*
   a. *wenig*
   b. *viel*
   c. *hier*

9. *Ich habe nicht* _____ (much) *Geld.*
   a. *wenig*
   b. *viel*
   c. *zu viel*

10. *Das ist* _____ (more) *als das.*
    a. *weniger*
    b. *mehr*
    c. *früh*

11. *Das ist nicht* _____ (cnough).
    a. *noch*
    b. *gut*
    c. *genug*

12. *Sie ist* _____ (beautiful).
    a. *gut*
    b. *schön*
    c. *nett*

13. _____ (as) *Sie wünschen.*
    a. *Nicht*
    b. *Wie*
    c. *Sehr*

14. *Wir sind* _____ (all) *da.*
    a. *wie*
    b. *genug*
    c. *alle*

15. _____ (Everyone) *weiß es.*
    a. *Alle*
    b. *Jeder*
    c. *Ganz*

16. *Ich* _____ (think) *nie daran.*
    a. *halte*
    b. *denke*
    c. *bin*

17. *Ich* _____ (hope) *nicht.*
    a. *helfe*
    b. *hoffe*
    c. *nehme an*

18. *Das macht* _____ (nothing).
    a. *nicht*
    b. *nichts*
    c. *schon*

19. *Das ist* _____ (the same).
    a. *dasselbe*
    b. *schon*
    c. *natürlich*

20. *Sind Sie* _____ (already) *fertig?*
    a. *selbst*
    b. *schöner*
    c. *schon*

ANSWERS

1—b; 2—b; 3—a; 4—b; 5—b; 6—c; 7—a; 8—a;
9—b; 10—b; 11—c; 12—b; 13—b; 14—c; 15—b;
16—b; 17—b; 18—b; 19—a; 20—c.

D. WORD STUDY

studieren	(to) study	*Bündel (das)*	bundle
hart	hard	*Karton (der)*	carton
Wagen (der)	wagon, car	*Farm (die)*	farm
Mitte (die)	middle		

SUPPLEMENTAL VOCABULARY 10:
NATURE

nature	*die Natur*
tree	*der Baum (die Bäume)*
flower	*die Blume (die Blumen)*
forest	*der Wald (die Wälder)*
mountain	*der Berg (die Berge)*
field	*das Feld (die Felder)*
river	*der Fluss (die Flüsse)*
lake	*der See (die Seen)*
ocean	*der Ozean (die Ozeane)*
sea	*das Meer (die Meere)*
beach	*der Strand (die Strände)*
desert	*die Wüste (die Wüsten)*
rock	*der Fels(en) (die Felsen)*
sand	*der Sand*
sky	*der Himmel*

sun	*die Sonne (die Sonnen)*
moon	*der Mond (die Monde)*
star	*der Stern (die Sterne)*
water	*das Wasser (die Wasser)*
land	*das Land (die Länder)*
plant	*die Pflanze (die Pflanzen)*
hill	*der Hügel (die Hügel)*
pond	*der Teich (die Teiche)*

LESSON 31

A. WHO? WHAT? HOW? ETC.

Wer?	Who?	
Was?	What?	Example: *Was hat er gesagt?*
		What did he say?

Wer is declined as follows:

wer	who	Example: *Wer hat das gesagt?*
		Who said that?
wessen	whose	*Wessen Geld ist das?*
		Whose money is that?
wem	to whom	*Wem haben Sie das gesagt?*
		To whom did you say that?
wen	whom	*Wen lieben Sie?*
		Whom do you love?

1. *Wer?* Who?

Wer ist da?
Who is it?

Wer sind Sie?
Who are you?

Wer weiß das?
Who knows that?

Wer kommt mit uns?
Who's coming with us?

Wem gehört das?
Whose is it? (To whom does it belong?)

Für wen ist das?
That is for whom? (Whom is that for?)

Mit wem sprechen Sie?
With whom are you talking?

Über wen sprechen Sie?
Whom are you speaking about?

Mit wem kommen Sie?
With whom are you coming?

Wen möchten Sie sehen?
Whom do you want to see?

Wen suchen Sie?
For whom are you looking?

2. *Was?* What

Womit?
With what?

Worüber?
About what?

Wozu?
To what? What for?

Was gibt es Neues?
What's new?

An wen denken Sie?
Whom are you thinking about?

Was brauchen Sie?
What do you need?

Was sagen Sie?
What are you saying?

Was sagen Sie dazu?
What do you say about that?

Was tun Sie?
What are you doing?

Was möchten Sie?
What do you want?
What would you like?

Was wollten Sie jetzt tun?
What did you want to do now?

Was möchten Sie sagen?
What do you mean?
What would you like to say?

Was suchen Sie?
What are you looking for?

Was haben Sie?
What do you have? What's the matter with you?
What's wrong with you?

Was hat er?
What does he have? What's the matter with him?

NOTES

These forms are used like nouns.

The masculine and feminine forms *wer,* etc., refer only to persons.

The neuter form *was* refers to things.

The masculine and feminine forms in the dative and accusative, *wem* and *wen,* do not change when preceded by a preposition.

Mit wem kommt er?	*Mit seinem Vater/seiner Mutter.*
With whom is he coming?	With his father/his mother.
Für wen kauft sie den Mantel?	*Für ihren Sohn/ihr Kind.*
For whom is she buying the coat?	For her son/her child.

However, the neuter form *was* changes to *wo* whenever it is connected with a preposition and it is contracted with that preposition.

mit was	becomes	*womit*	With what?
für was	becomes	*wofür*	For what?
zu was	becomes	*wozu*	To what?
über was	becomes	*worüber*	About what?
durch was	becomes	*wodurch*	By what?

Womit (Mit was) sehen wir?—Mit den Augen.
With what do we see?—With our (the) eyes.

Wofür (Für was) kämpfen sie?—Für die Freiheit.
What are they fighting for?—For (the) liberty.

3. *Welcher? Welche? Welches?* Which (one)?
   These interrogatives are used as adjectives or pronouns. They follow the same declension as the article *der, die, das.*

Welcher Garten ist der schönste?
Which garden is the most beautiful?

Welcher ist Ihr Garten?
Which one is your garden?

Welcher, welche, welches?
Which (one)?

Welcher Mann?
What man? (Which man?)

Welche Männer?
What men? (Which men?)

Welches Buch?
What book? Which book?

Welcher Tag ist heute?
What's today?

In welchem Monat sind wir?
What month is it? ("In which month are we?")

Welche Frau?
What woman?

Welche Frauen?
What women?

Welch ein Unterschied!
What a difference!

Welcher Unterschied besteht zwischen den beiden Dingen?
What's the difference between the two things?

4. *Was für ein, eine, ein?* What kind of?
   Was für remains unchanged. *Ein, eine, ein* follow
   the declension of the indefinite article. In the
   plural, *was für* stands without an article.

Was für ein Schuh ist das? Das ist ein schwarzer Schuh.
What kind of shoe is that? That is a black shoe.

Was für Schuhe sind das? Das sind schwarze Schuhe.
What kind of shoes are these? These are black shoes.

Das sind schwarze.
These are black ones.

Was für ein Mann ist das?
What kind of man is that?

Was für einen Film sehen Sie?
What kind of movie are you seeing?

Was für Menschen?
What kind of people (are they)?

5. *Wie?* How?

Wie?
How?

Aber wie?
But how?

Wie meinen Sie das?
How's that? What do you mean?

Wie heißen Sie?
What's your name?

Wie heißt diese Stadt?
What is the name of this town?

Wie geht's?
How are you?

Wie schreibt man das Wort auf Deutsch?
How do you write this word in German? How's this
word written in German?

Wie sagen Sie das auf Englisch?
How do you say that in English?

Wie sagen Sie "Thanks" auf Deutsch?
How do you say "Thanks" in German?

Wie ist das geschehen?
How did that happen?

Wie macht man das?
How do you do that?

Wie haben Sie das gemacht?
How did you do (accomplish) it?

Wie viel Uhr ist es?
What's the time?

Um wie viel Uhr?
What time?

   6. *Wann?* When?

Wann ist das?
When is it?

Wann kommen Sie?
When are you coming?

Bis wann bleiben Sie?
You're staying until when?

Wann gehen Sie?
When are you going?

Wann fahren Sie ab?
When are you leaving?

Wann kommt er?
When will he come? When is he coming?

Seit wann sind Sie hier?
How long have you been here?

7. *Warum?* Why?

Und warum nicht?
And why not?

Warum sagen Sie das?
Why do you say that?

Warum hat er das getan?
Why did he do it?

QUIZ 23

1. *Was tun Sie?*
2. *Was wünschen Sie?*
3. *Was gibt es?*
4. *Was möchten Sie sagen?*
5. *Was suchen Sie?*
6. *Wie heißt diese Straße?*
7. *Was macht das?*
8. *Welch ein Unterschied!*
9. *Welcher ist besser?*
10. *Wann fahren Sie ab?*
11. *Wer sind Sie?*
12. *Wen möchten Sie sehen?*

a. What's new?
b. What do you need?
c. And why not?
d. Why do you say that?
e. Why did he do it?
f. What's your name?
g. How are you?
h. But how?
i. When are you leaving?
j. Who are you?
k. Whom do you want to see?
l. What a difference!

13. *Was brauchen Sie?*   m. Which is the better one?

14. *Warum hat er es getan?*   n. What do you mean?

15. *Aber wie?*   o. What are you looking for?

16. *Wie geht's?*   p. What's going on?

17. *Warum sagen Sie das?*   q. How much is it?

18. *Und warum nicht?*   r. What's the name of this street?

19. *Was gibt es Neues?*   s. What are you doing?

20. *Wie heißen Sie?*   t. What do you wish?

ANSWERS

1—s; 2—t; 3—p; 4—n; 5—o; 6—r; 7—q; 8—l; 9—m; 10—i; 11—j; 12—k; 13—b; 14—e; 15—h; 16—g; 17—d; 18—c; 19—a; 20—f.

B. WORD STUDY

komisch	comical	*Land (das)*	land
Muskel (der)	muscle	*Juni (der)*	June
Fuss (der)	foot	*Boot (das)*	boat
Haar (das)	hair	*Offizier (der)*	officer
Hand (die)	hand		

C. HOW MUCH?

Der Preis?
The price?

Was ist der Preis?
What's the price? (How is the price?)

Wie viel?
How much?

Wie viel macht es?
How much is it?

Wie viel für alles?
How much for everything? How much does it all cost?

Wie viel für jedes?
How much each?

Wie viel pro Dutzend?
How much a dozen?

Wie viel wollen Sie dafür haben?
How much do you want for it?

D. How Many?

Wie viele?
How many?

Wie viel Geld?
How much (money)?

Wie viele Menschen?
How many people?

Wie viel Zeit?
How much time?

Wie viel Zeit braucht man, um dorthin zu kommen?
How long ("how much time") does it take to get there?

Wie viele sind dort?
How many are there?

Wie viele bleiben davon übrig?
How many of them are left?

Wie viele haben Sie davon?
How many of them ("of it") do you have?

Den Wievielten haben wir heute?
What's (the date) today? ("How many have we today?")

Der Wievielte ist Montag?
What's the date Monday? ("The how many will Monday be?")

QUIZ 24

1. *Wie viel gibt es davon?*
2. *Wie viel macht es?*
3. *Wie viel möchten Sie davon?*
4. *Welcher Preis?*
5. *Wie viel Zeit? Wie lange?*
6. *Den Wievielten haben wir?*
7. *Wie viel bleibt davon übrig?*
8. *Wie viele haben Sie davon?*
9. *Was ist der Preis?*
10. *Der Wievielte ist Montag?*

a. How much of it is left?
b. What's the date today? ("The how many?")
c. What's the date Monday?
d. What's the price?
e. What price?

  f. How much is it?
  g. How much do you want?
  h. How much time? How long?
  i. How many of them do you have?
  j. How many are there?

ANSWERS
1—j; 2—f; 3—g; 4—e; 5—h; 6—b; 7—a; 8—i;
9—d; 10—c.

LESSON 32

A. SOME, SOMEONE, SOMETHING,
  SOMETIMES

etwas
some, something

etwas Geld
some money

etwas Neues
something new

einige Menschen, einige Leute
some people

einige Wörter
some words, a few words

jemand
someone, somebody

Ist jemand hier, der das kann?
Is there anyone here who can do it?

manchmal
sometimes

Ich sehe ihn manchmal.
I see him sometimes.

B. ONCE, TWICE

einmal
once, one time

zweimal
twice, two times

das erste Mal
the first time

das nächste Mal
the next time

das letzte Mal
the last time

noch einmal
another time, again, once more

jedes Mal
every time, each time

dieses Mal, diesmal
this time

C. UP TO

bis
up to

bis jetzt
up to now

Bis jetzt hat er keine Arbeit gefunden.
Up to now he hasn't found any work.

bis dort
up to there

Wir fahren bis dorthin.
We are going (driving) up to that point.

Bis zum Ende
(up) to the end

Ich bleibe bis Ende August.
I'm staying until the end of August.

bis zum Bahnhof
(up) to (as far as) the station

Er fährt uns nur bis München.
He's driving us only as far as Munich.

Er fährt uns bis zum Bahnhof.
He's driving us (up) to the train station.

bis heute Abend
(up to) until this evening; see you this evening

Also, bis heute Abend!
Well then, see you this evening.

Der Film spielt bis heute Abend.
The movie is playing until tonight.

bis morgen
(up to) until tomorrow; see you tomorrow

bis Montag
(up to) until Monday; see you Monday

bis später
See you later.

bis bald
See you soon.

D. I Need It, It's Necessary

Ich brauche es.
I need it (that).

Das braucht er nicht.
He doesn't need it (that).

Brauchen Sie etwas?
Do you need anything?

Ich brauche nichts.
I don't need anything.

Ich brauche es überhaupt nicht.
I don't need it at all.

Sie brauchen es nicht zu kaufen.[1]
You do not need to (have to) buy it.

Es ist unbedingt notwendig, dass ich Sie spreche.
It's absolutely necessary that I speak to you.

---

[1] Note that the infinitive construction includes *zu* if *brauchen* is used in the negative with another verb.

Sie müssen es ihm sagen.
You have to (must) tell him.

Sie müssen früh nach Hause kommen.
You must come home early.

Sie müssen die Wahrheit sagen.
You must tell the truth.

N O T E

After a modal verb, the main verb is placed at the end
of the sentence in its infinitive form without *zu*. The
following are modal verbs: *dürfen* (to be allowed,
"may"); *mögen* (to like); *müssen* (to have to, "must");
sollen (ought to, is supposed to, "should"); *können* (to
be able to, "can"); and *wollen* (to want).

Er muss morgen arbeiten.	He has to work tomorrow.
Ich will heute nicht arbeiten.	I don't want to work today.
Sie darf nicht zu spät kommen.	She cannot come too late.

The model verb *müssen* (must) does not translate as
"must not" in the negative but rather as "don't/doesn't
have to."

Er muss morgen nicht arbeiten.	He doesn't have to work tomorrow.

E.   I FEEL LIKE . . .

Ich möchte es haben.
I'd like to have it. I feel like having it.

Ich möchte nicht dorthin gehen.
I don't feel like going there.

Ich möchte gern einen Apfel essen.
I feel like having (eating) an apple.

Möchten Sie gern den Film sehen?
Would you like to see this movie?

F.   AT THE HOME OF

zu Hause
at home

bei
at the home of

Fühlen Sie sich wie zu Hause!
Make yourself at home.

Wir waren bei Freunden.
We were at some friends' house.

Ich werde Sie bei Müllers sehen.
I'll see you at the Müllers'.

Er war beim (*bei dem*) **Arzt.**
He was at the doctor's.

Kommen Sie zu uns!
Come over to our place.

**Ich wohnte bei meinen Eltern, als ich die Stellung
bekam.**
I was living with my parents when I got the job.

Ist Herr Müller zu Hause?
Is Mr. Müller at home?

Ich muss zum Arzt gehen.
I have to go to the doctor's.

G. HERE IT IS, THERE IT IS

Hier ist es!
Here it is!

Hier bin ich.
Here I am.

Hier ist er.
Here he is.

Hier ist sie.
Here she is.

Hier sind sie.
Here they are.

Hier ist das Buch.
Here's the book.

Dort ist es!
There it is!

Dort ist er.
There he is.

Dort ist sie.
There she is.

Dort sind sie.
There they are.

QUIZ 25

1. *Ich brauche etwas Geld.*   a. to the end of May.
2. *einmal*   b. I need that.
3. *bis Ende Mai*   c. Here's the book.
4. *Ich brauche das.*   d. I need some money.
5. *Hier ist das Buch.*   e. Once

ANSWERS
1—d; 2—e; 3—a; 4—b; 5—c.

REVIEW QUIZ 4

1. _____ (What) *ist der Name dieser Stadt?*
   a. *Was*
   b. *Welches*
   c. *Wann*

2. _____ (Who) *sind Sie?*
   a. *Wer*
   b. *Welcher*
   c. *Wo*

3. _____ (When) *wird er kommen?*
   a. *Wenn*
   b. *Wann*
   c. *Welcher*

4. _____ (Why) *sagen Sie das?*
   a. *Wo*
   b. *Wann*
   c. *Warum*

5. *Das _____ (twelfth) Kapitel ist sehr lang.*
   a. *zwölfte*
   b. *siebzehnte*
   c. *sechste*

6. *Der Hut hat mich _____ (fifty-four) Euro gekostet.*
   a. *fünfundfünfzig*
   b. *fünfundvierzig*
   c. *vierundfünfzig*

7. *Ich wohne Friedrichstrasse. Nummer _____ (seventeen).*
   a. *dreiunddreissig*
   b. *siebzehn*
   c. *siebzig*

8. *Es ist _____ (noon).*
   a. *Mittag*
   b. *Mitternacht*
   c. *elf Uhr*

9. *Wir sehen uns um _____ (six) Uhr.*
   a. *fünf*
   b. *sieben*
   c. *sechs*

10. *Es ist _____ (time), es zu tun.*
    a. *Uhr*
    b. *Zeit*
    c. *Stunde*

11. *Wir haben heute _____ (Wednesday).*
    a. *Dienstag*
    b. *Mittwoch*
    c. *Montag*

12. *Er fährt* _____ (Tuesday) *ab*.
    a. *Dienstag*
    b. *Donnerstag*
    c. *Mittwoch*

13. *Heute ist der erste* _____ (June).
    a. *Juni*
    b. *Juli*
    c. *August*

14. *Er* _____ (need) *das nicht*.
    a. *macht*
    b. *braucht*
    c. *müssen*

15. _____ (How) *schreibt man das Wort auf Deutsch?*
    a. *Warum*
    b. *Wie*
    c. *Wann*

16. *Ich bin am* _____ (twelve) *April geboren*.
    a. *zwanzigsten*
    b. *elften*
    c. *zwölften*

17. _____ (Here's) *das Buch*.
    a. *Hier ist*
    b. *Dort ist*
    c. *Wo*

18. *Ich habe mein* _____ (money) *verloren*.
    a. *Tasche*
    b. *Geld*
    c. *Hof*

19. *Er arbeitet von* _____ (morning) *bis abends.*
    a. *morgens*
    b. *nachts*
    c. *nachmittags*

20. *An welcher Station muss ich* _____ (get off)?
    a. *gehen*
    b. *aussteigen*
    c. *anrufen*

ANSWERS
1—a; 2—a; 3—b; 4—c; 5—a; 6—c; 7—b; 8—a;
9—c; 10—b; 11—b; 12—a; 13—a; 14—b; 15—b;
16—c; 17—a; 18—b; 19—a; 20—b.

LESSON 33

A. ON THE ROAD

Verzeihung!
Pardon me.

Entschuldigen Sie!
Excuse me.

Wie heißt diese Stadt?
What is the name of this town (city)?

Wie weit sind wir von Berlin?
How far are we from Berlin?

Wie viele Kilometer sind es von hier bis Linz?
How many kilometers from here to Linz?

Von hier sind es zehn Kilometer.
It's ten kilometers from here.

Das ist zwanzig Kilometer von hier.
That's twenty kilometers from here.

Wie komme ich von hier nach Salzburg?
How do I get to Salzburg from here?

Fahren Sie diese Strasse entlang!
Follow this road.

Wo soll ich abbiegen?
Where should I turn?

Darf ich hier parken?
May I park here?

B. WALKING AROUND

Wie komme ich zu dieser Adresse?
How do I get to this address?

**Können Sie mir sagen, wie ich zu dieser Adresse
komme?**
Can you tell me how I can get to this address?

Können Sie mir sagen, wie ich dorthin komme?
Can you tell me how I can get to this place?

Haben Sie einen Stadtplan?
Do you have a map of the city?

Ich glaube, ich habe mich verlaufen.
I think I'm lost.

Wie heißt diese Straße?
What is the name of this street?

Können Sie mir sagen, wo sich diese Straße befindet?
Can you tell me where this street is?

Wo ist die Kaiserstraße?
Where is Kaiser Street?

Ist es weit von hier?
Is it far from here?

Wie weit ist es?
How far is it?

Kann ich zu Fuß gehen?
Can I get there by foot?

Ist es in der Nähe?
Is it near here?

Es ist die dritte Straße rechts.
It's the third street on the right.

Gehen Sie diesen Weg!
Go this way.

Gehen Sie geradeaus!
Go straight ahead.

Gehen Sie bis zur Ecke und dann links!
Go to the corner and turn left.

Nehmen Sie die erste Seitenstraße rechts!
Turn right ("Take the first side street to the right").

Wo befindet sich die Garage?
Where is the parking garage?

Wo befindet sich die Polizeistation?
Where is the police station?

Wo befindet sich das Museum?
Where is the museum?

C.   Bus, Train, Subway

Wo ist die Bushaltestelle?
Where is the bus stop?

Wie viel kostet eine Fahrt?
How much is the fare?

Sagen Sie mir bitte, wann ich austeigen muss.
Please tell me when to get off.

An welcher Station muss ich aussteigen?
What station do I get off at?

Wo muss ich aussteigen?
Where do I get off?

Wo ist der Bahnhof?
Where is the train station?

Wohin fährt dieser Zug?
Where does this train go?

Wo bekomme ich den Zug nach Berlin?
Where do I get the train for Berlin?

Auf Gleis zwei.
On track two.

Der Zug ist gerade abgefahren.
The train just left.

Um wie viel Uhr fährt der nächste Zug ab?
What time does the next train leave?

Könnte (*Kann*) ich eine Rückfahrkarte nach Berlin haben?
Could (Can) I have a round-trip ticket for Berlin?

Wie viel macht das?
How much is that?

Siebzig Euro fünfundzwanzig.
Seventy euros and twenty-five cents.

Wie lange dauert die Reise?
How long does it take to get there ("does the trip last")?

Etwas über eine Stunde.
A little over an hour.

Gibt es einen Taxistand in der Nähe?
Is there a taxi stand nearby?

Wo ist die nächste U-Bahn-Station?
Where is the nearest subway station?

D. WORD STUDY

Parfüm (das)	perfume	*neu*	new
falsch	false	*Australien (das)*	Australia
freundlich	friendly	*rund*	round
frisch	fresh	*März*	March
grün	green	*brechen*	(to) break

LESSON 34

A. WRITING AND MAILING LETTERS

Ich möchte einen Brief schreiben.
I'd like to write a letter.

Haben Sie einen Bleistift?
Do you have a pencil?

Haben Sie einen Kugelschreiber?
Do you have a ballpoint pen?

Haben Sie einen Stift?
Do you have a pen?

Haben Sie Schreibpapier?
Do you have writing paper?

Haben Sie einen Briefumschlag?
Do you have an envelope?

Haben Sie eine Briefmarke?
Do you have a stamp?

Wo kann ich eine Briefmarke kaufen?
Where can I buy a stamp?

Haben Sie eine Luftpostmarke?
Do you have an airmail stamp?

Wo befindet sich das Postamt?
Where is the post office?

Wie viele Briefmarken brauche ich für diesen Brief?
How many stamps do I need on this letter?

Ich möchte diesen Brief aufgeben.
I'd like to mail this letter.

Wo ist der Briefkasten?
Where is the mailbox?

An der Ecke.
At the corner.

B. FAXES AND E-MAIL

Ich möchte ein Fax schicken.
I'd like to send a fax.

Ich möchte etwas faxen.
I'd like to fax (something).

Wo kann ich ein Fax aufgeben?
Where can I send a fax?

Wie viel kostet ein Fax nach Berlin?
How much is a fax to Berlin?

Ich muss eine E-mail verschicken.
I need to send an e-mail.

Kann ich ins Internet gehen?
Can I get on the Internet?

Haben Sie eine Website?
Do you have a website.

Wo ist der Computer?
Where is the computer?

Mailen[1] Sie mir die Datei als Anlage. (*angehängte Datei*)
E-mail the file to me as an attachment.

Ich werde die Mail an Sie weiterleiten.
I'll forward the e-mail to you.

Brauche ich ein Codewort zum einloggen?
Do I need a code word to log in?

C. TELEPHONES

Gibt es ein Telefon hier?
Is there a phone here?

Wo kann ich telefonieren?
Where can I phone?

Wo befindet sich das Telefon?
Where is the telephone?

Wo ist ein öffentlicher Fernsprecher?
Where is the phone booth?

---

[1] The English word "mail" is used in German to mean e-mail. It can be a noun (*die Mail*) or a regular verb (*ich maile, du mailst*, etc.) *Die E-mail* and *e-mailen* also exist but are increasingly less common.

Wo bekomme ich eine Telefonkarte?
Where do I get a phone card?

Darf ich (Dürfte ich) Ihr Telefon benutzen?
May I (Might I) use your phone?

Selbstverständlich! Bitte sehr!
Of course! Go ahead!

Ein Ferngespräch, bitte.
May I have long distance, please?

Was kostet ein Gespräch nach Hamburg?
How much is a (telephone) call to Hamburg?

Darf ich Ihr Handy benutzen?
May I use your cell phone?

Ich habe hier keinen guten Empfang.
I don't have good reception here.

Ich brauche einen internationalen Handy-Service.
I need an international cell phone service provider.

Niemand hat geantwortet und ich habe eine Nachricht hinterlassen.
No one answered, so I left a message.

Ich muss meine Nachrichten abhören.
I have to check my voice mail/pick up my messages.

Er hat mir eine SMS geschickt.
He sent me a text message.

Einen Augenblick, bitte.
One moment, please.

Die Leitung ist besetzt.
The line's busy.

Sie haben mich falsch verbunden.
You gave me the wrong number.

Niemand antwortet.
There is no answer.

Kann ich bitte Herrn Wagner sprechen?
May I speak to Mr. Wagner, please?

Am Apparat.
Speaking.

Hier Lorenz.
This is Mr. Lorenz speaking.

SUPPLEMENTAL VOCABULARY 11: COMPUTERS AND THE INTERNET

computer and the internet	*Computer und Internet*
computer	*der Computer (die Computer)*
keyboard	*die Tastatur (die Tastaturen)*
monitor/screen	*der Monitor/der Bildschirm (die Monitore, die Bildschirme)*
printer	*der Drucker (die Drucker)*
mouse	*die Maus (die Mäuse)*
modem	*das Modem (die Modems)*
memory	*der Speicher (die Speicher)*
cd rom	*die CD-Rom (die CD-Roms)*

cd rom drive	*das CD-Rom-Laufwerk (die CD-Rom-Laufwerke)*
file	*die Datei (die Dateien)*
document	*das Dokument (die Dokumente)*
internet	*das Internet*
website	*die Website (die Websites)*
webpage	*die Webseite (die Webseiten)*
e-mail	*die E-mail (die E-mails), die Mail (die Mails)*
chatroom	*der Chatroom (die Chatrooms)*
log-in	*das Einloggen*
to log in	*einloggen*
to log off	*sich abmelden*
instant message	*die Sofortnachricht (die Sofortnachrichten)*
attachment	*die angehängte Datei (die angehängten Dateien), die Anlage (die Anlagen)*
to send an e-mail	*eine Mail schicken*
to send a file	*eine Datei schicken (beifügen)*
to forward	*weiterleiten*
to reply	*antworten*
to delete	*löschen*
to save a document	*ein Dokument abspeichern*
to open a file	*eine Datei öffnen*
to close a file	*eine Datei schließen*
to attach a file	*eine Datei anhängen*

LESSON 35

A. WHAT IS YOUR NAME?

Wie heißen Sie?
What is your name?

Ich heiße Hans Bauer.
My name is Hans Bauer.

Wie heißt er?
What is his name?

Er heißt Fritz Müller.
His name is Fritz Müller.

Wie heißt sie?
What is her name?

Sie heißt Lotte Schneider.
Her name is Lotte Schneider.

Wie heißen sie?
What are their names?

Er heißt Ludwig Schmitz und sie heißt Grete Meier.
His name is Ludwig Schmitz and hers is Grete Meier.

Was ist sein Vorname?
What's his first name?

Sein Vorname ist Mark.
His first name is Mark.

Was ist sein Familienname?
What is his last name?

Sein Familienname ist Pulver.
His last name is Pulver.

B. WHERE ARE YOU FROM?

Woher sind Sie?
Where are you from?

Woher kommen Sie?
Where do you come from?

Ich bin aus den Vereinigten Staaten.
I'm from the United States.

Ich komme aus Berlin.
I'm from Berlin.

Wo sind Sie geboren?
Where were you born?

Ich bin in Hamburg geboren.
I was born in Hamburg.

Ich wohne in England.
I live in England.

C. HOW OLD ARE YOU?

Wie alt sind Sie?
How old are you?

Ich bin zwanzig Jahre alt.
I'm twenty (years old).

Ich werde einundzwanzig im September.
I'll be twenty-one in September.

Ich wurde am neunzehnten August neunzehnhundertfünfundfünfzig geboren.
I was born August 19, 1955.

Wann ist Ihr Geburtstag?
When is your birthday?

Mein Geburtstag ist in zwei Wochen, am dreiundzwanzigsten Januar.
My birthday is in two weeks, January 23rd.

Wie viele Geschwister haben Sie?
How many brothers and sisters do you have?

Ich habe zwei Brüder.
I have two brothers.

Der Älteste ist zweiundzwanzig (Jahre alt).
The oldest is twenty-two (years old).

Er besucht die Universität.
He attends the university.

Der Jüngste ist siebzehn.
The youngest is seventeen.

Er ist das letzte Jahr auf dem Gymnasium.
He's in the last year of the "Gymnasium" (college prep school).

Wie viele Schwestern haben Sie?
How many sisters do you have?

Ich habe eine Schwester.
I have one sister.

Sie ist fünfzehn.
She's fifteen.

D. PROFESSIONS

Was machen Sie beruflich?
What's your occupation?

Was sind Sie von Beruf?
What's your profession?

Ich bin Arzt.
I'm a doctor. (male)

Ich bin Ärztin.
I'm a doctor. (female)

Was macht Ihr Vater beruflich?
What does your father do?

Was macht Ihre Mutter?
What does your mother do?

Was macht Ihr Mann?
What does your husband do?

Was macht Ihre Frau?
What does your wife do?

Sie ist Rechtsanwältin.
She's a lawyer.

Er ist Rechtsanwalt.
He's a lawyer.

Er ist Architekt.
He's an architect.

Sie ist Lehrerin.
She's a teacher.

Er ist Universitätsprofessor.
He's a university professor.

Sie ist Zahnärztin.
She's a dentist.

Sie ist Krankenpflegerin.
She's a nurse.

Er ist Geschäftsmann.
He's in business.

Er ist im Textilhandel.
He's in the textile business.

Er ist Landwirt.
He's a farmer.

Sie ist Beamtin.
She's a government employee.

Er ist Techniker.
He's a technician.

Er arbeitet in einer Automobilfabrik.
He works in an automobile factory.

NOTES

1. German does not use indefinite articles when speaking of professions: *Sie ist Verkäuferin*. She is a salesperson.
2. The feminine forms are derived in most cases by adding the suffix *-in* and (sometimes) placing an umlaut over the main vowel.

E. FAMILY MATTERS

Haben Sie Verwandte hier?
Do you have any relatives here?

Wohnt Ihre ganze Familie hier?
Does your whole family live here?

Meine ganze Familie außer meinen Großeltern.
All my family except my grandparents.

Sie wohnen auf einem Gut in Westfalen.
They live in a country home, in Westphalia.

Sind Sie mit Herrn Schneider verwandt?
Are you related to Mr. Schneider?

Er ist mein Onkel.
He's my uncle.

Er ist mein Vetter.
He's my cousin.

Sind Sie mit Frau Müller verwandt?
Are you related to Mrs. Müller?

Sie ist meine Tante.
She's my aunt.

Sie ist meine Kusine.
She's my cousin.

REVIEW QUIZ 5

1. *Wie heißt* _____ (this) *Stadt?*
   a. *dieser*
   b. *dieses*
   c. *diese*

2. _____ (How) *komme ich von hier nach Berlin?*
   a. *Wie viel*
   b. *Wie*
   c. *Welcher*

3. _____ (How) *heißt diese Straße?*
   a. *Was*
   b. *Wann*
   c. *Wie*

4. _____ (Where) *ist die Friedrichstraße?*
   a. *Wo*
   b. *Wann*
   c. *Dass*

5. _____ (go) *diesen Weg, Frau Meier?*
   a. *Gehen Sie*
   b. *Gehen wir*
   c. *Gehen sie*

6. *Gehen Sie zur Ecke und nehmen Sie die erste
   Straße* _____ (left).
   a. *links*
   b. *rechts*
   c. *weit*

7. _____ (How much) *macht es?*
   a. *Wie*
   b. *Wie viel*
   c. *Dass*

8. *Ich möchte einen Brief* _____ (to write).
   a. *zu schreiben*
   b. *schreiben*
   c. *schreibe*

9. *Wo kann ich eine* _____ (stamp) *kaufen?*
   a. *Briefmarke*
   b. *Post*
   c. *Stempel*

10. *An der Ecke dieser* _____ (street) *gibt es einen Briefkasten.*
   a. *Straße*
   b. *Bahnhof*
   c. *Allee*

11. _____ (Is there) *ein Telefon hier?*
   a. *Gibt es*
   b. *Es gibt*
   c. *Haben*

12. *Sie haben mich* _____ (wrong) *verbunden.*
   a. *falsch*
   b. *viel*
   c. *nicht*

13. *Was ist sein* _____ (first name)?
   a. *Vorname*
   b. *Familie*
   c. *nennt sich*

14. *Wo sind Sie* _____ (born)?
    a. *gewesen*
    b. *geboren*
    c. *gekommen*

15. *Der Jüngste ist siebzehn* _____ (years) *alt.*
    a. *Jahre*
    b. *Jahr*
    c. *jährlich*

16. *Er ist* _____ (lawyer).
    a. *Professor*
    b. *Rechtsanwalt*
    c. *Beamter*

17. *Er ist* _____ (worker).
    a. *Arbeiter*
    b. *Geschäftsmann*
    c. *Fabrik*

18. *Sie wohnen auf einem Gut,* _____ (near) *von Westfalen.*
    a. *in der Nähe*
    b. *in*
    c. *weit*

19.   (Follow) *dieser Straßenbahn!*
    a. *Gehen Sie*
    b. *Folgen Sie*
    c. *Nehmen Sie*

20. *Ist es* _____ (far) *von hier?*
    a. *weit*
    b. *geradeaus*
    c. *nahe*

21. *Auf _____ (track) zwei.*
    a. *Gleis*
    b. *Rückkehr*
    c. *Zug*

22. *Das bin _____ (I).*
    a. *mir*
    b. *mich*
    c. *ich*

23. *Das ist nicht _____ (free).*
    a. *früh*
    b. *falsch*
    c. *frei*

24. *Sind Sie mit Herrn Schneider _____ (related)?*
    a. *gekommen*
    b. *verwandt*
    c. *gefahren*

25. *Meine ganze Familie, _____ (except) meinen Großeltern, kommen aus Frankfurt am Main.*
    a. *außer*
    b. *aus*
    c. *davon*

ANSWERS
1—c; 2—b; 3—c; 4—a; 5—a; 6—a; 7—b; 8—b;
9—a; 10—a; 11—a; 12—a; 13—a; 14—b; 15—a;
16—b; 17—a; 18—a; 19—b; 20—a; 21—a; 22—c;
23—c; 24—b; 25—a.

SUPPLEMENTAL VOCABULARY 12: FAMILY AND RELATIONSHIPS

family and relationships	*Familie und Beziehungen*
mother	*die Mutter (die Mütter)*

father	*der Vater (die Väter)*
son	*der Sohn (die Söhne)*
daughter	*die Tochter (die Töchter)*
sister	*die Schwester (die Schwestern)*
baby	*das Baby (die Babys)*
brother	*der Bruder (die Brüder)*
husband	*der Ehemann (die Ehemänner)*
wife	*die Ehefrau (die Ehefrauen)*
aunt	*die Tante (die Tanten)*
uncle	*der Onkel (die Onkel)*
grandmother	*die Großmutter (die Großmütter), die Oma (die Omas)*
grandfather	*der Großvater (die Großväter), der Opa (die Opas)*
cousin (male)	*der Vetter (die Vettern)*
cousin (female)	*die Kusine (die Kusinen)*
mother-in-law	*die Schwiegermutter (die Schwiegermütter)*
father-in-law	*der Schwiegervater (die Schwiegerväter)*
stepmother	*die Stiefmutter (die Stiefmütter)*
stepfather	*der Stiefvater (die Stiefväter)*
stepson	*der Stiefsohn (die Stiefsöhne)*
stepdaughter	*die Stieftochter (die Stieftöchter)*
boyfriend	*der Freund (die Freunde)*
girlfriend	*die Freundin (die Freundinnen)*

fiancé(e)	*der/die Verlobte (die Verlobten)*
friend	*der Freund (die Freunde)*
relative	*der/die Verwandte (die Verwandten)*
to love	*lieben*
to know (a person)	*kennen*
to meet (a person)	*(sich) treffen*
to marry (someone)	*heiraten*
to divorce (someone)	*sich scheiden lassen (von)*
to get a divorce	*sich scheiden lassen, die Scheidung einreichen*
to inherit	*erben*

SUPPLEMENTAL VOCABULARY 13: ON THE JOB

jobs	*Berufe*
police man	*der Polizist (die Polizisten)*
police woman	*die Polizistin (die Polizistinnen)*
lawyer (male)	*der Rechtsanwalt (die Rechtsanwälte)*
lawyer (female)	*die Rechtsanwältin (die Rechtsanwältinnen)*
doctor (male)	*der Arzt (die Ärzte)*
doctor (female)	*die Ärztin (die Ärztinnen)*
engineer (male)	*der Ingenieur (die Ingenieure)*
businessman	*der Geschäftsman (die Geschäftsmänner)*
businesswoman	*die Geschäftsfrau (die Geschäftsfrauen)*
salesman	*der Verkäufer (die Verkäufer)*

saleswoman	*die Verkäuferin (die Verkäuferinnen)*
teacher (male)	*der Lehrer (die Lehrer)*
teacher (female)	*die Lehrerin (die Lehrerinnen)*
professor (male)	*der Professor (die Professoren)*
professor (female)	*die Professorin (die Professorinnen)*
banker	*der Bankier (die Bankiers)*
architect (male)	*der Archtekt (die Architekten)*
architect (female)	*die Architektin (die Archtektinnen).*
veterinarian (male)	*der Tierarzt (die Tierärzte)*
veterinarian (female)	*die Tierärztin (die Tierärztinnen)*
dentist (male)	*der Zahnarzt (die Zahnärzte)*
dentist (female)	*die Zahnärztin (dieZahnärztinnen)*
carpenter	*der Tischler (die Tischler)*
construction worker	*der Bauarbeiter (die Bauarbeiter)*
taxi driver (male)	*der Taxifahrer (die Taxifahrer)*
taxi driver (female)	*die Taxifahrerin (die Taxifahrerinnen)*
artist (male)	*der Künstler (die Künstler)*
artist (female)	*die Künstlerin (die Künstlerinnen)*
writer (male)	*der Schriftsteller (die Schriftsteller)*
writer (female)	*die Schriftstellerin (die Schriftstellerinnen)*

plumber	*der Klempner (die Klempner)*
electrician	*der Elektriker (die Elektriker)*
journalist (male)	*der Journalist (die Journalisten), der Reporter (die Reporter)*
journalist (female)	*die Journalistin (die Journalistinnen)*
actor	*der Schauspieler (die Schauspieler)*
actress	*die Schauspielerin (die Schauspielerinnen)*
musician (male)	*der Musiker (die Musiker)*
musician (female)	*die Musikerin (die Musikerinnen)*
farmer (male)	*der Landwirt (die Landwirte), der Bauer (die Bauern)*
farmer (female)	*die Bäuerin (die Bäuerinnen)*
secretary (male)	*der Sekretär (die Sekretäre)*
secretary (female)	*die Sekretärin (die Sekretärinnen)*
assistant (male)	*der Assistent (die Assistenten)*
assistant (female)	*die Assistentin (die Assistentinnen)*
unemployeed	*arbeitslos*
retired	*in Rente, pensioniert*
full-time	*Vollzeit-*
part-time	*Teilzeit-*
steady job	*das Angestelltenverhältnis (die Angestelltenverhältnisse)*

summer job   *der Sommerjob (die*
                              Sommerjobs)

LESSON 36

A. SHOPPING

Einkäufe
Purchases

1. **Wie viel kostet das?**
   How much is this?

2. **Zehn Euro.**
   Ten euros.

3. **Das ist zu teuer. Haben Sie nichts anderes?**
   That's too expensive. Don't you have anything
   else?

4. **Von derselben Sorte?**
   Of the same kind?

5. **Ja, dasselbe oder etwas Ähnliches.**
   Yes, the same kind or something similar.

6. **Wir haben so etwas.**
   We have something like it.

7. **Können Sie mir nichts anderes zeigen?**
   Don't you have anything else to show me?

8. **Etwas Billigeres?**
   Something less expensive?

9. **Wenn möglich.**
If possible.

10. **Möchten Sie so etwas?**
Would you like this?

11. **Das kommt auf den Preis an.**
That depends on the price.

12. **Das kostet acht Euro.**
This is eight euros.

13. **Und das hier? Ist es billiger oder teurer?**
How about this? Is it less expensive or more expensive?

14. **Teurer.**
More expensive.

15. **Haben Sie nichts anderes?**
Don't you have anything else?

16. **Im Moment nicht, aber ich erwarte einige Neuheiten.**
Not at the moment, but I'm expecting some new styles.

17. **Wann?**
When?

18. **Jeden Tag. Kommen Sie gegen Ende der Woche.**
Any day now. Drop in toward the end of the week.

19. **Ganz bestimmt. Übrigens, wieviel kostet es?**
I'll do that. By the way, how much is this?

20. **Sieben Euro das Paar.**
Seven euros a pair.

21. **Geben Sie mir ein Dutzend (davon)!**
Let me have a dozen (of them).

22. **Möchten Sie sie mitnehmen?**
Will you take them with you?

23. **Nein, bitte lassen Sie sie mir zuschicken!**
No, please have them delivered.

24. **Immer noch an dieselbe Adresse?**
Still at the same address?

25. **Ja, es ist immer noch dieselbe.**
Yes, it's still the same.

26. **Danke schön. Auf Wiedersehen!**
Thank you very much. Good-bye.

27. **Auf Wiedersehen!**
Good-bye.

NOTES

1. *Wieviel kostet es?* How much does it cost? *Was macht es?* How much does that make?
4. *Von:* always with the dative case.
5. *Ähnliches* (something similar) is a noun formed from an adjective, and it takes the same endings as an adjective. Here it is neuter, because it doesn't refer to a person but to "something."
6. *So etwas:* Something like this.
8. *Etwas Billigeres:* Something less expensive; neuter declension.
10. *Möchten Sie:* Would you like? polite form to express a want or wish; (conditional of *mögen*).

11. *ankommen (an-kommen):* separable prefix idio-
    matically, to depend on, or to arrive.
12. *Euro:* singular and plural.
13. Comparative: two examples of the comparative.
    Note that the second *e* in *teurer* is dropped in the
    comparative form.
16. *Im:* contraction of *in dem* (dative). *Einige* (a few,
    several): Use for *etwas* to express something pre-
    cise.
18. *Jeden Tag:* Accusative is generally used for
    expressions of time. *Gegen Ende* (idiomatic)
    toward the end; requires no article.
19. *Ganz bestimmt:* "Quite definite, certainly."
21. *mir:* Dative of the personal pronoun.
22. *mitnehmen (mit-nehmen):* separable prefix. *Ich
    nahm es mit.* I took it along.
23. *schicken lassen:* to have something sent. *machen
    lassen:* to have something done or made; *bauen
    lassen:* to have something built; etc.
24. *an* plus accusative (motion toward a destina-
    tion): *Er schickt es an mich.*

B. GENERAL SHOPPING EXPRESSIONS

Wo finde ich . . .
Where can I find . . .

Können Sie mir helfen?
Can you help me?

Ich schaue mich nur um.
I'm just browsing.

Ich suche eine Armbanduhr.
I'm looking for a wristwatch.

Zeigen Sie mir bitte einen Pullover.
Please show me a sweater.

Ich möchte etwas Billigeres.
I'd like something less expensive.

Ich möchte etwas Größeres.
I'd like something bigger.

Ich möchte etwas Kleineres.
I'd like something smaller.

Können Sie es mir bitte bestellen?
Can you please order it for me?

Ich nehme es.
I'll take it.

Wo ist die Kasse?
Where do I pay?

Kann ich das umtauschen?
Can I exchange this?

Kann ich mit Reiseschecks bezahlen?
Can I pay with traveler's checks?

QUIZ 26

1. _____ (How much) *macht das?*
     a. *Wie viel*
     b. *Wie*
     c. *Wann*

2. *Von derselben* _____ (kind).
     a. *Sorte*
     b. *Sache*
     c. *Abteilung*

3. *Ja, von derselben Sorte* _____ (or) *etwas Ähn-*
   liches.
   - a. *wann*
   - b. *oder*
   - c. *und*

4. *Es gibt* _____ (this).
   - a. *den*
   - b. *das*
   - c. *dies*

5. *Etwas* _____ (less).
   - a. *aber*
   - b. *weniger*
   - c. *nichts*

6. _____ (That) *kommt auf den Preis an.*
   - a. *Das*
   - b. *Dieses*
   - c. *Dem*

7. *Ich möchte etwas* _____ (less expensive).
   - a. *Kleineres*
   - b. *Billigeres*
   - c. *Grösseres*

8. _____ (When) *denn?*
   - a. *Wie*
   - b. *Wie viel*
   - c. *Wann*

9. *Geben Sie mir ein Dutzend* _____ (of them)!
   - a. *dort*
   - b. *davon*
   - c. *dann*

10. *Nein, schicken Sie* _____ (them) *mir, bitte!*
    a. *sie*
    b. *ihnen*
    c. *es*

ANSWERS
1—a; 2—a; 3—b; 4—c; 5—b; 6—a; 7—b; 8—c;
9—b; 10—a.

SUPPLEMENTAL VOCABULARY 14: CLOTHING

clothing	*Kleidung*
shirt	*das Hemd (die Hemden)*
pants	*die Hose (die Hosen)*
jeans	*die Jeans (die Jeans)*
tee shirt	*das T-Shirt (die T-Shirts)*
shoe	*der Schuh (die Schuhe)*
sock	*die Socke (die Socken)*
belt	*der Gürtel (die Gürtel)*
sneaker/tennis shoe	*der Turnschuh/ Tennisschuh (die Turnschuhe/ Tennisschuhe)*
dress	*das Kleid (die Kleider)*
skirt	*der Rock (die Röcke)*
blouse	*die Bluse (die Blusen)*
suit	*der Anzug (die Anzüge)*
hat	*der Hut (die Hüte)*
glove	*der Handschuh (die Handschuhe)*
scarf	*der Schal (die Schals)*
jacket (casual)	*die Jacke (die Jacken)*
jacket (formal)	*das Jackett (die Jacketts)*
coat	*der Mantel (die Mäntel)*

earring	*der Ohrring (die Ohrringe)*
bracelet	*das Armband (die Armbänder)*
necklace	*die Halskette (die Halsketten)*
eyeglasses	*die Brille (die Brillen)*
sunglasses	*die Sonnenbrille (die Sonnenbrillen)*
wrist watch	*die Armbanduhr (die Armbanduhren)*
ring	*der Ring (die Ringe)*
underpants	*die Unterhose (die Unterhosen)*
undershirt	*der Unterrock (die Unterröcke)*
bathing trunks	*die Badehose (die Badehosen)*
bathing suit	*der Badeanzug (die Badeanzüge)*
pyjamas	*der Schlafanzug (die Schlafanzüge)*
cotton	*die Baumwolle*
leather	*das Leder*
silk	*die Seide*
size	*die Größe (die Größen)*
to wear	*tragen*

LESSON 37

A. ORDERING BREAKFAST

1. *Es ist acht Uhr Sonntag Morgen. Martin Sandler aus den Vereinigten Staaten und seine deutsche Freundin Iris kommen in das Frühstücksrestaurant eines Hotels in Berlin.*
It is eight o'clock on Sunday morning. Martin Sandler from the United States and his German girlfriend Iris come into the breakfast restaurant of a hotel in Berlin.

2. *Iris:* **Du musst recht hungrig sein nach dem langen Flug, oder?**
Iris: You must be pretty hungry after that long flight, right?

3. *Martin:* **Ja, ein gutes Frühstück ist jetzt genau was ich brauche.**
Martin: Yes, a good breakfast is just what I need now.

4. *Iris:* **Hier soll man sehr gut frühstücken können.**
Iris: Breakfast is said to be very good here. (One should be able to eat breakfast very well here.)

5. *Iris und Martin setzen sich an einen freien Tisch. Kurz darauf kommt die Kellnerin und bringt die Speisekarte.*
Iris and Martin sit down at a free table. Shortly afterwards the waitress brings the menu.

6. *Kellnerin:* **Guten Morgen. Ich hoffe Sie haben ausgezeichnet geschlafen? Möchten Sie Kaffee, Tee oder heiße Schokolade zum Frühstück?**
Waitress: Good morning. I hope you slept very well. Would you like coffee, tea, or hot chocolate with your breakfast?

7. *Iris:* **Danke schön. Wir haben sehr gut geschlafen. Wir hätten beide gern Kaffee zum Frühstück.**
Iris: Thank you (nicely). We slept very well. We both would like coffee for breakfast.

8. *Martin schaut auf die Frühstückskarte und scheint ein wenig verwirrt.*
Martin looks at the breakfast menu, and seems a little confused.

9. *Martin:* **Eigentlich möchte ich Pfannkuchen, aber ich finde sie nicht hier auf der Karte, und auch kein Rührei mit Würstchen und Schinkenspeck.**
Martin: Actually, I would like pancakes, but I don't see any here on the menu, and also no scrambled eggs with sausages and bacon.

10. *Iris:* **Nun, ein typisch deutsches Frühstück besteht normalerweise aus Brötchen, Aufschnitt und verschiedene Sorten von Marmelade, vielleicht auch ein gekochtes Ei dazu. Du musst aber die verschiedenen Brötchen hier versuchen. Sie sind immer hervorragend.**
Iris: Well, a typical German breakfast normally consists of rolls, cold cuts, and different types of jams and preserves, perhaps also a boiled egg

with it. But you must try the different types of
rolls here. They are always great.

11. *Martin:* **Du weißt, ich esse nie Brot zum
Frühstück. Vielleicht haben sie auch etwas
anderes?**
Martin: You know, I never eat bread for breakfast. Perhaps they have something else, too?

12. *Iris:* **Keine Ahnung! Aber wir können ja die
Kellnerin fragen.**
Iris: I have no idea. But we can ask the waitress.

13. *Martin:* **Gute Idee!**
Martin: Good idea!

14. **Die Kellnerin kommt wieder zum Tisch mit
einer großen Kaffeekanne.**
The waitress comes back to the table with a large
pot of coffee.

15. *Kellnerin:* **Bitte sehr! Was darf ich Ihnen sonst
noch bringen?**
Waitress: Here you go! What else can I bring
you?

16. *Martin:* **Hätten Sie vielleicht auch Rührei
oder Pfannkuchen zum Frühstück?**
Martin: Would you by any chance also have
scrambled eggs or pancakes for breakfast?

17. *Kellnerin:* **Pfannkuchen haben wir leider nicht,
aber versuchen Sie doch das Bauernfrühstück.
Es ist Rührei mit Schinken, Champignons,
Zwiebeln und Käse.**

Waitress: Unfortunately, we don't have pancakes, but why don't you try the farmer's breakfast? It's scrambled eggs with prosciutto, mushrooms, onions, and cheese.

18. *Martin:* **Das hört sich gut an! Das nehme ich.**
Martin: That sounds good. I'll have that.

19. *Iris:* **Und ich hätte gern die Frühstücksplatte mit gemischtem Aufschnitt. Können Sie ein paar Brötchen extra bringen?**
Iris: And I would like the breakfast platter with mixed cold cuts. Could you bring a few extra rolls?

20. **Die Kellnerin lächelt und sagt: Selbstverständlich!**
The waitress smiles and says: Of course!

21. *Nach ein paar Minuten kommt die Kellnerin wieder mit dem Frühstück an den Tisch.*
After a few minutes, the waitress comes back to the table with breakfast.

21. *Ein paar Minuten später ...*
A few minutes later ...

22. *Iris:* **Wie schmeckt dir dein Rührei?**
Iris: How are your scambled eggs?

23. *Martin:* **Sehr gut, aber die Brötchen sind noch besser.**
Martin: Very good, but the rolls are even better.

24. *Nach weiteren fünfzehn Minuten kommt die Kellnerin zurück.*

After another fifteen minutes the waitress comes back.

25. *Kellnerin:* **Wie hat es Ihnen geschmeckt?**
    Waitress: Did you enjoy your breakfast?
    (Lit: How did it taste to you?)

26. *Martin:* **Ganz ausgezeichnet, besonders die hervorragenden Brötchen.**
    Martin: Really great, especially the outstanding rolls.

27. *Kellnerin:* **Vielen Dank. Dann brauche ich nur noch Ihre Schlüsselkarte.**
    Waitress: Thank you very much. Then all I need is your keycard.

28. *Iris:* **Hier bitte.**
    Iris: Here it is.

29. *Martin an Iris:* **Ich denke, morgen werde ich bestellen was du hattest.**
    Martin to Iris: I think tomorrow I'll order what you had.

30. *Iris (lächelnd):* **Du meinst, morgen werde ich auch frühstücken können?**
    Iris (smiling): You mean, tomorrow I'll be able to have breakfast as well?

NOTES

1. *Freund* (male friend) or *Freundin* (female friend) used with a possessive refers to boyfriend or girlfriend (*mein Freund, meine Freundin*). If you mean a general friend, you'd say *ein Freund von mir, eine Freundin von mir* (a friend of mine).

2. The preposition *nach* (after, to) is always followed by the dative case.

4. *Sollen* (should) can also refer to something that is assumed or supposed. *Morgen soll es regen.* (Tomorrow it's supposed to rain).

6. *Möchte* (would like) is a subjunctive form of *mögen* (to like). It is often used to order in a restaurant or to express any polite request to have or get something.

7. *Hätte* (would have) is another common subjunctive (of the verb *haben*) that is often used to indicate what you would like to have. It is commonly used in combination with the adverb *gern* (gladly).

10. It is uncommon to find a typical American breakfast in German hotels. Mostly larger hotels offer a breakfast buffet that increasingly offer cereal and other American breakfast items. In smaller hotels, a continental breakfast is usually served, and it consists of rolls, toast or bread, different types of cold cuts or cheese, and often a boiled egg. Of course, coffee or tea are always offered. You never have to order jam or marmelade. It always comes automatically with any breakfast.

12. *Ahnung* (idea) always refers to knowledge or a clue about something, never to a sudden creative thought or inspiration.

13. *Idee* (idea) is always a sudden creative thought or inspiration.

15. *Bitte sehr!* could mean "Here you go." or "You're welcome." or "Never mind." or "I beg your pardon." The situation and the tone of voice determine what is meant.

17. *Doch* after a verb (and a pronoun) often means "why don't you...?" in the sense of a polite request or suggestion. *Nehmen Sie doch Platz!* (Why don't you have a seat?)

21. *ein paar* (a few), *ein Paar* (a pair of, a couple)

27. Most hotels in Germany, like elsewhere, use the magnetic key card for the room *(die Schlüsselkarte)* to charge meals or other commodities within the hotel to your room. If the breakfast is included in the room price, you often just have to show your key card at the table.

B. A SAMPLE MENU

Speisekarte

KLEINE SPEISEN	SMALL DISHES
Schinkenbrot	Bread with Prosciutto
Gebackener Camembert	Baked Camembert with Fruit Jam
Bratwurst mit Kartoffelsalat	Roasted Sausage with Potato Salad
Currywurst mit Pommes Frites	Curry-Sausage with French Fries
Toast Hawai	Toast with Pineapple, Ham, and Melted Cheese

SUPPEN	SOUPS
Gemüsesuppe	Vegetable Soup
Zwiebelsuppe	Onion Soup
Goulaschsuppe	Beef Soup with Paprika
Leipziger Allerlei	Vegetable Soup with Sausage
Ochsenschwanzsuppe	Oxtail Soup
Erbsensuppe	Pea Soup
Linsensuppe	Lentil Soup

VORSPEISEN	APPETIZERS
Krabbensalat	Shrimp Cocktail
Räucherlachs auf Toast	Smoked Salmon with Toast
Spargel mit gekochtem Schinken	Asparagus Rolled in Baked Ham
Austern	Oysters
Gefüllte Paprikaschoten	Stuffed Green Peppers

SALATE	SALADS
Gemischter Salat	Mixed Green Salad
Tomatensalat	Tomato Salad
Bohnensalat	Green Bean Salad
Gurkensalat	Cucumber Salad

HAUPTGERICHTE	MAIN DISHES
Seelachs	Sea Salmon (Pollack)
Filetsteak	Filet Steak
Sauerbraten	Sweet and Sour Roast
Jägerschnitzel	Pork or Veal Cutlet with Mushroom Sauce
Kalbsragout	Veal Ragout
Brathähnchen	Grilled Chicken
Gegrillte Haxe	Grilled Leg of Pork

| *Wiener Schnitzel* | Breaded Veal Cutlet |
| *Forelle* | Trout |

HAUPT-BEILAGEN	MAIN SIDEDISHES
Bratkartoffeln	Fried Potatoes
Salzkartoffeln	Boiled Potatoes
Spätzle	Small Dumplings
Rösti	Fried Potato Pancakes
Knödel	Large Dumplings
Pommes Frites	French Fries

GEMÜSEBEILAGEN	VEGETABLE-SIDEDISHES
Rotkohl	Red Cabbage
Spargel	White Asparagus
Karotten	Carrots
Spinat	Spinach
Rosenkohl	Brussels Sprouts
Champignons	Mushrooms

NACHSPEISEN	DESSERTS
Schwarzwälder Kirschtorte	Black Forest Cherry Cake
Sacher Torte	Austrian Chocolate Cake
Apfelstrudel	Covered Apple Pie
Käseplatte	Cheese Platter
Gemischtes Eis	Mixed Icecream
Obstsalat	Fruit Salad

GETRÄNKE	DRINKS AND BEVERAGES
Mineralwasser	Mineral Water (carbonated)
Wasser Ohne	Mineral Water (noncarbonated)
Limonade	Lemonade (Soda)

Apfelsaft	Apple Juice
Orangensaft	Orange Juice
Bier	Beer
Weißwein	White Wine
Rotwein	Red Wine
Kaffee	Coffee
Tee	Tea

Note: In most lower and medium priced restaurants, it is common to leave just a few euros as a tip (*das Trinkgeld*). By law, all given prices everywhere including restaurants have to be final prices. Of course, waiters are not paid much more than they are here, and they often expect a tip. In higher priced restaurants, it is common to leave a ten percent tip; more is considered generous.

REVIEW QUIZ 6

1. *Du musst Hunger* _____ (have).
   a. *sein*
   b. *haben*
   c. *machen*

2. *Wir haben heute keine* _____ (butter).
   a. *Bier*
   b. *Butter*
   c. *Brot*

3. _____ (There is) *ein gutes Restaurant im Hotel.*
   a. *Es gibt*
   b. *Gibt es*
   c. *Das ist*

4. *Mein Kaffee ist* _____ (cold).
   a. *kalt*
   b. *warm*
   c. *mild*

5. *Geben Sie mir* _____ (the same)!
   a. *auch*
   b. *dasselbe*
   c. *viel mehr*

6. *Herr Ober, eine* _____ (napkin) *bitte!*
   a. *Gabel*
   b. *Messer*
   c. *Serviette*

7. *Würden Sie mir* _____ (also) *eine Gabel bringen?*
   a. *sehr*
   b. *nicht*
   c. *auch*

8. *Herr Ober,* _____ (the check).
   a. *der Tisch*
   b. *die Speisekarte*
   c. *die Rechnung*

9. *Etwas* _____ (more) *Zucker, bitte.*
   a. *gefällt*
   b. *mir*
   c. *mehr*

10. *Das ist in* _____ (okay)!
    a. *Rechnung*
    b. *Kleingeld*
    c. *Ordnung*

ANSWERS
1—b; 2—b; 3—a; 4—a; 5—b; 6—c; 7—c; 8—c;
9—c; 10—c.

LESSON 38

A. APARTMENT HUNTING

1. **Ich komme wegen der Wohnung.**
   I've come about the apartment.

2. **Welche, bitte?**
   Which one, please?

3. **Gibt es mehrere zu vermieten?**
   Are there several for rent?

4. **Es gibt zwei.**
   There are two.

5. **Können Sie mir eine Beschreibung geben?**
   Can you describe them?

6. **Die im fünften Stock ist unmöbliert.**
   The one on the fifth floor is unfurnished.

7. **Und die andere?**
   And the other?

8. **Die auf der zweiten Etage ist möbliert.**
   The one on the second floor is furnished.

9. **Wie viele Zimmer hat jede?**
   How many rooms does each one have?

10. **Die auf der fünften Etage hat vier Zimmer, Küche und Bad.**
The one on the fifth floor has four rooms, a kitchen, and bath.

11. **Die Wohnung hat auch eine gute Aussicht auf den Hof.**
The apartment also has a good view of the court-yard.

12. **Und die im zweiten Stock?**
And how about the one on the second floor?

13. **Sie hat fünf Zimmer, drei Schlafzimmer, ein Esszimmer und ein Wohnzimmer.**
It has five rooms, three bedrooms, a dining room, and a parlor.

14. **Liegt sie auch zum Hof hinaus?**
Is it also on the court?

15. **Nein, sie liegt zur Straße.**
No, it faces the street.

16. **Wie hoch ist die Miete?**
What's the rent?

17. **Die größere kostet zweitausend Euro mit Gas, Wasser und Strom.**
The larger one is two thousand euros with gas, water, and electricity.

18. **Und die möblierte Wohnung?**
And the furnished apartment?

19. **Zweitausendfünfhundert Euro. Gas, Wasser und Strom sind eingeschlossen.**
Two thousand five hundred euros. Gas, water, and electricity are included (in the price).

20. **Was für Möbel hat sie? Und in welchem Zustand sind sie?**
What kind of furniture does it have? And is it in good condition?

21. **Es sind antike Möbel in bestem Zustand.**
It's antique furniture (and) in excellent condition.

22. **Sind Wäsche und Silber einbegriffen?**
Are linens and silverware included?

23. **Sie finden alles, was man braucht, sogar eine vollständige Kücheneinrichtung.**
You'll find everything you need, even a complete set of kitchen utensils.

24. **Würde der Besitzer einen Mietvertrag mit mir machen? Und auf wie lange?**
Would the owner give me a lease? And for how long?

25. **Dafür müssen Sie sich an den Hausverwalter wenden.**
You'd have to see the renting agent for that.

26. **Wie sind die Bedingungen?**
What are the terms?

27. **Sie zahlen drei Monate im Voraus.**
You pay three months' rent in advance.

28. Sonst nichts?
Nothing else?

29. Referenzen, selbstverständlich.
References, of course.

30. Übrigens, ist ein Fahrstuhl vorhanden?
By the way, is there an elevator?

31. Nein, leider nicht.
No, unfortunately not.

32. Das ist schade.
That's too bad.

33. Davon abgesehen ist das Haus aber ganz modern.
Apart from that, though, the house is quite modern.

34. Wie meinen Sie das?
What do you mean?

35. Es hat neue Zentralheizung, Klimaanlage und Geschirrspüler.
It has a new central heating system, air conditioning, and a dishwasher.

36. Die Badezimmer wurden kürzlich renoviert.
Of course. The bathrooms were remodeled recently.

37. Sind eingebaute Schränke vorhanden?
Are there any closets?

38. Ja, einige große.
Yes, several large ones.

39. Wann kann man die Wohnungen sehen?
When can one see the apartments?

40. Nur am Morgen.
Only in the morning.

41. Sehr gut. Ich werde morgen früh kommen. Besten Dank.
Very well, I'll come tomorrow morning. Thanks a lot.

42. Keine Ursache.
Not at all.

NOTES

1. *Wegen:* because of (a preposition followed by the genitive).

5. *Können Sie mir eine Beschreibung geben?*—Can you give me a description?

6. *Die:* "the one"
   Auf der: (dative)
   In Germany the first floor is *das Erdgeschoss* ("ground floor").
   Therefore the first floor, *erster Stock,* is really the second floor for us.

9. *Jede* (standing alone) is "each one" and can also be used with a noun:
   jeder Mann—"each or every man"
   Here *jede* is feminine because it refers to the apartment: *die Wohnung.*

13. *Schlafzimmer:* bedroom ("sleeping room")
    Esszimmer: dining room ("eating room")
    Wohnzimmer: living room.

16. *Wie hoch ist die Miete?*—How high is the rent?
    Die Miete: the rent
    mieten: to rent
20. *Die Möbelstück:* furniture
    Das Möbelstück: a piece of furniture
22. *Die Wäsche:* linen; *also* laundry
    Die Wäscherei: laundry (place)
23. *Was man braucht:* "What one needs" *man* is
    used much more frequently than the English
    "one"
41. *Ich werde kommen:* Future of *kommen,* to come
42. *Keine Ursache*—("no cause, no reason")

B. At Home

Wir haben eine Wohnung.
We have an apartment.

Wir haben eine Eigentumswohnung.
We have a condominium.

Wir haben ein Haus.
We have a house.

Fühlen Sie sich wie zu Hause.
Make yourself at home.

Machen Sie es sich bequem.
Make yourself comfortable.

Was für ein schönes Haus haben Sie!
What a lovely house you have!

QUIZ 27

1. _____ (How many) *Zimmer haben Sie?*
   a. *Anderes*
   b. *Wie viele*
   c. *Jede*

2. *Die Wohnung hat eine Aussicht auf die* _____
   (street)?
   a. *Hof*
   b. *Wohnzimmer*
   c. *Straße*

3. *Was ist der* _____ (price)?
   a. *Preis*
   b. *Miete*
   c. *Art*

4. *Man* _____ (pays) *drei Monate im Voraus.*
   a. *sind*
   b. *kauft*
   c. *zahlt*

5. *Das* _____ (house) *ist sehr modern.*
   a. *Halle*
   b. *Haus*
   c. *Bad*

6. *Sind die* _____ (furniture) *modern.*
   a. *Möbel*
   b. *Teppiche*
   c. *Heizung*

7. *Ist eine* _____ (air conditioner) *auch vorhan-den?*
   a. *Klimaanlage*
   b. *Zimmer*
   c. *Geschirrspüler*

8. _____ (Only) *morgens*.
   a. *Besuchen Sie*
   b. *Nur*
   c. *Auch*

9. *Ich komme* _____ (tomorrow) *früh*.
   a. *morgen*
   b. *gestern*
   c. *heute*

10. _____ (Thank you) *vielmals*.
   a. *Morgen*
   b. *Dienst*
   c. *Danke*

ANSWERS

1—b; 2—c; 3—a; 4—c; 5—b; 6—a; 7—a; 8—b;
9—a; 10—c.

REVIEW QUIZ 7

1. *Ich ziehe diese Wohnung* (prefer) _____.
   a. *um*
   b. *vor*
   c. *an*

2. *Was kann* (this) _____ *heißen?*
   a. *das*
   b. *der*
   c. *diesem*

3. *Ich weiß nicht* _____ (how).
   a. *noch*
   b. *wo*
   c. *wie*

4. *Er kommt _____* (never).
    a. *auch*
    b. *niemals*
    c. *wie*

5. *Er hat _____* (nothing) *gesagt.*
    a. *kein*
    b. *nicht*
    c. *nichts*

6. *Ihr Buch ist besser als _____* (his) *Buch.*
    a. *Ihr*
    b. *sein*
    c. *mein*

7. *Ich bin _____* (glad), *Sie kennenzulernen.*
    a. *erfreut*
    b. *vorstellen*
    c. *Bekanntschaft*

8. *Bis nächste _____* (week)!
    a. *Monat*
    b. *Woche*
    c. *Jahr*

9. *Bis zum _____* (next) *Mal!*
    a. *neulich*
    b. *nächsten*
    c. *heute*

10. *Es geht gut, _____* (thanks).
    a. *denke*
    b. *danke*
    c. *sage*

11. *Rufen Sie mich diese* _____ (week) *an!*
    a. *Woche*
    b. *Tage*
    c. *Monat*

12. _____ (Know) *Sie meinen Freund?*
    a. *Kennen*
    b. *Treffen*
    c. *Wissen*

13. *Nein, ich* _____ (think) *nicht.*
    a. *will*
    b. *denke*
    c. *kenne*

14. *Ich* _____ (hope), *Sie bald wiederzusehen.*
    a. *erfreut*
    b. *gemacht*
    c. *hoffe*

15. *Ich werde es Ihnen* _____ (write).
    a. *haben*
    b. *schreiben*
    c. *sehen*

16. *Sie können mich*   (in the morning)
    anrufen.
    a. *nachmittags*
    b. *abends*
    c. *morgens*

17. *Ich habe ihn* _____ (met).
    a. *erfreut*
    b. *getroffen*
    c. *angerufen*

18. _____ (give) *Sie mir Ihre Adresse!*
    a. *Gehen*
    b. *Geben*
    c. *Rufen*

19. *Das ist sehr* _____ (good).
    a. *gut*
    b. *bald*
    c. *ganz*

20. *Auf* _____ (soon).
    a. *bald*
    b. *morgen*
    c. *auch*

ANSWERS
1—b; 2—a; 3—c; 4—b; 5—c; 6—b; 7—a; 8—b;
9—b; 10—b; 11—a; 12—a; 13—b; 14—c; 15—b;
16—c; 17—b; 18—b; 19—a; 20—a.

SUPPLEMENTAL VOCABULARY 15: IN THE KITCHEN

in the kitchen	*in der Küche*
refrigerator	*der Kühlschrank (die Kühlschränke)*
(kitchen) sink	*die Spüle (die Spülen)*
counter	*die Arbeitsflächen*
stove	*der Herd (die Herde)*
oven	*der Backofen (die Backöfen)*
microwave	*der Mikrowellenherd (die Mikrowellenherde)*
cupboard	*der Geschirrschrank (die Geschirrschränke)*

drawer	*die Schublade (die Schubladen)*
plate	*der Teller (die Teller)*
cup	*die Tasse (die Tassen)*
bowl	*die Schüssel (die Schüsseln)*
glass	*das Glas (die Gläser)*
spoon	*der Löffel (die Löffel)*
knife	*das Messer (die Messer)*
can	*die Dose (die Dosen)*
box	*die Schachtel (die Schachteln)*
bottle	*die Flasche (die Flaschen)*
carton	*der Karton (die Kartons)*
coffee maker	*die Kaffeemaschine (die Kaffeemaschinen)*
tea kettle	*der Teekessel (die Teekessel)*
blender	*der Mixer (die Mixer)*
iron	*das Bügeleisen (die Bügeleisen)*
ironing board	*das Bügelbrett (die Bügelbretter)*
broom	*der Besen (die Besen)*
dishwasher	*die Spülmaschine (die Spülmaschinen)*
washing machine	*die Waschmaschine (die Waschmaschinen)*
dryer	*der Trockner (die Trockner)*
to cook	*kochen*
to do the dishes	*abwaschen/spülen*
to do the laundry	*waschen*
dishwashing detergent	*das Geschirrspülmittel (die Geschirrspülmittel)*

laundry detergent	*das Waschpulver (die Waschpulver)*
bleach	*das Bleichmittel (die Bleichmittel)*
clean/dirty	*sauber/schmutzig*

SUPPLEMENTAL VOCABULARY 16: IN THE BATHROOM

in the bathroom	*im Badezimmer*
toilet	*die Toilette (die Toiletten)*
sink (wash basin)	*das Waschbecken (die Waschbecken)*
bath tub	*die Badewanne (die Badewannen)*
shower	*die Dusche (die Duschen)*
mirror	*der Spiegel (die Spiegel)*
medicine cabinet	*der Badezimmerschrank (die Badezimmer-schränke)*
towel	*das Handtuch (die Handtücher)*
toilet paper	*das Toilettenpapier*
shampoo	*das Shampoo*
soap	*die Seife (die Seifen)*
bath gel	*das Bademittel (die Bademittel)*
shaving cream	*die Rasiercreme*
razor	*der Rasierapparat (die Rasierapparate)*
to wash (oneself)	*sich waschen*
to take a shower/bath	*duschen/baden*
to shave	*sich rasieren*
cologne	*das Parfüm (die Parfüms), das Kölnischwasser,*
perfume	*das Parfüm (die Parfüms)*

deodorant	*das Deodorant (die Deodorants)*
bandage	*die Binde (die Binden)*
powder	*der Puder (die Puder)*

LESSON 39

A. To Come: *KOMMEN*

ich komme	I come	*wir kommen*	we come
du kommst	you come	*ihr kommt*	you come
er kommt	he comes	*Sie kommen*	you come
sie kommt	she comes	*sie kommen*	they come
es kommt	it comes		

Komm!	Come! (*fam.*)
Kommen Sie!	Come! (*pol.*)
Kommen Sie hierher!	Come (over) here!
Kommen Sie mit mir mit!	Come with me!
Kommen Sie wieder!	Come again!
Kommen Sie nach Hause!	Come home!
Kommen Sie zu Besuch!	Come for a visit!
Kommen Sie nicht!	Don't come!
Woher kommen Sie?	Where do you come from? Where are you coming from?
Ich komme aus Berlin.	I come from Berlin. I'm coming from Berlin.
Ich komme aus dem Theater.	I'm coming from the theater.
Ich komme sofort.	I'm coming right away.

B. To Say: *SAGEN*

ich sage	I say	*wir sagen*	we say
du sagst	you say	*ihr sagt*	you say
er sagt	he says	*sie sagen*	they say
sie sagt	she says	*Sie sagen*	you say
es sagt	it says		

Man sagt, dass . . .	It's said that . . . People say that . . . They say that . . .
Man hat es mir gesagt.	I've been told (it).
Das ist schwer zu sagen.	That's hard to say.
Sagen Sie!	Say (it)!
Sagen Sie es!	Say it!
Sagen Sie es noch einmal!	Say it again!
Sagen Sie es auf Deutsch!	Say it in German!
Sagen Sie es langsam!	Say it slowly!
Sagen Sie es nicht!	Don't say it!
Sagen Sie das nicht!	Don't say that!
Sagen Sie mir . . .	Tell me. Well, tell me. Say, . . .
Sagen Sie, ist das Ihr Ernst?	Say, you're not serious, are you?
Sagen Sie mir.	Tell me.
Sagen Sie es mir.	Say it to me. Tell me (it).
Sagen Sie ihm.	Tell him.
Sagen Sie es ihm.	Tell it to him.
Sagen Sie ihm, er soll kommen!	Tell him to come!

Sagen Sie es ihm nicht.	Don't tell it to him. Don't tell him.
Sagen Sie ihm nichts.	Don't tell him anything. Tell him nothing.
Sagen Sie es niemand.	Don't tell it to anybody.
Was sagen Sie?	What did you say? ("What say you?")
sozusagen	so to say, so to speak
Können Sie mir sagen, wo ein Hotel ist?	Can you tell me where there's a hotel?
Was möchten Sie sagen?	What do you mean? ("What do you want [would you like] to say?")
Er hat nichts gesagt.	He hasn't said anything.

QUIZ 28

1. *Ich komme aus dem Theater.*	a. Come with me.
2. *Ich komme sofort.*	b. Where are you coming from?
3. *Ich komme später.*	c. Come for a visit.
4. *Woher kommen Sie?*	d. I'm coming right away.
5. *Sagen Sie mir!*	e. I'm coming from the theater.
6. *Sagen Sie es auf Deutsch!*	f. Say it in German.
7. *Das ist schwer zu sagen.*	g. So to say, so to speak.
8. *Kommen Sie mit mir mit!*	h. That's hard to say.

9. *Kommen Sie zu Besuch!*   i. I'll come later.
10. *Sozusagen.*   j. Tell me.

ANSWERS
1—e; 2—d; 3—i; 4—b; 5—j; 6—f; 7—h; 8—a;
9—c; 10—g.

C. To Do: *Tun*

Ich tue	I do	*wir tun*	we do
du tust	you do	*ihr tut*	you do
er tut	he does	*Sie tun*	you do
sie tut	she does	*sie tun*	they do
es tut	it does		

Ich tue es.	I do it. I'm doing it.
Ich tue es nicht.	I don't do it. I'm not doing it.
Was tun Sie?	What are you doing?
Wie tun Sie das?	How do you do it?
Was haben Sie getan?	What have you done?
Tun Sie es nicht.	Don't do it.
Tun Sie es nicht mehr.	Don't do it anymore.
Das ist getan.	It's done. It's over.
Das tut mir weh.	That hurts me.
Das tut mir Leid.	I'm sorry.
Ich tue nichts.	I'm not doing anything. I'm doing nothing.
Tun Sie das nicht!	Don't do that!
Tun Sie es noch einmal.	Do it again.
Tun Sie es schnell!	Do it quickly!
Tun Sie nichts!	Don't do anything!
Sie dürfen das nicht tun.	You may not do that.

Ich habe es gerade getan.	I've just done it. I just did it.
Was ist zu tun?	What's to be done? (What should one do?)
Was kann man tun?	What can one do? ("What to do?")
Wie sollen wir es tun?	How shall we do it?
Wer hat das getan?	Who did that?
Ich weiß nicht, was ich tun soll.	I don't know what to do.
So etwas tut man nicht.	That isn't done. ("One doesn't do that.")

QUIZ 29

1. *Was haben Sie getan?* a. I'm sorry.
2. *Tun Sie es nicht!* b. Do it quickly.
3. *Das ist getan.* c. What are you doing?
4. *Ich habe es getan.* d. What have you done?
5. *Was ist zu tun?* e. Don't do it!
6. *Tun Sie es noch einmal!* f. That's done. It's over.
7. *Wer hat das getan?* g. Do me a favor.
8. *Ich habe es gerade getan.* h. You are hurting me!
9. *Tun Sie mir einen Gefallen.* i. That isn't done. You don't do that. ("One does not do that.")
10. *Du tust mir weh!* j. I have done it. I did it.
11. *Das tut mir Leid.* k. What are we doing tomorrow?
12. *Was tun Sie?* l. What's to be done?
13. *Tun Sie es schnell.* m. I've just done it. I just did it.
14. *So etwas tut man nicht.* n. Do it again.

15. *Was tun wir morgen?*   o. Who has done that?
                              Who did that ?

ANSWERS
1—d; 2—e; 3—f; 4—j; 5—l; 6—n; 7—o; 8—m;
9—g; 10—h; 11—a; 12—c; 13—b; 14—i; 15—k.

REVIEW QUIZ 8

1. *Ich* _____ (am coming) *sofort.*
    a. *kenne*
    b. *komme*
    c. *sehe*

2. *Das ist schwer zu* _____ (say).
    a. *kommen*
    b. *antworten*
    c. *sagen*

3. *Was* _____ (do) *Sie?*
    a. *sagen*
    b. *tun*
    c. *macht*

4. *Ich weiß nicht, was ich* _____ (do) *soll.*
    a. *sagen*
    b. *kommen*
    c. *tun*

5. _____ (Take) *Sie es nicht!*
    a. *Nehmen*
    b. *Schicken*
    c. *Versuchen*

6. _____ (Stop) *Sie sofort* _____!
   a. *Halten . . . an*
   b. *Hören . . . an*
   c. *Helfen . . . mit*

7. *Ich* _____ (hope), *bald von Ihnen zu hören.*
   a. *komme*
   b. *hoffe*
   c. *helfe*

8. *Ich* _____ (see) *nicht gut ohne Brille.*
   a. *spreche*
   b. *weiß*
   c. *sehe*

9. *Ich werde Sie heute Abend* _____ (see).
   a. *sehen*
   b. *können*
   c. *gesehen*

10. *Er* _____ (holds, is holding) *seinen Hut in der Hand.*
    a. *haltet*
    b. *kann*
    c. *hält*

11. *Ich weiß nicht, wie wir das machen* _____ (can).
    a. *könnt*
    b. *können*
    c. *mögen*

12. *Er* _____ (understand) *einfach nicht.*
    a. *besucht*
    b. *versteht*
    c. *stellt*

13. _____ (Take) *Sie Ihr Buch.*
    a. *Stellen*
    b. *Nehmen*
    c. *Geben*

14. *Sie* _____ (owe) *mir nichts.*
    a. *schulden*
    b. *fragen*
    c. *brauchen*

15. *Er* _____ (ask) *mich, wo der Laden ist.*
    a. *fährt*
    b. *fragt*
    c. *darf*

ANSWERS
1—b; 2—c; 3—b; 4—c; 5—a; 6—a; 7—b; 8—c;
9—a; 10—c; 11—b; 12—b; 13—b; 14—a; 15—b.

D. COULD YOU GIVE ME SOME INFORMATION?

  1. Verzeihung, mein Herr.
  I beg your pardon, sir.

  2. Bitte sehr.
  Not at all.

  3. Können Sie mir eine Auskunft geben?
  Could you give me some information?

4. Gewiss, mit Vergnügen.
Certainly, I'd be glad to.

5. Ich kenne die Stadt nicht. Ich finde mich nicht zurecht.
I don't know the town. I can't find my way around.

6. Das ist doch ganz einfach.
It's quite simple.

7. Sehen Sie, ich bin fremd hier.
You see, I'm a stranger here.

8. Das macht nichts.
That's nothing. No problem.

9. Könnten Sie mir erklären, wo die wichtigsten Gebäude sind?
Could you tell me (explain to me) where the most important buildings are (located)?

10. Natürlich. Passen Sie gut auf!
Certainly. Pay careful attention!

11. Ich passe gut auf und schreibe alles auf.
I'll pay careful attention and write everything down.

12. Fangen wir mit der Post an!
Let's begin with the post office.

13. Schön. Das ist eine gute Idee.
Fine! That's a good idea.

14. Sehen Sie das Gebäude an der Ecke?
Do you see the building at the corner?

15. Das mit der blauen Laterne?
The one with the blue lantern?

16. Ja, das ist es. Das Postamt ist im Erdgeschoss.
Yes, that's the one. The post office is on the ground floor.

17. Der Laden mit der Fahne—was ist das?
The store with the flag—what's that?

18. Das ist unsere Polizei.
That's our police station.

19. Dort ist ein anderes Gebäude mit einer Fahne.
There's another building with a flag.

20. Das ist das Rathaus.
That's the City Hall.

21. Wie heißt diese Strasse?
What's the name of this street?

22. Das ist die Marktstrasse. Sehen Sie das Geschäft?
This is Market Street. Do you see that store?

23. Welches? Das auf der rechten Seite?
Which one? The one on the right?

24. Ja. Das mit der großen grünen Kugel im Fenster.
Yes. The one with a large green globe in the window.

25. Und einer roten in dem andern?
And a red one in the other?

26. Richtig. Das ist die Apotheke.
That's right. That's the pharmacy.

27. Ah, ich verstehe.
Oh, I see.

28. Der Arzt wohnt nebenan.
The doctor lives right next door.

29. Ist er ein guter Arzt?
Is he a good doctor?

30. Er ist auch Herzspezialist und ist jeden Morgen im Krankenhaus.
He's also a heart specialist and is at the hospital every morning.

31. Wo befindet sich das Krankenhaus?
Where's the hospital?

32. Zwei Straßen von hier, links, gerade bevor Sie auf die Landstraße kommen.
Two streets from here, to your left, just before you come to the main highway.

33. Gibt es ein Schreibwarengeschäft hier in der Nähe?
Is there a stationery store around here?

34. Natürlich. Das ist nicht weit von hier in der Hauptstraße, gegenüber von Ihrem Hotel.
Of course. It's not far from here, on Main Street, across from your hotel.

35. Jetzt weiß ich Bescheid.
I know my way around.

36. Kaufen Sie sich doch einen Stadtplan!
Why don't you go and buy yourself a map of the city?

37. Das ist eine gute Idee! Wo bekomme ich einen?
That's a good idea. Where can I get one?

38. Entweder am Bahnhof oder am Zeitungsstand.
Either at the station or at the newspaper stand.

39. Wo ist der Bahnhof?
Where is the station?

40. Der Bahnhof ist am Ende der Marktstraße.
The station is at the end of Market Street.

41. Und wo ist ein Zeitungsstand?
And where's there a newspaper stand?

42. An der nächsten Ecke.
At the next corner.

43. Ich hatte Glück, Sie zu treffen. Sie scheinen die Stadt sehr gut zu kennen.
I was lucky to meet you. You seem to know the town very well.

44. Das ist selbstverständlich. Ich bin der Bürgermeister der Stadt.
It's quite natural. ("It is obvious.") I'm the mayor of the town.

45. Besten Dank.
Thank you very much.

46. Ich hoffe, dass Sie in unserer Stadt einen guten Aufenthalt haben.
I hope you have an enjoyable stay in our city.

NOTES

1. *Verzeihung, Entschuldigen Sie, Entschuldigung:* I beg your pardon; Excuse me; I am sorry.
6. *Doch* gives emphasis to the sentence.
8. *Das macht nichts:* "That's nothing." *Das ist unwichtig:* "That's unimportant."
10. *Aufpassen:* "to listen to" or "to watch out" (separable prefix).
12. *Die Post or Das Postamt:* the post office.
14. *An der Ecke:* (dative) (no motion toward anything).
20. *Das Rathaus:* "the council house" (city hall). *Der Bürgermeister:* "the mayor."
25. *Einer roten:* (feminine, dative) because of *mit* in sentence 24.
28. Physicians are called *Doktor* or *Arzt* and are addressed as *Herr Doktor.*
31. *Befindet sich* is located. ("Where does it find itself?") *finden:* to find, *sich befinden:* to be.
32. Note verb transposition. *Bevor* is a subordinating conjunction.
33. *Das Schreibwarengeschäft:* another example of compound nouns; "store for merchandise to write" or "stationery store."
35. *Jetzt bin ich . . .* (inverted word order)
38. *Entweder . . . oder* either . . . or; *weder . . . noch* neither . . . nor.

44. *Selbstverständlich:* "That understands itself"; "That is self-evident." (Another polite expression: *Gern geschehen:* "It happened with pleasure.")
45. *Besten Dank* ("best thanks").

QUIZ 30

1. _____ (Not at all).
    a. *Bitte sehr!*
    b. *Das tut mir Leid!*
    c. *Keine Ursache!*

2. *Können Sie mir einige Auskünfte* _____ (give)?
    a. *besorgen*
    b. *sprechen*
    c. *geben*

3. *Sie müssen mir alles* _____ (explain).
    a. *hören*
    b. *erklären*
    c. *anfangen*

4. *Sehen Sie das* _____ (house) *an der Ecke?*
    a. *Büro*
    b. *Gebäude*
    c. *Laterne*

5. *Wie heißt diese* _____ (Street)?
    a. *Geschäft*
    b. *Straße*
    c. *Ecke*

6. *Der Arzt* _____ (lives) *nebenan.*
    a. *wohnt*
    b. *singt*
    c. *macht*

7. *Bei* _____ (green) *Licht dürfen Sie gehen.*
   a. *roten*
   b. *grünem*
   c. *gelbes*

8. *Er ist jeden* _____ (morning) *im Krankenhaus.*
   a. *Nachmittag*
   b. *Morgen*
   c. *Abend*

9. *Ich hatte* _____ (luck), *Sie zu treffen.*
   a. *Pech*
   b. *Spass*
   c. *Glück*

10. *Wo befindet sich* _____ (the train station)?
   a. *das Postamt*
   b. *der Bahnhof*
   c. *das Rathaus*

ANSWERS
1—c; 2—c; 3—b; 4—b; 5—b; 6—a; 7—b; 8—b;
9—c; 10—b.

SUPPLEMENTAL VOCABULARY 17: AROUND TOWN

around town	*in der Stadt*
town	*der Ort (die Orte)*
city	*die Stadt (die Städte)*
village	*das Dorf (die Dörfer)*
car	*das Auto (die Autos)*
bus	*der Bus (die Busse)*
train	*der Zug (die Züge)*
taxi	*das Taxi (die Taxis/Taxen)*

subway / metro	*die U-Bahn (die U-Bahnen)*
traffic	*der Verkehr*
building	*das Gebäude (die Gebäude)*
apartment building	*das Wohngebäude (die Wohngebäude)*
library	*die Bibliothek (die Bibliotheken)*
restaurant	*das Restaurant (die Restaurants)*
store	*das Geschäft (die Geschäfte)*
shop, small store	*der Laden (die Läden)*
street	*die Straße (die Straßen)*
park	*der Park (die Parks)*
train station	*der Bahnhof (die Bahnhöfe)*
airport	*der Flughafen (die Flughäfen)*
airplane	*das Flugzeug (die Flugzeuge)*
intersection	*die Kreuzung (die Kreuzungen)*
lamp post	*der Laternenpfahl (die Laternenpfähle)*
street light	*die Straßenlaterne (die Straßenlaternen)*
bank	*die Bank (die Banken)*
church	*die Kirche (die Kirchen)*
temple	*der Tempel (die Tempel)*
mosque	*die Moschee (die Moscheen)*
sidewalk	*der Gehsteig (die Gehsteige)*

bakery	*die Bäckerei (die Bäckereien)*
butcher shop	*der Metzgerladen (die Metzgerläden)*
café/coffee shop	*das Café (die Cafés)*
drugstore/pharmacy	*die Apotheke (die Apotheken)*
supermarket	*der Supermarkt (die Supermärkte)*
market	*der Markt (die Märkte)*
shoe store	*das Schuhgeschäft (die Schuhgeschäfte)*
clothing store	*das Bekleidungsgeschäft (die Bekleidungsgeschäfte)*
electronics store	*das Elektrogeschäft (die Elektrogeschäfte)*
bookstore	*die Buchhandlung (die Buchhandlungen)*
department store	*das Kaufhaus (die Kaufhäuser)*
mayor	*der Bürgermeister (die Bürgermeister)*
city hall/municipal building	*das Rathaus (die Rathäuser)*
to buy	*kaufen*
to go shopping	*einkaufen gehen*
near/far	*nah / weit*
urban	*städtisch, urban*
suburban	*vorstädtisch*
rural	*ländlich*

LESSON 40

A. The Most Common Verb Forms

In the present tense, German verbs may be regular or irregular. Both types of verbs take certain endings in the different conjugated forms, but irregular verbs also have a vowel change in the stem. In the past tense, verbs may be weak or strong. Weak verbs take endings on their basic stems, and strong verbs undergo vowel changes. In the table below, *fragen* is regular and weak, and *sprechen* is irregular and strong.

INFINITIVE

PRESENT

| *fragen* | to ask | *sprechen* | to speak |

PAST

| *gefragt haben* | | *gesprochen haben* |
| to have asked | | to have spoken |

PARTICIPLES

PRESENT

| *fragend* | asking | *sprechend* | speaking |

PAST

| *gefragt* | asked | *gesprochen* | spoken |

INDICATIVE

PRESENT

frage	*spreche*
fragst	*sprichst*
fragt	*spricht*
fragen	*sprechen*

fragt   *sprecht*
fragen   *sprechen*

SIMPLE PAST

fragte   *sprach*
fragtest   *sprachst*
fragte   *sprach*

fragten   *sprachen*
fragtet   *spracht*
fragten   *sprachen*

FUTURE

werde fragen   *werde sprechen*
wirst fragen   *wirst sprechen*
wird fragen   *wird sprechen*

werden fragen   *werden sprechen*
werdet fragen   *werdet sprechen*
werden fragen   *werden sprechen*

CONDITIONAL

würde fragen   *würde sprechen*
würdest fragen   *würdest sprechen*
würde fragen   *würde sprechen*

würden fragen   *würden sprechen*
würdet fragen   *würdet sprechen*
würden fragen   *würden sprechen*

CONVERSATIONAL PAST
(PRESENT PERFECT)

habe gefragt   *habe gesprochen*
hast gefragt   *hast gesprochen*
hat gefragt   *hat gesprochen*

haben gefragt	haben gesprochen
habt gefragt	habt gesprochen
haben gefragt	haben gesprochen

PAST PERFECT
(PLUPERFECT)

hatte gefragt	hatte gesprochen
hattest gefragt	hattest gesprochen
hatte gefragt	hatte gesprochen
hatten gefragt	hatten gesprochen
hattet gefragt	hattet gesprochen
hatten gefragt	hatten gesprochen

FUTURE PERFECT

werde gefragt haben	werde gesprochen haben
wirst gefragt haben	wirst gesprochen haben
wird gefragt haben	wird gesprochen haben
werden gefragt haben	werden gesprochen haben
werdet gefragt haben	werdet gesprochen haben
werden gefragt haben	werden gesprochen haben

PAST CONDITIONAL

würde gefragt haben	würde gesprochen haben
würdest gefragt haben	würdest gesprochen haben
würde gefragt haben	würde gesprochen haben
würden gefragt haben	würden gesprochen haben
würdet gefragt haben	würdet gesprochen haben

würden gefragt haben   *würden gesprochen*
                                           haben

IMPERATIVE

frage!   *sprich!*
fragt!   *sprecht!*
fragen wir!   *sprechen wir!*
fragen Sie!   *sprechen Sie!*

SUBJUNCTIVE

PRESENT

dass ich frage   *dass ich spreche*
dass du fragest   *dass du sprechest*
dass er frage   *dass er spreche*

dass wir fragen   *dass wir sprechen*
dass ihr fraget   *dass ihr sprechet*
dass sie fragen   *dass sie sprechen*

IMPERFECT

dass ich fragte   *dass ich spräche*
dass du fragtest   *dass du sprächest*
dass er fragte   *dass er spräche*

dass wir fragten   *dass wir sprächen*
dass ihr fragtet   *dass ihr sprächet*
dass sie fragten   *dass sie sprächen*

PRESENT PERFECT

dass ich gefragt habe   *dass ich gesprochen*
                                            habe

dass du gefragt habest   *dass du gesprochen*
                                            habest

dass er gefragt habe	*dass er gesprochen habe*
dass wir gefragt haben	*dass wir gesprochen haben*
dass ihr gefragt habet	*dass ihr gesprochen habet*
dass sie gefragt haben	*dass sie gesprochen haben*

PAST PERFECT

dass ich gefragt hätte	*dass ich gesprochen hätte*
dass du gefragt hättest	*dass du gesprochen hättest*
dass er gefragt hätte	*dass er gesprochen hätte*
dass wir gefragt hätten	*dass wir gesprochen hätten*
dass ihr gefragt hättet	*dass ihr gesprochen hättet*
dass sie gefragt hätten	*dass sie gesprochen hätten*

2. Some common forms of common verbs:

   a. I have gone, etc.

I have gone

ich bin gegangen	*wir sind gegangen*
du bist gegangen	*ihr seid gegangen*
er ist gegangen	*sie (Sie) sind gegangen*

Compare: *Ich habe gegeben* ("I have given") and *ich bin gegangen* ("I have gone").

Notice that most verbs use *ich habe, du hast, er hat,* etc., but that a few (chiefly verbs of motion) have *ich bin, du bist, er ist,* as a helping verb.

The most common verbs which have the latter form are:

ich bin eingetreten	I have entered, I entered
ich bin ausgegangen	I have gone out, I went out
ich bin angekommen	I have arrived, I arrived
ich bin abgereist	I have left, I left
ich bin hinaufgegangen	I have gone up, I went up
ich bin hinunterge-gangen	I have gone down, I went down
ich bin geblieben	I have remained, I remained
ich bin zurückgekommen	I have returned, I returned
ich bin gefallen	I have fallen, I fell
ich bin geboren	I was born
ich bin geworden	I have become, I became
ich bin hingefahren	I went (traveled) there

b. I had given, had gone, etc.

I had given

ich hatte gegeben	*wir hatten gegeben*
du hattest gegeben	*ihr hattet gegeben*
er hatte gegeben	*Sie (sie) hatten gegeben*

Other examples:

ich hatte gesprochen	I had spoken
ich hatte gefragt	I had asked
ich hatte gebracht	I had brought

I had gone

ich war gegangen	*wir waren gegangen*
du warst gegangen	*ihr wart gegangen*
er war gegangen	*Sie (sie) waren gegangen*

Other examples:

ich war angekommen	I had arrived
ich war gekommen	I had gone
ich war eingetreten	I had entered
ich war ausgegangen	I had gone out
ich war abgereist	I had left
ich war hinaufgegangen	I had gone up
ich war gefallen	I had fallen
ich war gewesen	I had been

c. Help! Bring!

Helfen Sie mir!	Help me!
Bringen Sie mir noch mehr . . . !	Bring me some more . . . !
Bringen Sie es mir!	Bring it to me!
Halten Sie an!	Stop!
Halten Sie sofort an!	Stop right away!
Halten Sie dort!	Stop there!
Halten Sie ihn!	Stop him!

Setzen Sie sich!	Sit down! Have a seat!
Glauben Sie mir!	Believe me!
Hören Sie!	Listen!
Hören Sie mir zu!	Listen to me!
Hören Sie mir gut zu!	Listen to me carefully!
Hören Sie sich das an!	Listen to this (that)!
Hören Sie gut zu!	Listen carefully!

The *Sie* form corresponds to the polite, that is, the formal form.

The familiar form, that is, the *du* form, is as follows:

	To give: *geben*
du gibst	you give
Gib!	Give!

	To speak: *sprechen*
du sprichst	you speak
Sprich!	Speak!

	To take: *nehmen*
du nimmst	you take
Nimm!	Take!

d. Giving, Speaking

gebend	giving
sprechend	speaking
kommend	coming
sehend	seeing
fliessendes Wasser	running water
den Sitten folgend (dative plural)	following the custom

Notice that the German *-end* form corresponds to our *-ing* form in English.

e. Let's go! Listen! (Polite)

Gehen wir dorthin!	Let's go over there.
Sehen wir einmal!	Let's see.
Gehen wir!	Let's leave!
Versuchen wir!	Let's try!
Warten wir!	Let's wait!
Nehmen wir etwas!	Let's take some!
Hören Sie ihm zu!	Listen to him.
Hören Sie ihm nicht zu!	Don't listen to him.
Nehmen Sie das fort!	Take that away.
Herein!	Come in!
Treten Sie ein!	Go in! Come in! Enter!
Schicken Sie es ihm!	Send it to him.
Schicken Sie sie mir!	Send them to me.
Schicken Sie ihm einige!	Send him some!
Schicken Sie mir einige!	Send me some!
Versuchen Sie!	Try!
Versuchen Sie nicht!	Don't try!
Versuchen Sie nicht, das zu tun!	Don't try to do that!
Waschen Sie sich!	Wash yourself!
Stehen Sie auf!	Get up! Stand up!
Lesen Sie das!	Read that!
Führen Sie mich dorthin!	Take me there!
Gehen Sie dort hinauf!	Go up there!
Zeigen Sie mir!	Show me!
Zeigen Sie mir das!	Show me it (that)!
Zeigen Sie ihm!	Show him!
Zeigen Sie es ihm nicht!	Don't show it to him!
Vergessen Sie nicht!	Don't forget!

Gehen Sie fort!	Leave!
Gehen Sie schnell fort!	Leave quickly! Go right away!
Gehen Sie hinein!	Go in!
Denken Sie daran!	Think of it!
Tragen Sie das dorthin!	Carry this over there!
Nehmen Sie!	Take!
Nehmen Sie es!	Take it!
Nehmen Sie es nicht!	Don't take it!
Nehmen Sie noch eins!	Take another one!
Nehmen Sie den Zug!	Take the train!
Nehmen Sie ein Taxi!	Take a taxi!
Sehen Sie!	Look!
Sehen Sie noch einmal!	Look again!
Sehen Sie hierher!	Look (over) here!
Sehen Sie mich an!	Look at me!
Sehen Sie das an!	Look at this (that)!
Sehen Sie nicht hier-her!	Don't look [over here].
Geben Sie es mir wieder!	Return it to me!
Gehen Sie nach Hause!	Go home!
Gehen Sie früher nach Hause!	Go home earlier!
Wiederholen Sie!	Repeat! Say it again!
Wiederholen Sie das!	Repeat it (this, that). Say it (this, that) again.
Bleiben Sie!	Stay!
Bleiben Sie hier!	Stay here!
Bleiben Sie ruhig!	Be still! (quiet, calm)
Gehen Sie hinaus!	Go out!
Folgen Sie!	Follow!
Folgen Sie mir!	Follow me!
Folgen Sie ihm!	Follow him!
Berühren Sie es nicht!	Don't touch it!

Schenken Sie mir Kaf-   Pour me some coffee.
fee ein.

QUIZ 31

1. *Zeigen Sie mir!*	a. Look at (that).
2. *Treten Sie ein!*	b. Look here.
3. *Darf ich mal?*	c. Take a taxi.
4. *Denken Sie daran.*	d. Take another one.
5. *Zeig mir das Buch!*	e. Show me the book!
6. *Führen Sie mich dorthin.*	f. Take me there.
7. *Nehmen Sie ein Taxi.*	g. May I?
8. *Nehmen Sie noch eins.*	h. Think of it.
9. *Sehen Sie her.*	i. Go in!
10. *Sehen Sie das an.*	j. Show me.

ANSWERS
1—j; 2—i; 3—g; 4—h; 5—e; 6—f; 7—c; 8—d;
9—b; 10—a.

B. AT A SPA

Herr Wirth und Herr Kuhn treffen sich in einem Kurort.
Mr. Wirth and Mr. Kuhn meet at a spa.

1. *W:* **Herr Kuhn, schön, Sie zu treffen. Erholen Sie sich gut?**
   W: Mr. Kuhn, how nice to see you. Are you recuperating?

2. *K:* **Ja, danke. Leider müssen wir am Sonntag zurück und wieder einen Tag im Bus sitzen.**
   K: Yes, thanks. Unfortunately, we have to return home on Sunday and spend another day on the bus.

3. *W:* **Schade! Wie verbringen Sie die Tage hier?**
   W: Too bad. How are you spending your days here?

4. *K:* **Meine Frau macht eine Kur. Jeden Morgen und Abend trinkt sie das Heilquellenwasser. Vormittags schwimmt sie im Mineralbad.**
   K: My wife is taking treatments. She drinks the medicinal spring water every morning and evening. Before noon, she swims in the mineral pool.

5. *W:* **Bekommt sie auch Massagen und Lehmpackungen?**
   W: Does she also get massages and mud packs?

6. *K:* **Ja, ja. Danach ruht sie sich in der Liegehalle aus. Ich mache während dieser Zeit Gymnastik und promeniere in der Wandelhalle. Laufen tut mir gut.**
   K: Oh yes. After that, she rests in the lounge. I do exercises (calisthenics) during this time and go for a stroll in the indoor promenade. Walking is good for me.

7. *W·* **Wir hören gern das Kurkonzert und waren auch zweimal wöchentlich im Spielkasino. Aber am Abend und in der Nacht wird es zu kühl, nicht?**
   W: We like to listen to the concerts and also went to the casino twice a week. But it gets too cool in the evenings and at night, doesn't it?

8. *K:* **Ja. Vor zwei Jahren war es hier genau so kalt. Irgendwann einmal fahren wir in einen Kurort weiter südlich.**
K: Yes. Two years ago it was just as cold here. Someday we'll go to a health resort further south.

NOTES

2. *Leider müssen wir zurück (reisen.)* The *reisen* is understood in this sentence. Also notice the use of the accusative case (*einen Tag*) and the dative case (*im Bus.*) The accusative is used in a time expression without a preposition, "a day," and the dative is used to indicate location, "in the bus."

4. *Die Kur* means "treatment." A "cure" is *eine Heilung.*

6. Notice the use of the dative case in the following instances: *in der Liegehalle* (location) and *in der Wandelhalle* (location). The last example would be in the accusative if it involved direction or motion toward: *Ich gehe in die Wandelhalle.* "I'm going into the indoor promenade." Also notice that the preposition *während* is followed by the genitive.

C. Sightseeing

Laura und Olga sind in der Altstadt.
Laura and Olga are in the Old Town.

1. *L:* **Wie hübsch die Wandmalereien an den Häusern sind. Und es ist so angenehm, dass es keinen Verkehr gibt.**
L: How pretty the murals on the houses are. And it's so pleasant without any traffic.

2. *O:* **Hast du nicht gewusst, dass viele Stadt-zentren Fußgängerzonen sind? Deshalb haben wir ja auch außerhalb der Stadtmauer geparkt.**
O: Didn't you know that many inner cities are pedestrian zones? That's why we parked outside the city walls.

3. *L:* **Ach, so. Hast du jetzt Lust, den Markt-platz, das Rathaus, den Dom und das Kloster zu besichtigen?**
L: Oh, I see. Do you feel like looking at the mar-ketplace, the city hall, the cathedral, and the cloister now?

4. *O:* **Klar. Sie liegen ja alle nah zusammen. Wir können zuerst auf den Domturm steigen, um einen Überblick über die ganze Stadt zu bekommen. Das empiehlt auch der Reise-führer. Hast du ihn mitgebracht?**
O: Sure. They're all close together. We can climb the cathedral tower first in order to get an overview of the whole city. The guidebook rec-ommends it also. Did you bring it?

5. *L:* **Wie dumm von mir, ihn nicht mitzu-bringen! Wie kommen wir denn jetzt ohne Stadtplan zur Stadtmitte?**
L: How stupid of me not to bring it along. How will we get to the center without the city map?

6. *O:* **Wir können fragen oder uns an der Domspitze orientieren. Wir gehen jetzt zuerst geradeaus, später müssen wir dann irgendwo links abbiegen. Und im Dom sind jede halbe Stunde Führungen.**

O: We can ask or orient ourselves by the top of the steeple. First we'll walk straight ahead, later we'll have to turn to the left. And there are guided tours of the cathedral every half hour.

7. *L:* **Gut.**

L: Good.

NOTES

2. The past participle of *wissen* is *gewusst.*

3. *Hast du Lust, den Marktplatz zu besichtigen?* "Do you feel like looking at the market place?" To express that you feel like doing something, use *Lust haben* with *zu* plus an infinitive. *Ich habe Lust, ein gutes Buch zu lesen.* I feel like reading a good book.

4. *Um . . . zu . . .* is translated as "in order to." *Um einen Überblick über die ganze Stadt zu bekommen.* "In order to get a an overview of the whole city." Also notice: *Hast du ihn mitgebracht?* "Did you bring it?" "It" is translated as *ihn* because it refers to *der Reiseführer,* which is masculine. *Ihn* is the accusative form of *er.*

5. Notice that *zu* is inserted between the separable prefix *mit* and the root *bringen* of the infinitive *mitbringen: mitzubringen.*

6. *Sich orientieren* means to orient oneself, but in this sentence *uns* is used because the infinitive refers to *wir. Wir können uns orientieren,* "we

can orient ourselves." *Ich kann mich orientieren,*
"I can orient myself."

QUIZ 32

1. _____ (Running) *tut mir gut.*
    a. *Ich laufe*
    b. *Laufend*
    c. *Laufen*

2. *Danach ruht sie sich* _____ (in the lounge) *aus.*
    a. *in die Liegehalle*
    b. *in der Liegehalle*
    c. *im Liegehalle*

3. *Und es ist so* _____ (pleasant), *daß es keinen
   Verkehr gibt.*
    a. *angenehm*
    b. *bequem*
    c. *hübsch*

4. *Wie dumm von mir, ihn nicht* _____ (to bring
   along)!
    a. *mitzubringen*
    b. *zu mitbringen*
    c. *um mitzubringen*

5. *Hast du jetzt Lust, den Marktplatz, das Rathaus,
   den Dom und das Kloster* _____ (to visit)?
    a. *zu besichtigen*
    b. *besichtigen*
    c. *besichtigt*

6. *Hast du nicht* _____ (known), *dass viele Stadtzentren Fußgängerzonen sind?*
   a. *weißt*
   b. *gewusst*
   c. *wissend*

7. *Aber am Abend und* _____ (at night) *wird es zu kühl, nicht?*
   a. *in die Nacht*
   b. *in Nachts*
   c. *in der Nacht*

8. *Leider müssen wir am Sonntag zurück und wieder* _____ (a day) *im Bus sitzen.*
   a. *eines Tages*
   b. *einen Tag*
   c. *ein Tag*

9. *Wir können zuerst auf den Domturm* (climb) _____ , *um einen Überblick über die ganze Stadt zu bekommen.*
   a. *steigen*
   b. *umsteigen*
   c. *einsteigen*

10. *Ich mache* _____ (during this time) *Gymnastik oder promeniere in der Wandelhalle.*
    a. *während diese Zeit*
    b. *während diesen Zeit*
    c. *während dieser Zeit*

ANSWERS
1—c; 2—b; 3—a; 4—a; 5—b; 6—b; 7—c; 8—b; 9—a; 10—c

D. Commonly Used Verbs

1. To see, to look: *sehen*

ich sehe	*wir sehen*
du siehst	*ihr seht*
er sieht	*Sie (sie) sehen*
sie sieht	
es sieht	

Sehen wir einmal nach!
Let's see. (Let's take a look.)

Ich sehe nicht.
I don't see.

Er sieht alles.
He sees everything.

Haben Sie ihn gesehen?
Have you seen him? Did you see him?

Ich habe sie gerade gesehen.
I've just seen her.

Wen sehen Sie?
Whom do you see?

2. To know: *wissen*

ich weiß	*wir wissen*
du weißt	*ihr wisst*
er weiß	*Sie (sie) wissen*
sie weiß	
es weiß	

Ich weiß es.
I know it.

Ich weiß es nicht.
I don't know it.

Ich weiß es sehr gut.
I know it very well.

Er weiß nichts.
He doesn't know anything.

Ich weiß nichts darüber.
I don't know anything about it.

Ich weiß, dass er hier ist.
I know that he is here.

Wissen Sie das?
Do you know that?

Wissen Sie, wo er ist?
Do you know where he is?

Wer weiß?
Who knows?

Wir wissen nicht, ob er kommt.
We don't know whether he is coming.

3. To hold: *halten*

ich halte	*wir halten*
du hältst	*ihr haltet*
er hält	*Sie (sie) halten*
sie hält	
es hält	

Halten Sie mir das einen Moment!
Hold this for me a minute.

Er hält seinen Hut in der Hand.
He's holding his hat in his hand.

Halten Sie sich fest!
Hold on firmly!

Bleiben Sie am Apparat!
Hold the phone a minute.

Halten Sie still!
Keep still! Don't move!

Er hält es für selbstverständlich.
He takes it for granted.

Was halten Sie davon?
What do you think about it?

Ich halte nicht viel davon.
I don't think much of it.

Halten Sie sich rechts!
Keep to your right!

Halten Sie Ihr Versprechen!
Keep your promise!

4. To be able, can: *können*

ich kann	*wir können*
du kannst	*ihr könnt*
er, sie, es kann	*Sie (sie) können*

Ich kann nicht.
I can't.

Ich kann es tun.
I can do it.

Können Sie mir sagen, ob . . .
Can you tell me whether . . .

Können Sie kommen?
Can you come?

Ich verstehe nicht, wie er das kann.
I don't see how he can do that.

Ich kann nicht auf die Frage antworten.
I can't answer the question.

Sie können es ohne Schwierigkeit tun.
You can do it without any difficulty.

Ich kann nicht dorthin gehen.
I can't go there.

Wann können wir gehen?
When can we leave?

Sie können dorthin gehen.
You can go there.

Können Sie mir helfen?
Can you help me?

5. To understand: *verstehen*

ich verstehe	*wir verstehen*
du verstehst	*ihr versteht*
er, sie, es versteht	*Sie (sie) verstehen*

Er versteht nicht.
He doesn't understand.

Ich verstehe sehr gut.
I understand very well.

Ich verstehe Sie nicht.
I don't understand you.

Verstehen Sie mich nicht?
Don't you understand me?

Verstehen Sie?
Do you understand?

Verstehen Sie Deutsch?
Do you understand German?

Verstehen Sie Englisch?
Do you understand English?

Verstehen Sie alles, was er Ihnen sagt?
Do you understand everything he's saying to you?

Ich habe nicht verstanden.
I don't understand, ("I haven't understood. I didn't understand.")

Haben Sie verstanden?
Did you understand? ("Have you understood?")

Er versteht nichts vom Geschäft.
He doesn't understand anything about business.

Verstanden?
Did you understand? Do you understand? ("Is that understood?")

Ich verstehe es überhaupt nicht.
I don't understand it at all.

6. *legen* — to put in a prone position
   stellen — to put in a standing position
   hinstellen — to put down

Stellen Sie es dorthin!
Put it there (in an upright position).

Wo haben Sie es hingestellt?
Where did you put it?

Legen Sie es hin!
Lay it down.

Er weiß nie, wo er seine Sachen hinlegt.
He never knows where he puts his things.

Stellen Sie den Schirm in die Ecke!
Put the umbrella in the corner.

Legen Sie das Buch auf den Tisch.
Put the book on the table.

7. To know, to be acquainted with: *kennen*

ich kenne	*wir kennen*
du kennst	*ihr kennt*
er, sie, es kennt	*Sie (sie) kennen*

Ich kenne ihn.
I know him.

Ich kenne es nicht.
I don't know it.

Kennen Sie dieses Wort?
Do you know this word?

Ich kenne seine Familie.
I know his family.

Jeder kennt ihn.
Everybody knows him.

Ich kenne ihn dem Aussehen nach.
I know him by sight (according to the way he looks).

Ich kenne ihn dem Namen nach.
I know him by name.

Das ist sehr bekannt.
It's very well known.

Das ist nicht sehr bekannt in Deutschland.
That's not very well known in Germany.

Das ist unbekannt.
It's unknown.

8. To want: *wollen*

ich will	*wir wollen*
du willst	*ihr wollt*
er, sie, es will	*Sie (sie) wollen*

Ich will es.
I want it.

Ich will es nicht.
I don't want it.

Ich will nichts.
I don't want anything.

Ich will etwas.
I want some ("something").

Er will nichts davon.
He doesn't want any of it.

Er kann es tun, aber er will nicht.
He can do it but he doesn't want to.

Wollen Sie?
Do you want to?

Was wollen Sie?
What do you want? (not very polite)

Was möchten Sie?
What do you want (wish)? What would you like?

Wollen Sie kommen?
Do you want to come?

Wollen Sie mit uns kommen?
Do you want to come with us?

Wollen Sie Samstag kommen?
Do you want to come Saturday?

Wollen Sie mit uns zu Mittag essen?
Will you have lunch with us?

Wer will das?
Who wants that?

Was wollen Sie sagen?
What do you want to say?

Wollen Sie mir folgen?
Will you follow me?

Wie Sie wollen.
As you wish.

Wenn Sie wollen, kann ich es Ihnen bringen.
If you wish, (If you want to) I'll bring it to you.

9. To have to, to be obliged to, must: *müssen*

ich muss	*wir müssen*
du musst	*ihr müsst*
er, sie, es muss	*Sie (sie) müssen*

Ich muss jetzt gehen.
I must (have to) go now.

Er muss kommen.
He must (has to) come.

Er muss hier sein.
He must (has to) be here.

Sie müssen dort sein.
They have to (should, ought to) be there.

Müssen Sie dort hingehen?
Do you have to go (there)?

Was muss ich tun?
What do I have to do?

10. To wait: *warten*

Warten Sie hier!
Wait here.

Warten Sie dort!
Wait there.

Warten Sie auf mich!
Wait for me!

Warten Sie ein wenig!
Wait a little!

Warten Sie einen Moment!
Wait a minute!

Warten Sie nicht auf ihn!
Don't wait for him!

Ich warte auf ihn.
I'm waiting for him.

Sie wartet auf die andern.
She's waiting for the others.

Auf wen warten Sie?
Whom are you waiting for?

Warum warten Sie?
Why are you waiting?

Es tut mir Leid, dass ich Sie habe warten lassen.
I'm sorry I kept you waiting.

11. To ask: *fragen*

Fragen Sie dort drüben!
Ask over there.

Was fragt er?
What's he asking? What does he want?

Fragen Sie nach dem Weg, wenn Sie sich verlaufen.
Ask your way if you get lost.

Fragen Sie ihn, wie spät es ist!
Ask him the time (what time it is).

Gehen Sie und fragen Sie ihn!
Go and ask him!

Ich komme gleich zurück, falls jemand nach mir fragt.
I'll be right back if someone asks for me.

Er hat gefragt, wo es ist.
He asked where it is.

Was man weiß, soll man nicht fragen.
What one knows, one should not ask.

Stellen Sie nicht so viele Fragen!
Don't ask so many questions.

Jemand fragt nach Ihnen.
Someone is asking for you. You're wanted.

Ich frage mich, ob das wahr ist.
I wonder if it's true. ("I ask myself if . . .")

Ich frage mich, warum er nicht kommt.
I wonder why he doesn't come.

Das frage ich mich selbst.
I wonder about that. ("That's what I am asking myself.")

12. To love: *lieben*

gern haben   to like
lieber haben   to prefer

Er liebt sie.
He loves her.

Er ist in sie verliebt.
He's in love with her.

Haben Sie ihn gern?
Do you like him?

Das habe ich nicht gern.
I don't like that.

Ich habe das andere lieber.
I like the other better. (I prefer the other.)

Ich gehe lieber heute Abend dorthin.
I'd rather go there this evening.

13. To be worth: *wert sein*

Wie viel ist das wert?
How much is that worth?

Das ist keinen Pfennig wert.
That's not worth a cent.

Das ist nichts wert.
That's not worth anything. That's no good.

Das ist es nicht wert.
It's not worth that.

Das ist nicht viel wert.
That's not worth much.

Das ist preiswert.
That's reasonable. ("It's worth its price.")

Das ist viel Geld wert.
That's worth a lot of money.

Das ist nicht der Mühe wert.
That's not worth the effort.

E. COMMON NOTICES AND SIGNS

Bekanntmachung	Public Notice
Herren	Gentlemen
Damen	Ladies
Herrentoilette	Men's Room
Damentoilette	Ladies' Room
W.C.	Toilet
Nichtraucher	Nonsmokers
Rauchen verboten!	No smoking
Geöffnet	Open
Geschlossen	Closed
Eingang	Entrance
Ausgang	Exit
Notausgang	Emergency Exit
Fahrstuhl	Elevator
Erdgeschoss	Ground Floor
Drücken	Push

Ziehen	Pull
Drehen	Turn
Bitte klingeln	Please Ring
Durchgang verboten!	Keep Out! No Thoroughfare!
Flugplatz	Airport
Herein!	Come In!
Herein ohne zu klopfen	Come In Without Knocking
Vor Eintritt klopfen	Knock Before Entering
Wegen Umbau geschlossen	Closed For Repairs
Unter neuer Leitung	Under New Management
Eintritt verboten!	No Admittance!
Eröffnung in Kürze	Will Open Shortly
Ganze Nacht geöffnet	Open All Night
Es ist verboten, auf den Boden zu spucken!	No Spitting!
Füsse abputzen	Wipe Your Feet
Hunde an der Leine	Keep Dogs On Leash
Für Fussgänger verboten!	Pedestrians Keep Out!
Betreten des Geländes verboten	No Trespassing
Beschwerdebüro	Complaint Department
Am Schalter fragen	Apply at the Window
Geldwechsel	Money Exchanged (at a bank)
Zu verkaufen	For Sale
Zu vermieten	For Rent
Wohnung zu vermieten	Apartment to Let
Möblierte Wohnung zu vermieten	Furnished Apartment to Let
Preisnachlass	(Reductions) Prices Slashed!

Ausverkauf	Sale
Garderobe	Checkroom (in a hotel, restaurant, or cafe)
Passkontrolle	Passport Checkpoint
Portier	Doorman
Abstellraum	Cloakroom
Umleitung	Detour
Straßenarbeiten	Road under Repair
Achtung: Kurve	Attention: Curve
Parken verboten	No Parking
Einbahnstraße	One-Way Street
Überschreiten der Gleise verboten!	Do Not Cross the Tracks!
Eisenbahnkreuzung	Railroad Crossing
Eisenbahnstrecke	Railroad (Rail Route)
Unterführung	Underpass
Halt!	Stop!
Vorsicht!	Caution!
Fußgänger	Pedestrian Crossing
Kreuzung	Crossroads
Bushaltestelle	Bus Stop
Plakate ankleben verboten!	Post No Bills!
Höchstgeschwindigkeit 30 Stundenkilometer	Maximum Speed 30 Kilometers Per Hour
Langsam fahren!	Go Slow!
Schule	School Go Slow
Gefahr!	Danger!
Frisch gestrichen	Wet Paint
Haltestelle	(Bus) Stops Here (Bus Stop)
Nicht aus dem Fenster lehnen!	Don't Lean Out of the Window!
Alarmsignal	Alarm Signal
Hochspannung	High Voltage

Untergrundbahn	Subway
Gepäckaufbewahrung	Baggage Room, Check-room (in a railroad station)
Garderobe	Coatroom
Wartesaal	Waiting Room
Erster Klasse	First Class
Zweiter Klasse	Second Class
Gaststätte	Restaurant
Altstadt	Old Part of the City
Ankunft	Arrival
Abfahrt	Departure
Bahnsteig	Platform
Auskunft	Information
Auskunftsschalter	Information Booth
Theaterkasse	Box Office
Postamt	Post Office
Briefkasten	Mailbox
Kartenschalter	Ticket Office
Feuerlöscher	Fire Box
Bibliothek	Public Library
Polizeiwache	Police Station
Tankstelle/Benzin	Gas Station
Buchhandlung	Bookstore
Rathaus	City Hall
Herren- und Damenfrisör	Barbershop and Hair-dresser
Friseuse	Ladies' Hairdresser
Arzt	Physician
Zahnarzt	Dentist
Schuhmacher	Shoe Repair
Matinee	Matinee
Abendvorstellung um 8:30	Evening Performance at 8:30
Abendkleidung	Formal Dress

Laufende Vorstellung	**Continuous Performance**
Programmwechsel	**Change of Program**
Erfrischungen	**Refreshments**

FINAL QUIZ

1. _____ (How) *geht es Ihnen?*
   a. *Wann*
   b. *Wie*
   c. *Wenn*

2. _____ (Speak) *Sie langsam!*
   a. *Sprechen*
   b. *Sprecht*
   c. *Sprich*

3. _____ (Have) *Sie Zeit?*
   a. *Habe*
   b. *Hast*
   c. *Haben*

4. *Bringen Sie* _____ (me) *die Speisekarte, bitte.*
   a. *mir*
   b. *mich*
   c. *es*

5. _____ (I'd like) *eine Tasse Kaffee.*
   a. *Ich will*
   b. *Ich möchte*
   c. *Ich gehe*

6. *Wir möchten für drei Personen* _____ (break-fast).
   a. *Mittagessen*
   b. *Frühstück*
   c. *Abendessen*

7. _____ (Bring) *Sie mir einen Teelöffel!*
   a. *Geben*
   b. *Bringen*
   c. *Können*

8. *Wo befindet sich* _____ (the train station)?
   a. *der Weg*
   b. *der Bahnhof*
   c. *das Büro*

9. _____ (Are you) *sicher?*
   a. *Machen Sie*
   b. *Sagen Sie*
   c. *Sind Sie*

10. _____ (I have) *genug Zeit.*
    a. *Ich bin*
    b. *Ich habe*
    c. *Ich hatte*

11. _____ (Does he have) *Geld?*
    a. *Gibt es*
    b. *Ist er*
    c. *Hat er*

12. _____ (Are there) *Briefe für mich?*
    a. *Es gibt*
    b. *Gibt es*
    c. *Hat er*

13. _____ (Understand) *Sie gut Deutsch?*
    a. *Verstehe*
    b. *Verstehen*
    c. *Hören*

14. *Es* _____ (I'm glad) *Sie kennenzulernen.*
    a. *glücklich*
    b. *freut mich*
    c. *geehrt*

15. *Wollen Sie davon wenig oder* _____ (a lot)?
    a. *noch*
    b. *viel*
    c. *mehr*

16. *Was* _____ (say) *Sie?*
    a. *machen*
    b. *sagen*
    c. *gesagt*

17. *Wie* _____ (does one say) *das auf Deutsch?*
    a. *sagen Sie*
    b. *sagt man*
    c. *schreibt man*

18. *Ihre Adresse ist* _____ (Castle Street 132).
    a. *Schlosser Straße einhundertdreiundzwanzig*
    b. *Schlossstraße einhundertzweiunddreißig*
    c. *Schloss Straße hundertdreizwei*

19. _____ (I need) *das.*
    a. *Ich möchte*
    b. *Ich habe davon*
    c. *Ich brauche*

20. *Ich komme* _____ (tomorrow morning).
    a. *Nachmittag*
    b. *morgen früh*
    c. *gestern Abend*

21. _____ (Must one) *den Hausmeister deshalb sehen?*
    a. *Müssen*
    b. *Muss man*
    c. *Musst du*

22. *Ich* _____ (beg) *Sie um Verzeihung.*
    a. *bitte*
    b. *frage*
    c. *sage*

23. *Wie* _____ (is your name) *Sie?*
    a. *heißen*
    b. *nennen*
    c. *sind*

24. _____ (The check), *bitte.*
    a. *Die Butter*
    b. *Das Geld*
    c. *Die Rechnung*

25. *Könnten Sie mir eine Serviette* _____ (give)?
    a. *bestellen*
    b. *geben*
    c. *gehen*

ANSWERS
1—b; 2—a; 3—c; 4—a; 5—b; 6—b; 7—b; 8—b; 9—c; 10—b; 11—c; 12—b; 13—b; 14— b; 15—b; 16—b; 17—b; 18—b; 19—c; 20—b; 21—b; 22—a; 23—a; 24—c; 25—b.

Supplemental Vocabulary 18: Entertainment

entertainment	*Unterhaltung*
movie/film	*der Film (die Filme)*
to go to the movies	*ins Kino gehen*
to see a movie	*einen Film sehen*
theater	*das Theater (die Theater)*
to see a play	*ein Theaterstück sehen*
opera	*die Oper (die Opern)*
concert	*das Konzert (die Konzerte)*
club	*der Club (die Clubs), der Klub (die Klubs)*
circus	*der Zirkus (die Zirkusse)*
ticket (for an event)	*die Eintrittskarte (die Eintrittskarten)*
museum	*das Museum (die Museen)*
gallery	*die Galerie (die Galerien)*
painting	*das Gemälde (die Gemälde)*
sculpture	*die Skulptur (die Skulpturen)*
television program	*das Fernsehprogramm (die Fernsehprogramme)*
to watch television	*fernsehen*
comedy	*die Kommödie (die Kommödien)*
documentary	*der Dokumentarfilm (du Dokumentarfilme)*
drama	*das Drama (die Dramen)*
book	*das Buch (die Bücher)*
magazine	*die Zeitschrift (die Zeitschriften)*
to read a book	*ein Buch lesen*
to read a magazine	*eine Zeitschrift lesen*

to listen to music	*Musik hören*
song	*der Song (die Songs), das Lied (die Lieder)*
band	*die Band (die Bands), die Musikgruppe (die Musikgruppen)*
the news	*die Nachrichten*
talk show	*die Talk-Show (die Talk-Shows)*
to flip channels	*die Sender wechseln*
to have fun	*Vergnügen haben, Spaß haben*
to be bored	*gelangweilt sein*
funny	*lustig, witzig*
interesting	*interessant*
exciting	*aufregend, spannend, fesselnd*
scary	*gruselig, schaurig*
party	*die Party (die Partys)*
restaurant	*das Restaurant (die Restaurants)*
to go to a party	*auf eine Party gehen*
to have a party	*eine Party haben*
to dance	*tanzen*

SUMMARY OF GERMAN GRAMMAR

1. THE ALPHABET

LETTER	NAME	LETTER	NAME	LETTER	NAME
a	ah	j	yot	s	ess
b	beh	k	kah	t	teh
c	tseh	l	ell	u	oo
d	deh	m	em	v	fauh
e	eh	n	en	w	veh
f	eff	o	oh	x	iks
g	geh	p	peh	y	üpsilon
h	hah	q	ku	z	tsett
i	ee	r	err		

2. THE VOWELS

long **a**	as in *ah:* "father"	*Vater*
short **a**	as in *a:* "matter"	*Ratte*
long **ä**	as in "hair"	*spät*
short **ä**	as in "men"	*Männer*
long **e**	as in "dare"	*gehen*
short **e**	as in "bent"	*Adresse*
e	at end of a word as in "pocket"	*heute*
long **i, ie**	as in "meet"	*Liebe*
short **i**	as in "ship"	*Mitte*
long **o**	as in "lone"	*Bohne*
short **o**	as in "off"	*kommen*
long **ö**	similar to *e* in *geben* but with rounded lips}	*König*
short **ö**	similar to short *u* but with rounded lips}	*können*
long **u**	as in "mood"	*Buch*
short **u**	as in "bush"	*dumm*

long **ü**	as in long *i* with rounded lips	*früh*
short **ü**	as in short *i* but with rounded lips	*Brücke*
y	pronounced as long or short *ü*	*Typ,*
		Mystik

3. THE DIPHTHONGS

⎧ **ai**	*y* "by"	*Kai*
⎩ **ei**		*Leine*
au	as in *ou* "house"	*Haus*
⎧ **äu**	as in *oy* "boy"	*häufig*
⎩ **eu**		*Freund*

4. THE CONSONANTS

b	as in *b* "bed" and at the end of a word as in *p* "trap"
c	as in *k* "keep" and rather rarely like *ts*
d	as in *d* "date" at the end of a word like *t* as in "but"
f	as in *f* "fly"
g	as in *g* "garden"
h	as in *h* "hundred" sometimes not pronounced at all as in *Schuh*—"shoe"
j	as in *y* "York"
k	as in *c* "cut"
l	as in *l* "life"
m	as in *m* "man"
n	as in *n* "never"
p	as in *p* "painter"
q	like English *kv*
r	a little more rolled than in English.
s	at the beginning of a word as in *z* "zoo" at the end of a word or syllable as in *s* "son"
t	as in *t* "tea"

v	as in *f* "fair"
w	as in *v* "vain"
x	as in *x* "mix"
z	like the English combination *ts*

5. SPECIAL LETTER COMBINATIONS

ch	as in *k* "character" *Charakter*
chs	as in *ks Fuchs*—fox
ch	a sound near the English *h* in "hue": *Kirche*—church
ch	a guttural sound not existing in English but close to the Scotch "loch"; *e.g., ach!*—"ah!"
ck	in final position pronounced *k:* *Scheck*—check
ig	as sound of *h* in "hue"
sch	as in *sh* "shoe"
sp or **st**	when placed at the beginning of the word also gives the initial sound of the *sh* as in "shoe" *e.g., Spanien*—Spain
ng	as in *ng* "sing"
tz	is similar to the English *ts, e.g., Blitz*—lightning

6. THE GERMAN DECLENSION

1. Nominative (subject, noun)

Das Buch ist hier.   The book is here.

2. Genitive (possessive case)

der Name des Lehrers   The name of the teacher

3. Dative (indirect object)

Er gibt dem Kind einen   He gives an apple to the
  Apfel.   child.

4. Accusative (direct object)

Sie hält den Stift.   She is holding the pen.

7. PLURAL OF NOUNS

1. Masculine

    a. nominative plus *e*

der Abend   *die Abende*
der Freund   *die Freunde*

    b. nominative plus *er*

der Geist   *die Geister*
der Leib   *die Leiber*

    c. nominative plus *e* and ¨ (Umlaut) on the last
       vowel

der Hut   *die Hüte*
der Fall   *die Fälle*

    d. nominative plus *er* and ¨ (Umlaut) on the last
       vowel

der Mann   *die Männer*
der Rand   *die Ränder*

e. masculine nouns ending in *el, en, er* do not change.

der Schlüssel	*die Schlüssel*
der Kuchen	*die Kuchen*
der Maler	*die Maler*

2. Feminine

a. Most feminine nouns form their plural by adding *n* or *en*

die Tür	*die Türen*
die Frage	*die Fragen*

b. Some add *e* or Umlaut on the last vowel and an *e*. Note: An *s* ending will double in the plural.

die Kenntnis	*die Kenntnisse*
die Frucht	*die Früchte*

c. Feminine words ending in *in* form their plural with *innen*

die Schülerin	*die Schülerinnen*
die Freundin	*die Freundinnen*

3. Neuter
Most neuter nouns form their plural like the masculine, the majority of them in *e* or *er.*

das Heft	*die Hefte*
das Licht	*die Lichter*

8. GENDER

German nouns can be masculine, feminine, or neuter. However, there is no rule to determine their gender. Here are a few helpful hints:

1. Masculine are:

   a. designations of trade or profession:
      der Maler, der Arzt, der Künstler

   b. titles of nobility:
      der Fürst, der Graf, der König

   c. nouns ending in *ling:*
      der Sperling, der Jüngling

   d. days of the week and months:
      der Montag, der April

2. Feminine are:

   a. feminine designations of trade:
      die Malerin, die Ärztin

   b. feminine titles of nobility:
      die Königin, die Fürstin

   c. names of numbers:
      die Drei, die Null

   d. many names of trees:
      die Tanne, die Eiche

   e. nouns ending in *ei, heit, keit, schaft, sucht, ung:*
      die Freiheit, die Gesellschaft, die Ahnung

3. Neuter are:

   a. the diminutives in *chen* or *lein:*
      das Mädchen, das Büchlein

b. many nouns ending in *tum:*
das Altertum

c. most names of metals:
das Gold, das Eisen

d. most cities:
das schöne Berlin

e. most countries:
das schöne Amerika

f. colors:
das Rot

g. most collective nouns beginning with *ge:*
das Gebirge (mountains)

THE STRESS: German words generally have one strongly accented syllable or even two if the word is very long.

1. *Short words:* The accent is generally on the first syllable:
Example: *Vater, Mutter, Bruder*

2. *Long words:* The accent is generally on the root of the word:
Empfehlung Gebirge Gebäude

3 Separable prefixes are always accented:
abmachen zugeben mitgohen

4. Inseparable prefixes (*be, emp, ent, er, ge, ver, zer*) are never accented. The accent always falls on the following syllable.
erhalten vergessen zerbrechen

9. THE DEFINITE ARTICLE

1. Unlike English usage, the definite article can be used in front of a first name (*familiar*)
Der Hans und die Margarete   John and Margaret

2. In front of a title:
Ist der Herr Doktor da? Is the (Mr.) doctor at home? *Nein, aber die Frau Doktor ist zu Hause.* No, but the (Mrs.) Doctor is at home.

Remember the declension of the articles:

MASCULINE	FEMININE	NEUTER
N. *der*	N. *die*	N. *das*
G. *des*	G. *der*	G. *des*
D. *dem*	D. *der*	D. *dem*
A. *den*	A. *die*	A. *das*

PLURAL FOR ALL
N. *die*
G. *der*
D. *den*
A. *die*

10. THE INDEFINITE ARTICLE

Notice that in a negation *ein* becomes *kein*.

Er war kein Arzt, sondern ein Zahnarzt.
He was not a physician but a dentist.

MASCULINE	FEMININE	NEUTER
N. *ein*	*eine*	*ein*
G. *eines*	*einer*	*eines*
D. *einem*	*einer*	*einem*
A. *einen*	*eine*	*ein*

Masculine, feminine, and
neuter singular of *kein,*
same as *ein.*

PLURAL
N. *keine*
G. *keiner*
D. *keinen*
A. *keine*

11. THE ADJECTIVES

Adjectives are declined in three ways:

1. Without article or pronoun (Strong Declension):

MASCULINE	FEMININE	NEUTER
*rot**er** Wein*	*rot**e** Tinte*	*rot**es** Licht*
*rot**en** Weines*	*rot**er** Tinte*	*rot**en** Lichtes*
*rot**em** Wein*	*rot**er** Tinte*	*rot**em** Licht*
*rot**en** Wein*	*rot**e** Tinte*	*rot**es** Licht*

PLURAL (M.F.N.)

Nom. *rot**e** Weine*
Gen. *rot**er** Weine*
Dat. *rot**en** Weine**n***
Acc. *rot**e** Weine*

2. With the definite article (Weak Declension):

SINGULAR

N. *der rot**e** Wein*   N. *die rot**e** Tinte*
G. *des rot**en** Weines*   G. *der rot**en** Tinte*
D. *dem rot**en** Wein*   D. *der rot**en** Tinte*
A. *den rot**en** Wein*   A. *die rot**e** Tinte*

PLURAL

N. *das rot**e** Licht*   N. *die rot**en** Weine*
G. *des rot**en** Lichtes*   G. *der rot**en** Weine*
D. *dem rot**en** Licht*   D. *den rot**en** Weine**n***
A. *das rot**e** Licht*   A. *die rot**en** Weine*

3. With the indefinite article, possessive adjective, or (italicized) *kein* words (Mixed Declension):

MASCULINE

N. *ein roter Wein*
G. *eines roten Weines*
D. *einem roten Wein*
A. *einen roten Wein*

FEMININE

N. *seine rote Tinte*
G. *seiner roten Tinte*
D. *seiner roten Tinte*
A. *seine rote Tinte*

NEUTER

N. *kein rotes Licht*
G. *keines roten Lichtes*
D. *keinem roten Licht*
A. *kein rotes Licht*

PLURAL

N. *meine roten Weine*
G. *meiner roten Weine*
D. *meinen roten Weinen*
A. *meine roten Weine*

12. COMPARATIVE AND SUPERLATIVE

1. The comparative and the superlative are formed as in English by adding *er* for the comparative and *st* (or *est*) for the superlative to the adjective.

   Some short adjectives also take an Umlaut on their vowels.

schlecht, schlechter, schlechtest   bad, worse, worst
alt, älter, ältest   old, older, oldest

2. There are a few adjectives which have an irregular comparative. Here are the most common ones:

POSITIVE	COMPARATIVE	SUPERLATIVE
gut	*besser*	*der (die, das) beste, am besten*
groß	*größer*	*der (die, das) größte, am größten*
hoch	*höher*	*der (die, das) höchste, am höchsten*
nahe	*näher*	*der (die, das) nächste, am nächsten*
viel	*mehr*	*der (die, das) meiste, am meisten*
gern	*lieber*	*der (die, das) liebste, am liebsten*

13. THE PARTITIVE

1. Generally not translated:

   Example:
   Geben Sie mir Brot!   Give me some bread.
   Geben Sie mir ein Glas Wein.   Give me a glass of wine.

2. *Etwas* can also be used to mean a part of something:

   Example:
   Ich gebe ihm etwas zu trinken.
   I am giving him something to drink.

   Ich gebe ihm etwas davon.
   I give him some of it.

3. The negative *kein* is declined like the indefinite article.

   Example:
   Ich habe ein Messer, aber keine Gabel.
   I have a knife but no fork.

14. POSSESSIVE ADJECTIVES

1. Possessive adjectives agree in gender and number with the thing possessed:

NOMINATIVE

Before Singular nouns:

MASCULINE AND NEUTER	FEMININE	PLURAL	
mein	meine	meine	my
dein	deine	deine (fam.)	your
sein	seine	seine	his, its
ihr	ihre	ihre	her
unser	unsere	unsere	our
euer	eure	eure	your (fam. pl.)
Ihr	Ihre	Ihre	your (polite)
ihr	ihre	ihre	their

2. Examples:

mein Hund	my dog
meine Tante	my aunt
ihr Vater	her father
seine Mutter	his mother
Ihr Buch	your (polite) book
ihre Bleistife	their pencils

3. Notice that these adjectives agree in gender not only with the possessor but also with the noun they modify. *Sein* and *seine* may mean "his" or "its":

Hans spricht mit seiner Mutter.
John is talking to his mother.

Das Bier hat seinen Geschmack verloren.
The beer has lost its taste.

Sie liest ihren Roman.
She is reading her (their) novel.

15. POSSESSIVE PRONOUNS

NOMINATIVE

MASCULINE	FEMININE	NEUTER	
meiner	*meine*	*meines*	mine
deiner	*deine*	*deines*	yours (*fam.*)
seiner	*seine*	*seines*	his
ihrer	*ihre*	*ihres*	hers
unser	*unsere*	*unseres*	ours
euer	*eure*	*eures*	yours (*fam.*)
Ihrer	*Ihre*	*Ihres*	yours (*pol.*)
ihrer	*ihre*	*ihres*	theirs

Ist das mein Hut?—Ja, das ist Ihrer. (deiner)
Is that my hat?—Yes, that is yours.

Ist das deine Krawatte?—Ja, das ist meine.
Is that your tie?—Yes, that is mine.

Ist das sein Buch?—Nein, das ist meins. (Note: The *e*
of the neuter *-es* can be dropped.)
Is that his book?—No, that is mine.

Ist das ihr Schirm?—Nein, das ist seiner.
Is that her umbrella?—No, that is his.

16. DEMONSTRATIVE ADJECTIVES

SINGULAR

N. *dieser*	*diese*	*dieses*	this or that[1]
G. *dieses*	*dieser*	*dieses*	
D. *diesem*	*dieser*	*diesem*	
A. *diesen*	*diese*	*dieses*	

PLURAL (M, F, N)
N. *diese*
G. *dieser*
D. *diesen*
A. *diese*

Examples:

Dieses Haus ist schön.
This (that) house is beautiful.

Er sieht diesen Mann.
He sees this man.

Das Haus ist hässlich.
That house is ugly.

Er gibt dieser Frau ein Geschenk.
He gives this woman a present.

17. DEMONSTRATIVE PRONOUNS

Although these forms exist in German, they are not commonly used.

SINGULAR

MASCULINE	FEMININE	NEUTER
N. *derjenige*	N. *diejenige*	N. *dasjenige*
G. *desjenigen*	G. *derjenigen*	G. *desjenigen*

---

[1] *jen (-er, -e, -es)* may also be used, but is less common in conversation.

D. *demjenigen*   D. *derjenigen*   D. *demjenigen*
A. *denjenigen*   A. *diejenige*   A. *dasjenige*

PLURAL

N. *diejenigen*
G. *derjenigen*
G. *denjenigen*
A. *diejenigen*

Mein Buch ist blau. Dasjenige meiner Schwester ist grün.
My book is blue. The one of my sister (My sister's) is green.

18. RELATIVE PRONOUNS

The relative pronoun is like the demonstrative pronoun but its declension varies in the Genitive singular of all genders, and in the Genitive and Dative plural.

SINGULAR

MASCULINE	FEMININE	NEUTER	
N. *der*	N. *die*	N. *das*	who
G. *dessen*	G. *deren*	G. *dessen*	whose
D. *dem*	D. *der*	D. *dem*	to whom
A. *den*	A. *die*	A. *das*	whom

PLURAL

N. *die*	who
G. *deren*	whose
D. *denen*	to whom
A. *die*	whom

Examples:

Der Junge, dessen Vater ich kenne, heißt Richard.
The boy whose father I know is named Richard.

Die Frau, deren Tochter die Universität besucht,
arbeitet in einen Kaufhaus.
The woman whose daughter attends the university
works in a department store.

Welcher can also be used and is declined in the same
way as the article *der*.

Examples:

Der Freund, welcher morgen kommt, heißt Max.
The friend who is coming tomorrow is named Max.

NOTES

1. These pronouns must agree in gender and number with the noun they refer to.

   Das Mädchen, das auf der Straße spielt.
   The little girl who is playing on the street.

2. A comma should always be used before them.

3. The verb is always placed at the end of the
   clause that a relative pronoun introduces.

4. Relative pronouns can never be omitted as in
   English.

   Das Buch, das ich lese . . .
   The book (that) I am reading . . .

19. PERSONAL PRONOUNS

SINGULAR

N.	*ich*	*du*	*er*	*sie*	*es*	*Sie*	(pol.)
G.	*meiner*	*deiner*	*seiner*	*ihrer*	*seines*	*Ihrer*	(pol.)

| D. *mir* | *dir* | *ihm* | *ihr* | *ihm* | *Ihr* | (pol.) |
| A. *mich* | *dich* | *ihm* | *sie* | *es* | *Sie* | (pol.) |

PLURAL

N. *wir*	*ihr*	*sie*	*Sie*
G. *unserer*	*eurer*	*ihrer*	*Ihrer*
D. *uns*	*euch*	*ihnen*	*Ihnen*
A. *uns*	*euch*	*sie*	*Sie*

Examples:

Wir geben ihr Blumen.
We are giving her flowers.

Du sprichst mit ihm.
You are speaking with him.

Wir sprechen von Ihnen.
We're talking about you (*polite*).

Diese Geschenke sind für dich.
These presents are for you.

20. INDEFINITE PRONOUNS

man	one
Jeder (man)	everybody, everyone
jemand	somebody, someone
niemand	nobody
etwas	something, some

Examples:

Jemand steht vor der Tür.
Someone is standing (before) in front of the door.

Es muss etwas geschehen.
Something has to be done.

Man spricht hier nur Deutsch.
One speaks only German here.

21. POSITION OF PRONOUNS

In a German sentence, the subject pronoun usually comes first and the indirect object generally precedes the direct object.

1. *Er   gibt   dem Bruder   einen Roman.*
   Subj.   Indir. Obj.   Dir. Obj.
   He   gives   the brother   a novel.

2. *Sie schenkt der Mutter eine Ledertasche.*
   She gives her mother a leather handbag.

Dem Bruder and *der Mutter* are the indirect objects. If we substituted indirect object pronouns for each indirect object, the sentences would read as follows:

Er gibt <u>ihm</u> einen Roman.
He gives <u>him</u> a novel.
(He gives a novel to <u>him.</u>)

Er schenkt <u>ihr</u> eine Ledertasche.
He gives <u>her</u> a leather handbag.
(He gives a leather handbag to <u>her.</u>)

3. If we substituted a direct object pronoun for each direct object, the two sentences would read as follows:

Er gibt <u>ihn</u> dem Bruder.
He gives it to the brother.

Er schenkt <u>sie</u> der Mutter.
He gives it to (his) mother.

4. If we substitute pronouns for both objects in each sentence, we get:

Er gibt ihn ihm.
He gives it to him.

Er schenkt sie ihr.
He gives it to her.

22. THE NEGATIVE

A sentence is made negative by using the word *nicht,* generally following the verb. Words may come between the verb and *nicht.*

Ich weiß.	I know.
Ich weiß nicht.	I do not know.
Ich weiß es nicht.	I don't know it.

The negative of *ein* is *kein.*

23. ADVERBS

1. Almost all adjectives can be used as adverbs.

2. Their comparative is formed the same way as the adjectives.
   Their superlative is preceded by *am* instead of the article, and has the ending *-en.*

Fritz ist ein guter Tänzer.
Fritz is a good dancer.

Fritz tanzt gut.
Fritz dances well.

Karl ist ein besserer Tänzer als Fritz.
Karl is a better dancer than Fritz. Karl dances better than Fritz.

Fred Astaire ist der beste Tänzer.
Fred Astaire is the best dancer.

Fred Astaire tanzt am besten.
Fred Astaire dances the best.

3. A few adverbs have an irregular comparative and superlative. Here are the most common ones:

viel	*mehr*	*am meisten*	much, more, most
gern	*lieber*	*am liebsten*	gladly, preferably most preferably
bald	*eher*	*am ehesten*	soon, sooner, soonest

4. Adverbs of place:

hier	here
dort	there
fort	away
links	on the left
rechts	on the right
vorne	in front of
nirgends	nowhere
irgendwo	somewhere
weg	aside, away

hinten	behind, in the back
unten	down(stairs)
drinnen	inside
draußen	outside
überall	everywhere
nirgendwo, nirgends	nowhere
weit	far
nahe	near
dort oben	up there
dort drüben	over there

5. Adverbs of time:

heute	today
bald	soon
ab und zu	now and then
gerade	just
morgen	tomorrow
gestern	yesterday
vorgestern	the day before yesterday
übermorgen	the day after tomorrow
jetzt	now
dann	then
vorher	before
damals	once, at that time
einmal, ehemals	once, formerly
früh	early
spät	late
oft	often
niemals, nie	never
immer, je, jemals	always, ever
lang, lange	long, for a long time
sofort	at once, right away
manchmal	sometimes

noch	still, yet
nicht mehr	no longer, no more
nachher	afterwards

6. Adverbs of manner:

deshalb	therefore
fast	almost
genau	exactly
sehr	very
sogar	even
überhaupt	at all
sowieso	anyway
gut	well
schlecht	ill, badly
so, somit	thus, so
ähnlich	similarly
andererseits	on the other hand
zusammen	together
viel	much
besonders	above all, especially
absichtlich	on purpose, purposely
ausdrücklich	expressly
gewöhnlich	usually

7. Adverbs of quantity or degree:

viel	much, many
genug	enough
auf einmal	all of a sudden
kaum	not much, hardly
wenig	little
mehr	more
nicht mehr	no more

weniger	less
noch mehr	more, even more
zu viel	too much, too many
so viel	so much, so many

8. Particles and intensifiers

allerdings	certainly
also	so, well
doch	yes, indeed
eben	exactly, just
ja	certainly, to be sure
mal	just, simply
nämlich	namely
nur	only
schon	already, I (we) suppose
wohl	probably
zwar	to be sure

24. PREPOSITIONS

1. With the Genitive:

während	during
wegen	because of
statt, unstatt	instead of
trotz	in spite of

2. With the Accusative:

durch	through, by
für	for
gegen	against, toward
ohne	without
um	round, about, at (time)

3. With the Dative:

aus	from, out of
bei	at, by, near, with
außer	besides, except
mit	with
nach	after, to (a place)
seit	since
von	of, from, by
zu	to, at

4. With the Dative or Accusative:

an	at, to
auf	on, upon, in
hinter	behind
in	in, into, at
neben	beside, near
über	over, across
unter	under, among
vor	before, ago
zwischen	between

25. CONTRACTIONS

am	for	*an dem*
ans	for	*an das*
im	for	*in dem*
ins	for	*in das*
beim	for	*bei dem*
vom	for	*von dem*
zum	for	*zu dem*
zur	for	*zu der*
ins	for	*in das*
fürs	for	*für das*
aufs	for	*auf das*

26. Prefixes

Many German verbs have certain prefixes. These often correspond to English prefixed verbs (*over*come, *re*make) or phrasal verbs (come out, do over, go in). They are divided into three groups:

1. *The inseparable prefixes,* which remain attached to the verb and are never accented (just like the English verbs overthrow, understand, etc.). The past participles of these verbs do not take the prefix *ge*. These prefixes are: *be, emp, ent, er, ge, miss, ver, zer, hinter, wider:* Ex.: *empfehlen, gefallen, verstehen*

2. *The separable prefixes,* which are linked to the verb in the compound tenses; in the other tenses they are separated and generally placed at the end of the sentence. Their past participles place the *ge* between the prefix and the verb form. Ex.: *mitgegangen.* They are always accented. The most common such prefixes are: *ab, an, auf, aus, bei, ein, fort, mit, nach, vor, weg, zu, frei, los, wahr, statt.* There are also compound separable prefixes added to verbs, such as: *hinaus, herauf, hinein, herein, zurück, zusammen:* Ex.: *mitkommen, weggehen, zuschliessen*
Her indicates a movement toward the person who is speaking:

Kommen Sie herunter!   Come down.

Hin indicates a movement away from the person speaking:

Geh hinaus!   Go out!

The separable prefix is so important in the sentence that the verb is sometimes omitted in short statements:

Herein!   (Come) in!

3. Some prefixes are sometimes separable and sometimes inseparable, depending on the meaning of the verb. They are:

wieder, voll, durch, um, unter, über.

Examples: *Der Schüler wiederholt seine Lektion.*
          The student repeats his lesson.

Holen Sie das wieder!
Take it back!

Die Polizei hat das ganze Hause durchsucht.
The police searched whole house.

27. THE TENSES OF THE INDICATIVE

SIMPLE TENSES

1. The present tense expresses an uncompleted action in the present. It has several English translations:

ich spreche   I speak, I am speaking, I do speak
ich esse   I eat, I am eating, I do eat

Remember that regular verbs are conjugated with a set
of endings, and irregular verbs take the same endings
but also have a vowel change.

2. The simple past (narrative past) is mostly used in
   writing. It sometimes indicates an action that
   was happening when something else happened.
   The weak verbs add the following endings to
   their stems: *te, test, te, tet, ten.*
      The strong verbs usually change their stem
   vowels. The first and third person singular have
   no ending. The others are as in the present.

Er schlief, als Hans ein-   He was sleeping when
trat.   John entered.
Er sprach oft davon.   He often spoke about
                               that.
Es war dunkel, als er   It was night (dark) when
ausging.   he went out.

COMPOUND TENSES

1. The future tense is formed by using the auxiliary
   werden plus the infinitive of the verb. It indicates
   a future action:

Er wird morgen ankom-   He'll arrive tomorrow.
men.
Ich werde ihm morgen   I'll write him (to him)
schreiben.   tomorrow.

2. The conversational past tense (also known as the present perfect) is formed by adding the past participle to the present indicative of *haben* or, in some cases, *sein*. It is usually used in spoken German to indicate a past action.

Er hat mir nichts gesagt.	He didn't tell me anything.
Ich habe meine Arbeit beendet.	I finished my work. I have finished my work.
Haben Sie ihn gesehen?	Have you seen him? Did you see him?
Sie sind angekommen.	They arrived.

3. The pluperfect tense is formed by adding the past participle to the imperfect of *haben* or, in some cases, *sein:*

Er hatte es getan.	He had done it.
Als ich zurückkam, war er schon fort gewesen.	When I came back, he had already left.

4. The future perfect tense is formed by adding the past participle to the future of *haben* or, in some cases, *sein*. It translates the English future perfect:

Er wird bald seine Arbeit beendet haben.	He will soon have finished his work.
In zwei Wochen wird er schon in Spanien gewesen sein.	In two weeks he already will have been in Spain.

Sometimes it indicates probability:

Er wird es ihm zweifellos gesagt haben.	No doubt he will have told him.
Er wird krank gewesen sein.	He probably was sick.
Ich werde mich geirrt haben.	I must have been mistaken.

haben AND *sein* IN THE COMPOUND PAST TENSES

1. Most compound past tenses are made up of *haben* and the past participle. Some verbs use *sein* instead, namely intransitive verbs of motion and verbs that express a state of being or a change of state.

Er hat gesprochen.	He has spoken.
Sie haben gegessen.	You have eaten.
Ich habe ein Geschenk erhalten.	I received a present.
Er hat zuviel getrunken.	He drank too much.

2. The most common intransitive verbs conjugated with the verb *sein* are:
   gehen, ankommen, absteigen, eintreten, einsteigen, sterben, abreisen, bleiben, kommen, fallen, zurückkommen, laufen, geboren.

Examples:

Ich bin gekommen.	I have come.
Er ist angekommen.	He has come.
Wir sind abgereist.	We have left.
Sie ist geboren.	She was born.

Er ist durch ganz Europa gefahren.
He traveled through Europe.

The verb *fahren* can also be used as a transitive verb, requiring a direct object. In that case it is conjugated with *haben*.

Er hat den Mercedes nach Hamburg gefahren.
He drove the Mercedes to Hamburg (the Mercedes is the direct object of the verb, *fahren*).

28. THE PAST PARTICIPLE

The first syllable of the past participle of the weak and strong verbs is usually *ge* when the verbs have no prefix whatsoever. If they do have a separable prefix, then the syllable *ge* stands between the prefix and the past participle. If the verbs have an inseparable prefix, the past participle has no additional *ge*. Most verbs that end in *-ieren* have no *ge* in the past participle.

Infinitive	*Past Participle*
(strong verb without prefix)	
ziehen to pull	*gezogen*
(strong with a separable prefix)	
vorziehen to prefer	*vorgezogen*
(weak without prefix)	
warten to wait	*gewartet*
(weak with a separable prefix)	
abwarten to wait and see	*abgewartet*
(strong verb with an inseparable prefix)	
verlieren to lose	*verloren*
(weak with an inseparable prefix)	
entdecken to discover	*entdeckt*

(-*ieren* verb)
  studieren to study   *studiert*

In the weak verbs, the past participle ends in *t* or *et*.

arbeiten   *gearbeitet*
lernen   *gelernt*

In the strong verbs the past participle ends in *en*, but the vowel of the infinitive stem generally changes. Therefore, when you study the verbs, do not forget to memorize the past participle as well as the other tenses. See table of irregular verbs, page 353.

29. USE OF THE AUXILIARIES *HABEN* AND *SEIN*

Notice that most verbs form the perfect, pluperfect, and future perfect with the auxiliary *haben:*

Ich habe gesehen.   I have seen.
Du hast gesehen.   You have seen.
Ich habe mich gewaschen.   I have washed myself.

However, quite a few verbs, chiefly intransitive, form these tenses with the auxiliary *sein:*

1. The verbs *sein, werden, bleiben.*

2. Verbs indicating a change of place (chiefly, verbs of motion, as: *gehen, kommen, eilen, fallen, fließen, laufen, reisen, rollen, steigen, sinken, aufstehen, fliegen, begegnen,* etc.)

3. Verbs indicating a change in the condition of a thing or a person, as: *aufwachen, einschlafen,*

wachsen, aufbleiben, verblühen, vergehen, verschwinden, sterben, erhalten, platzen, erkranken.

30. THE SUBJUNCTIVE

Present of *haben, sein, werden* "to have, to be, to become."

ich habe	*ich sei*	*ich werde*
(hätte)		*(würde)*
du habest	*due seiest*	*du werdest*
er, sie, es habe	*er, sie, es sei*	*er, sie, es werde*
wir haben (hätten)	*wir seien*	*wir werden (würden)*
ihr habet	*ihr seiet*	*ihr werdet*
Sie, sie haben (hätten)	*Sie, sie seien*	*Sie, sie werden (würden)*

The endings of both weak and strong verbs are *e, est, e, en, et, en*. The strong verbs keep the stem vowel in each person.

When the present subjunctive verb forms are identical to the indicative, the imperfect subjunctive verb forms can be used: *Er sagte, dass ich ihn nicht begrüsst hätte* (instead of *begrüsst habe*).

IMPERFECT

ich hätte	*ich wäre*	*ich würde*
du hättest	*du wärest*	*du würdest*
er, sie, es hätte	*er, sie, es wäre*	*er, sie, es würde*
wir hätten	*wir wären*	*wir würden*
ihr hättet	*ihr wäret*	*ihr würdet*
Sie, sie hätten	*Sie, sie wären*	*Sie, sie würden*

Notice that the imperfect tense of the weak verbs is identical in both the indicative and subjunctive. When this occurs, the structure *würde* and a main verb are used. The substitution is therefore with the present conditional tense. Examples:

Indirect Discourse:
Er sagte, dass er es nicht lernen würde.
He said that he would not learn it.

Unreal Conditions:
Wenn er mit mir ins Kino ginge, dann würde ich mich freuen.
If he went with me to the movies, I'd be happy.

Strong verbs have the same endings as the present subjunctive, but take the *Umlaut* if their stem vowel is *a, e,* or *u.*

ich tat	I did	*ich täte*	that I did

The past tenses: The past, pluperfect, and the future are formed with the past participle of the indicative of the verb plus the auxiliaries *haben, sein,* and *werden* in their respective subjunctive forms. The subjunctive is used to express "doubt, wish, eventuality, unreality." It is also used:

1. in indirect discourse

2. after certain conjunctions and expressions, such as:

als ob	as if
es sei denn, dass	unless

Examples:

Er glaubte, dass er käme.	He believed that he was coming.
Wir helfen ihm, damit er gesund werde.	We help him, so that he may be healthy again.

3. A contrary-to-fact condition in reference to present or future time is usually introduced by the conjunction *wenn* (if) and the imperfect subjunctive followed by the result clause in the present conditional:

Example: *Wenn er morgen käme, dann würde ich mit ihm in die Stadt fahren.*
If he came tomorrow, I would go to the city with him.

The "if" clause (*wenn* clause) has transposed word order (verb in last position), and the main clause has inverted word order (subject after the verb) whenever it stands after the subordinate clause. The above sentence may also be expressed as follows:

a. *Ich würde mit ihm in die Stadt fahren, wenn er morgen käme.*

b. *Ich führe mit ihm in die Stadt, wenn er käme.*

c. *Ich würde mit ihm in die Stadt fahren, wenn er kommen würde.*

Sentence "c" is employed less frequently, since it employs one conditional verb form in each clause.

4. To express a wish:

Mögen Sie glücklich sein!   May you be happy!
Wärest du doch hier!   Wish you were here!

5. Unreal conditions in reference to past time are formed by the past perfect subjunctive in the *wenn* clause, followed by the conditional perfect. In modern German, the conditional perfect is usually replaced by the pluperfect subjunctive. Note that the helping verb may be a form of *haben* or *sein*. Examples:

Wenn ich Zeit gehabt hätte, wäre ich mit dir zum Strand gekommen.
If I had had the time, I would have come to the beach with you.

Wenn ich die Bahn genommen hätte, (dann) hätte ich ihn rechtzeitig getroffen.
If I had taken the train, (then) I would have met him on time.

31. THE CONDITIONAL

The conditional is most often formed with the auxillary *werden* in its imperfect subjunctive form.

ich würde   *wir würden*
du würdest   *ihr würdet*
er, sie, es würde   *sie (Sie) würden*

It is generally used in connection with the conjunction *wenn* instead of the subjunctive to express a condition.

Wenn wir Geld hätten, würden wir eine lange Reise machen.
If we had any money, we would go on a long trip.

The past conditional is formed like the past future, but using *würde* instead of *werde*.

32. THE PASSIVE VOICE

The passive voice is formed with the past participle of the verb and the auxiliary *werden* used in the present and in the past.

Die Erde wird von der Sonne beleuchtet.

The earth is lit by the sun. "By" is translated by the German *von* (plus dative):

Amerika wurde von Kolumbus entdeckt.
America was discovered by Columbus.

In the past tense (perfect tense) the participle of the auxiliary *werden, geworden,* drops the prefix *ge-* and becomes simply *worden.*
Example:

Das Buch ist von ihm geschrieben worden.
The book has been written by him.

Er war von ihr gesehen worden.
He had been seen by her.

33. THE IMPERATIVE

The imperative of the verbs is formed from the present indicative tense.

2nd person singular: Drop the ending *n* from the infinitive. However, strong verbs that change the vowel *e* to *i* or *ie* in the present indicative form their imperative by dropping the *st* from this tense.

Lerne! (du lernst)
Nimm! (du nimmst)

1st person plural: Invert the infinitive form with the personal pronoun:

Singen wir! (wir singen)

2nd person plural: Simply insert the second person plural of the present indicative tense and omit the pronoun.

Gebt! (ihr gebt)

Polite 2nd person: Same as the 1st person plural.

Nehmen Sie! Geben Sie!

To express the imperative, the verb *lassen* can also be used; it corresponds to the English "let."

Example:

Lassen Sie das sein!   Let it be!

Imperative of *sein* and *haben:*

sein to be	*haben* to have
sei (fam.)! be!	*habe* (fam.)! have!
seid (fam. pl.)! be!	*habt* (fam. pl.)! have!
seien wir! let us be!	*haben wir!* let us have!
seien Sie! (pol.) be!	*haben Sie!* have! (pol.)

34. THE INFINITIVE

The infinitive is usually preceded by *zu* when used in connection with another verb; however, *zu* is in most instances omitted when the infinitive is used in connection with the following verbs:

werden, können, dürfen, wollen, mögen, müssen, sollen, lassen, machen, hören, sehen, heißen, helfen, lehren, lernen

Examples:

Er bittet ihn, den Brief zu schreiben.	He asks him to write the letter.
Ich werde ihr schreiben.	I shall write to her (future).
Ich helfe ihm den Wagen waschen.	I'm helping him wash the car.
Er lehrt uns schwimmen.	He teaches us to swim.

The infinitive is also used after certain prepositions in connection with *zu:*

um . . . zu (in order to)	
ohne . . . zu (without)	the *zu* can be used alone
anstatt . . . zu (instead of)	

Examples:

Wir gehen zur Schule, um zu lernen.	We go to school to learn.
Ich kann nicht essen, ohne etwas zu trinken.	I cannot eat without drinking something.
Er faulenzt, anstatt uns zu helfen.	He is lazy instead of helping us.

Words with a separable prefix have the *zu* between the prefix and the infinitive.

Example: *aufmachen*

Er bittet ihn, die Tür aufzumachen.
He asks him to open the door.

35. COMPLEMENTS OF VERBS

Verbs can be followed by:

a. a preposition: Their complement should be put in the case required by the preposition; for example: *bedecken mit*—"to cover with" (always dative)

Der Tisch ist mit Staub   The table is covered
  bedeckt.   with dust.

b. an object without a preposition: The genitive, accusative, or dative is used, depending on the verb.
Examples:

Er ist des Mordes beschuldigt.   He is accused of
(Genitive)   murder.

Sie glauben mir nicht.   You don't believe
(Dative)   me.

Wir lieben ihn.   We love him.
(Accusative)

36. Changes in the Normal Sequence of Words Within a Sentence

1. *By Transposition:* putting the verb at the end of a sentence.

In a subordinate clause, that is, a clause beginning with a relative pronoun or a subordinating conjunction, the verb is always placed at the end of the clause.

Die Sprache, die wir lernen, ist Deutsch.
The language that we are learning is German.

Ich kann nicht sehen, weil es dunkel ist.
I cannot see because it is dark.

Ich glaube, dass das Essen in diesem Restaurant gut ist.
I believe that the food in this restaurant is good.

Notice also that a comma is always used before the relative pronoun or conjunction. If the verb is in a compound tense, the *auxiliary* is placed at the end of the sentence.

Ich glaube nicht, dass es morgen regnen wird.
I do not believe that it will rain tomorrow.

In the case of an indirect question or subordinate clause introduced by an interrogative word, such as the pronouns: *wer, was,* or *welcher,* or the adverbs: *wo, wann,* etc., or the conjunction: *ob,* the verb is also placed at the end of the sentence.

Wir wissen nicht, ob er morgen kommt.
We don't know whether he is coming tomorrow.

Können Sie mir sagen, wie weit es von hier bis zum Bahnhof ist?
Can you tell me how far it is from here to the train station?

2. *By Inversion:*   putting the verb before the subject. The inversion is necessary:

   a. Usually when a question is asked.

(affirmative)
Er schreibt den Brief.   He writes the letter.
   (interrogative)
Schreibt er den Brief?   Does he write the letter?

   b. In the main clause of any sentence when it is preceded by a subordinate clause.

Wenn wir die Augen schließen, können wir nicht sehen.
If we close our eyes, we cannot see.

   c. Whenever the main clause opens with a word other than the subject.

Morgen werden die Kinder ins Kino gehen.
Tomorrow the children will go to the movies.

Here we have inversion because the sentence does not start with its subject, *die Kinder,* but with an adverb: *morgen.*

Die Kinder werden morgen ins Kino gehen.
The children will go to the movies tomorrow.

The above does not take any inversion because the sentence is started by its subject, *die Kinder.*

37. INDIRECT DISCOURSE

When you want to tell a story or make an indirect quotation in German, you use indirect discourse:

Direct Discourse:
Hans sagt: "Ich gehe zum Bahnhof."
Hans says: "I am going to the station."

Indirect Discourse:
Hans sagt, dass er zum Bahnhof gehe.
Hans says that he is going to the station.

Imperfect:
Hans sagte, dass er zum Bahnhof ginge.
Hans said that he was going to the station.

NOTES

1. The subjunctive should be used (even though you can use the indicative, as many Germans do).

2. The conjunction *dass*—"that" can be used or omitted.

If it is used, the verb should be placed at the end of the sentence, as in the regular case of transposition.

Er sagt, dass er zum Bahnhof gehe.

3. If it is omitted, the order of the words remains unchanged.

Hans sagt, er gehe zum Bahnhof.
Hans says he is going to the station.

Hans sagte, er ginge zum Bahnhof.
Hans said he was going to the station.

The tense of the verb in indirect discourse does not affect the tense of the inflected verb form in the indirect statement. Examples:

Er berichtet, er nehme (nähme) den Bus. (action in present)
Er berichtet, er habe (hätte) den Bus genommen. (action in past)
Er erzählt uns, er sei (wäre) eine Meile gelaufen. (action in past with an intransitive verb)
Er berichtet, er werde (würde) den Bus nehmen. (action in future)

The subjunctive of indirect discourse is normally used after the following verbs: *behaupten* (to claim), *berichten* (to report), *erklären* (to explain), *glauben* (to believe), *meinen* (to mean), *sagen* (to say), and *schreiben* (to write).

4. Notice that in both instances, a comma is used at the beginning of the second clause.

5. The following sequence of tenses is generally observed in expressing conditional sentences:

For Real Conditions:

The If Clause (*Wenn-Clause*)	Result Clause
Present Indicative	Future or Present Indicative

*For Unreal Conditions in Reference to Present or
    Future Time:*

The If Clause (*Wenn-Clause*)	Result Clause
Imperfect Subjunctive	Present Conditional or Imperfect Subjunctive

For Unreal Conditions in Reference to Past Time:

The If Clause (*Wenn-Clause*)	Result Clause
Pluperfect Subjunctive	Pluperfect Subjunctive or Conditional Perfect

38. CONSTRUCTION OF THE SENTENCE
(SUMMARY)

1. Main Clauses or Simple Sentences:

   a. Affirmative sentence:

Das Buch ist rot.	The book is red.

   b. Interrogative:

Ist das Buch rot?	Is the book red?

   c. Negative:

Das Buch ist nicht rot.	The book is not red.

   d. Past tenses:

Ich habe ein Gedicht gelernt.	I have learned a poem.
Ich lernte ein Gedicht.	I learned a poem.
Ich hatte ein Gedicht gelernt.	I had learned a poem.

e. Infinitive:

Sie brauchen das nicht zu wissen.	You do not need to know that.

2. Subordinate clauses:

a. Transposition:

Ich sehe, dass das Buch rot ist.	I see that the book is red.
Ich kenne den Schüler, der das Gedicht liest.	I know the student who is reading the poem.

b. Inversion:

Wenn das Wetter schön ist, gehe ich gern spazieren.
(The second clause has inverted word order).
When the weather is fine, I like to take a walk.

c. Indirect discourse:

Sie antwortet ihm, dass sie eine Schülerin $\begin{cases} sei. \\ ist. \end{cases}$

Sie antwortet ihm, sie $\begin{cases} sei \\ ist \end{cases}$ *eine Schülerin.*

She answers (him) that she is a pupil.

39. THE MOST COMMON IRREGULAR VERBS

sein   to be

INFINITIVE

PRESENT	PAST
sein	*gewesen sein*

PARTICIPLES

PRESENT	PAST
seiend	*gewesen*

INDICATIVE

PRESENT	CONVERSATIONAL PAST
ich bin	*bin gewesen*
du bist	*bist gewesen*
er, sie, es ist	*ist gewesen*
wir sind	*sind gewesen*
ihr seid	*seid gewesen*
sie (Sie) sind	*sind gewesen*

SIMPLE PAST	PAST PERFECT
ich war	*war gewesen*
du warst	*warst gewesen*
er, sie, es war	*war gewesen*
wir waren	*waren gewesen*
ihr wart	*wart gewesen*
sie (Sie) waren	*waren gewesen*

FUTURE	PAST FUTURE
ich werde sein	*werde gewesen sein*
du wirst sein	*wirst gewesen sein*
er, sie, es wird sein	*wird gewesen sein*
wir werden sein	*werden gewesen sein*
ihr werdet sein	*werdet gewesen sein*
sie (Sie) werden sein	*werden gewesen sein*

CONDITIONAL

PRESENT	CONDITIONAL PERFECT
ich würde sein	*würde gewesen sein*
du würdest sein	*würdest gewesen sein*
er, sie, es würde sein	*würde gewesen sein*

wir würden sein	*würden gewesen sein*
ihr würdet sein	*würdet gewesen sein*
sie (Sie) würden sein	*würden gewesen sein*

IMPERATIVE

sei!
seien wir!
seid!
seien Sie!

SUBJUNCTIVE

PRESENT	PRESENT PERFECT
ich sei	*ich sei gewesen*
du seiest	*du seiest gewesen*
er, sie, es sei	*er sei gewesen*
wir seien	*wir seien gewesen*
ihr seiet	*ihr seiet gewesen*
sie (Sie) seien	*sie seien gewesen*

IMPERFECT	PAST PERFECT
ich wäre	*ich wäre gewesen*
du wärest	*du wärest gewesen*
er, sie, es wäre	*er wäre gewesen*
wir wären	*wir wären gewesen*
ihr wäret	*ihr wäret gewesen*
sie (Sie) wären	*sie (Sie) wären gewesen*

haben to have

INFINITIVE

PRESENT	PAST
haben	*gehabt haben*

PARTICIPLES

PRESENT

habend

PAST

gehabt

INDICATIVE

PRESENT

ich habe
du hast
er, sie, es hat
wir haben
ihr habt
sie, Sie haben

CONVERSATIONAL PAST

habe gehabt
hast gehabt
hat gehabt
haben gehabt
habt gehabt
haben gehabt

SIMPLE PAST

ich hatte
du hattest
er hatte
wir hatten
ihr hattet
sie (Sie) hatten

PAST PERFECT

hatte gehabt
hattest gehabt
hatte gehabt
hatten gehabt
hattet gehabt
hatten gehabt

FUTURE

ich werde haben
du wirst haben
er, sie, es wird haben
wir werden haben
ihr werdet haben
sie (Sie) werden haben

FUTURE PERFECT

werde gehabt haben
wirst gehabt haben
wird gehabt haben
werden gehabt haben
werdet gehabt haben
werden gehabt haben

CONDITIONAL

ich würde haben
du würdest haben
er, sie, es würde haben
wir würden haben
ihr würdet haben
sie (Sie) würden haben

PAST CONDITIONAL

würde gehabt haben
würdest gehabt haben
würde gehabt haben
würden gehabt haben
würdet gehabt haben
würden gehabt haben

IMPERATIVE

Habe!
Haben wir!
Habt!
Haben Sie!

SUBJUNCTIVE

When the subjunctive forms are identical to the indicative forms, you have to use an alternate subjunctive form. These alternates are in parentheses.

PRESENT	PAST
ich habe	*ich habe (hätte) gehabt*
du habest	*du habest gehabt*
er, sie, es habe	*er, sie, es habe gehabt*
wir haben	*wir haben (hätten) gehabt*
ihr habet	*ihr habet gehabt*
sie (Sie) haben	*sie (Sie) haben (hatten) gehabt*

IMPERFECT	PAST PERFECT
ich hätte	*ich hätte gehabt*
du hättest	*du hättest gehabt*
er, Sie, es hätte	*er, Sie, es hätte gehabt*
wir hätten	*wir hatten gehabt*
ihr hättet	*ihr hättet gehabt*
sie (Sie) hätten	*sie (Sie) hätten gehabt*

werden   to become

INFINITIVE

PRESENT	PAST
werden	*geworden sein*

PARTICIPLES

PRESENT

werdend

PAST

geworden

INDICATIVE

PRESENT

ich werde
du wirst
er, sie, es wird
wir werden
ihr werdet
sie (Sie) werden

CONVERSATIONAL PAST

bin geworden
bist geworden
ist geworden
sind geworden
seid geworden
sind geworden

SIMPLE PAST

ich wurde
du wurdest
er, sie, es wurde
wir wurden
ihr wurdet
sie (Sie) wurden

PAST PERFECT

war geworden
warst geworden
war geworden
waren geworden
wart geworden
waren geworden

FUTURE

ich werde werden
du wirst werden
er, sie, es wird werden
wir werden werden
ihr werdet werden
sie (Sie) werden werden

FUTURE PERFECT

werde geworden sein
wirst geworden sein
wird geworden sein
werden geworden sein
werdet geworden sein
werden geworden sein

CONDITIONAL

ich würde werden
du würdest werden

er, sie, es würde werden
wir würden werden

CONDITIONAL PERFECT

würde geworden sein
würdest geworden
    sein

würde geworden sein
würden geworden sein

ihr würdet werden   *würdet geworden sein*
sie (Sie) würden werden   *würden geworden sein*

IMPERATIVE

werde!
werden wir!
werdet!
werden Sie!

SUBJUNCTIVE

PRESENT	PRESENT PERFECT
ich werde (würde)	*ich sei geworden*
du werdest	*du seiest gewordeen*
er, sei, es werde	*er, sie, es sei geworden*
wir werden (würden)	*wir seien geworden*
ihr werdet	*ihr seiet geworden*
sie (Sie) werden (würden)	*sie (Sie) seien geworden*

IMPERFECT	PAST PERFECT
ich würde	*ich wäre geworden*
du würdest	*du wärest geworden*
er, sie, es würde	*er, sie, es wäre geworden*
wir würden	*wir wären geworden*
ihr würdet	*ihr würet geworden*
sie (Sie) würden	*sie (Sie) wären geworden*

können   to be able to

INFINITIVE

PRESENT	PAST
können	*gekonnt haben*

PARTICIPLES

PRESENT
könnend

PAST
gekonnt (können)*

INDICATIVE

PRESENT	CONVERSATIONAL PAST
ich kann	*habe gekonnt**
du kannst	*hast gekonnt*
er, sie, es kann	*hat gekonnt*
wir können	*haben gekonnt*
ihr könnt	*habt gekonnt*
sie (Sie) können	*haben gekonnt*

SIMPLE PAST	PAST PERFECT
ich konnte	*hatte gekonnt*
du konntest	*hattest gekonnt*
er, sie, es konnte	*hatte gekonnt*
wir konnten	*hatten gekonnt*
ihr konntet	*hattet gekonnt*
sie (Sie) konnten	*hatten gekonnt*

FUTURE	FUTURE PERFECT
ich werde können	*werde gekonnt haben*
du wirst können	*wirst gekonnt haben*
er, sie, es wird können	*wird gekonnt haben*
wir werden können	*werden gekonnt haben*
ihr werdet können	*werdet gekonnt haben*
sie (Sie) werden können	*werden gekonnt haben*

* The model verbs *können, dürfen, müssen, sollen,* and *wollen* appear in the past in their infinitive forms when used with another verb, for example: *er muss es tun* (he has to do it) becomes *er hat es tun müssen* (he had to do it), with a double infinitive, in the past.

CONDITIONAL	CONDITIONAL PERFECT
ich würde können	*würde gekonnt haben*
du würdest können	*würdest gekonnt haben*
er, sie, es würde können	*würde gekonnt haben*
wir würden können	*würden gekonnt haben*
ihr würdet können	*würdet gekonnt haben*
sie (Sie) werden können	*würden gekonnt haben*

SUBJUNCTIVE

PRESENT	PRESENT PERFECT
ich könne	*ich (habe) hätte gekonnt*
du könnest	*du habest gekonnt*
er, sie, es könne	*er habe gekonnt*
wir können (könnten)	*wir (haben) hätten gekonnt*
ihr könnet	*ihr habet gekonnt*
sie (Sie) können (könnten)	*sie (Sie) (haben) hätten gekonnt*

IMPERFECT	PAST PERFECT
ich könnte	*ich hätte gekonnt*
du könntest	*du hättest gekonnt*
er, sie, es könnte	*er, sie, es hätte gekonnt*
wir könnten	*wir hätten gekonnt*
ihr könntet	*ihr hättet gekonnt*
sie (Sie) könnten	*sie (Sie) hätten gekonnt*

dürfen   to be allowed to

INFINITIVE

PRESENT	PAST
dürfen	*gedurft haben*

PARTICIPLES

PRESENT   PAST
dürfend   *gedurft (dürfen)**

INDICATIVE

PRESENT	CONVERSATIONAL PAST
ich darf	*habe gedurft**
du darfst	*hast gedurft*
er, sie, es darf	*hat gedurft*
wir dürfen	*haben gedurft*
ihr dürft	*habt gedurft*
sie, Sie dürfen	*haben gedurft*

SIMPLE PAST	PAST PERFECT
ich durfte	*hatte gedurft*
du durftest	*hattest gedurft*
er, sie, es durfte	*hatte gedurft*
wir durften	*hatten gedurft*
ihr durftet	*hattet gedurft*
sie (Sie) durften	*hatten gedurft*

FUTURE	FUTURE PERFECT
ich werde dürfen	*werde gedurft haben*
du wirst dürfen	*wirst gedurft haben*
er, sie, es wird dürfen	*wird gedurft haben*
wir werden dürfen	*werden gedurft haben*
ihr werdet dürfen	*werdet gedurft haben*
sie (Sie) werden dürfen	*werden gedurft haben*

CONDITIONAL	CONDITIONAL PERFECT
ich würde dürfen	*würde gedurft haben*
du würdest dürfen	*würdest gedurft haben*
er, sie, es würde dürfen	*würde gedurft haben*
wir würden dürfen	*würden gedurft haben*

* See note under *Können*.

ihr würdet dürfen *würdet gedurft haben*
sie (Sie) würden dürfen *würden gedurft haben*

SUBJUNCTIVE

PRESENT	PRESENT PERFECT
ich dürfe	*ich habe (hätte) gedurft*
du dürfest	*du habest gedurft*
er, sie, es dürfe	*er habe gedurft*
wir dürfen (dürften)	*wir haben (hätten) gedurft*
ihr dürfet	*ihr habet gedurft*
sie (Sie) dürfen (dürften)	*sie (Sie) haben (hätten) gedurft.*

IMPERFECT	PAST PERFECT
ich dürfte	*ich hätte gedurft*
du dürftest	*du hättest gedurft*
er, sie, es dürfte	*er hätte gedurft*
wir dürften	*wir hätten gedurft*
ihr dürftet	*ihr hättet gedurft*
sie (Sie) dürften	*sie hätten gedurft*

müssen to be obliged to, to have to

INFINITIVE

PRESENT	PAST
müssen	*gemusst haben*

PARTICIPLES

PRESENT	PAST
müssend	*gemusst (müssen)**

* See note under *Können*.

INDICATIVE

PRESENT	CONVERSATIONAL PAST
ich muss	*habe gemusst**
du musst	*hast gemusst*
er, sie, es muss	*hat gemusst*
wir müssen	*haben gemusst*
ihr müsst	*habt gemusst*
sie, (Sie) müssen	*haben gemusst*

SIMPLE PAST	PAST PERFECT
ich musste	*hatte gemusst*
du musstest	*hattest gemusst*
er, sie, es musste	*hatte gemusst*
wir mussten	*hatten gemusst*
ihr musstet	*hattet gemusst*
sie (Sie) mussten	*hatten gemusst*

FUTURE	FUTURE PERFECT
ich werde müssen	*werde gemusst haben*
du wirst müssen	*wirst gemusst haben*
er, sie, es wird müssen	*wird gemusst haben*
wir werden müssen	*werden gemusst haben*
ihr werdet müssen	*werdet gemusst haben*
sie (Sie) werden müssen	*werden gemusst haben*

CONDITIONAL	CONDITIONAL PERFECT
ich würde müssen	*würde gemusst haben*
du würdest müssen	*würdest gemusst haben*
er, sie, es würde müssen	*würde gemusst haben*
wir würden müssen	*würden gemusst haben*
ihr würdet müssen	*würdet gemusst haben*
sie (Sie) würden müssen	*würden gemusst haben*

* See note under *Können*.

SUBJUNCTIVE

PRESENT	PRESENT PERFECT
ich müsse	*ich habe (hätte) gemusst*
du müssest	*du habest gemusst*
er, sie, es müsse	*er, sie, es habe gemusst*
wir müssen (müssten)	*wir haben (hätten) gemusst*
ihr müsset	*ihr habet gemusst*
sie, Sie müssen (müssten)	*sie, Sie haben (hätten) gemusst*

IMPERFECT	PAST PERFECT
ich müsste	*ich hätte gemusst*
du müsstest	*du hättest gemusst*
er, sie, es müsse	*er, sie, es hätte gemusst*
wir müssten	*wir hätten gemusst*
ihr müsstet	*ihr hättet gemusst*
sie, Sie müssten	*sie (Sie) hätten gemusst*

wissen   to know

INFINITIVE

PRESENT	PAST
wissen	*gewusst haben*

PARTICIPLES

PRESENT	PAST
wissend	*gewusst*

INDICATIVE

PRESENT	CONVERSATIONAL PAST
ich weiß	*habe gewusst*
du weißt	*hast gewusst*

er, sie, es weiß	hat gewusst
wir wissen	haben gewusst
ihr wisst	habt gewusst
sie, Sie wissen	haben gewusst

SIMPLE PAST	PAST PERFECT
ich wusste	hatte gewusst
du wusstest	hattest gewusst
er, sie, es wusste	hatte gewusst
wir wussten	hatten gewusst
ihr wusstet	hattet gewusst
sie (Sie) wussten	hatten gewusst

FUTURE	FUTURE PERFECT
ich werde wissen	werde gewusst haben
du wirst wissen	wirst gewusst haben
er, sie, es wird wissen	wird gewusst haben
wir werden wissen	werden gewusst haben
ihr werdet wissen	werdet gewusst haben
sie (Sie) werden wissen	werden gewusst haben

CONDITIONAL	CONDITIONAL PERFECT
ich würde wissen	würde gewusst haben
du würdest wissen	würdest gewusst haben
er, sie, es würde wissen	würde gewusst haben
wir würden wissen	würden gewusst haben
ihr würdet wissen	würdet gewusst haben
sie (Sie) würden wissen	würden gewusst haben

IMPERATIVE

wisse!
wissen wir!
wisst!
wissen Sie!

SUBJUNCTIVE

PRESENT	PRESENT PERFECT
ich wisse	*ich habe hätte gewusst*
du wissest	*du habest gewusst*
er, sie, es wisse	*er habe gewusst*
wir wissen (wüssten)	*wir haben (hätten) gewusst*
ihr wisset	*ihr habet gewusst*
sie (Sie) wissen	*sie (Sie) haben (hätten)*
(wüssten)	*gewusst*

IMPERFECT	PAST PERFECT
ich wüsste	*ich hätte gewusst*
du wüsstest	*du hättest gewusst*
er, sie, es wüsste	*er, sie, es hätte gewusst*
wir wüssten	*wir hätten gewusst*
ihr wüsstet	*ihr hättet gewusst*
sie (Sie) wüssten	*sie (Sie) hätten gewusst*

gehen   to go

INFINITIVE

PRESENT	PAST
gehen	*gegangen sein*

PARTICIPLES

PRESENT	PAST
gehend	*gegangen*

INDICATIVE

PRESENT	CONVERSATIONAL PAST
ich gehe	*bin gegangen*
du gehst	*bist gegangen*

er, sie, es geht	ist gegangen
wir gehen	sind gegangen
ihr geht	seid gegangen
sie (Sie) gehen	sind gegangen

SIMPLE PAST	PAST PERFECT
ich ging	war gegangen
du gingst	warst gegangen
er, sie, es ging	war gegangen
wir gingen	waren gegangen
ihr gingt	wart gegangen
sie (Sie) gingen	waren gegangen

FUTURE	FUTURE PERFECT
ich werde gehen	werde gegangen sein
du wirst gehen	wirst gegangen sein
er, sie, es wird gehen	wird gegangen sein
wir werden gehen	werden gegangen sein
ihr werdet gehen	werdet gegangen sein
sie (Sie) werden gehen	werden gegangen sein

CONDITIONAL	CONDITIONAL PERFECT
ich würde gehen	würde gegangen sein
du würdest gehen	würdest gegangen sein
er, sie, es würde gehen	würde gegangen sein
wir würden gehen	würden gegangen sein
ihr würdet gehen	würdet gegangen sein
sie (Sie) würden gehen	würden gegangen sein

IMPERATIVE

gehe!
gehen wir!
geht!
gehen Sie!

SUBJUNCTIVE

PRESENT	PRESENT PERFECT
ich (gehe) ginge	*ich sei gegangen*
du gehest	*du seiest gegangen*
er, sie, es gehe	*er sei gegangen*
wir (gehen) gingen	*wir seien gegangen*
ihr gehet	*ihr seid gegangen*
sie (Sie) (gehen) gingen	*sie (Sie) seien gegangen*

IMPERFECT	PAST PERFECT
ich ginge	*ich wäre gegangen*
du gingest	*du wärest gegangen*
er, sie, es ginge	*er wäre gegangen*
wir gingen	*wir wären gegangen*
ihr ginget	*ihr wäret gegangen*
sie (Sie) gingen	*sie wären gegangen*

kommen   to come

INFINITIVE

PRESENT	PAST
kommen	*gekommen sein*

PARTICIPLES

PRESENT	PAST
kommend	*gekommen*

INDICATIVE

PRESENT	CONVERSATIONAL PAST
ich komme	*bin gekommen*
du kommst	*bist gekommen*
er, sie, es kommt	*ist gekommen*
wir kommen	*sind gekommen*

| ihr kommt | seid gekommen |
| sie, Sie kommen | sind gekommen |

SIMPLE PAST	PAST PERFECT
ich kam	war gekommen
du kamst	warst gekommen
er, sie, es kam	war gekommen
wir kamen	waren gekommen
ihr kamt	wart gekommen
sie (Sie) kamen	waren gekommen

FUTURE	FUTURE PERFECT
ich werde kommen	werde gekommen sein
du wirst kommen	wirst gekommen sein
er, sie, es wird kommen	wird gekommen sein
wir werden kommen	werden gekommen sein
ihr werdet kommen	werdet gekommen sein
sie (Sie) werden kommen	werden gekommen sein

CONDITIONAL	CONDITIONAL PERFECT
ich würde kommen	würde gekommen sein
du würdest kommen	würdest gekommen sein
er, sie, es würde kommen	würde gekommen sein
wir würden kommen	würden gekommen sein
ihr würdet kommen	würdet gekommen sein
sie (Sie) würden kommen	würden gekommen sein

IMPERATIVE

komm!
kommen wir!
kommt!
kommen Sie!

SUBJUNCTIVE

PRESENT	PRESENT PERFECT
ich (komme) käme	ich sei gekommen
dass du kommest	du seiest gekommen

er, sie, es komme *er, sie, es sei gekommen*
wir (kommen) kämen *wir seien gekommen*
ihr kommet *ihr seid gekommen*
sie (Sie) (kommen) *sie seien gekommen*
  kämen

IMPERFECT	PAST PERFECT
ich käme	*ich wäre gekommen*
du kämest	*du wärest gekommen*
er, sie, es käme	*er, sie, es wäre gekommen*
wir kämen	*wir wären gekommen*
ihr kämet	*ihr wäret gekommen*
sie (Sie) kämen	*sie wären gekommen*

40. OTHER IRREGULAR VERBS

When the present subjunctive form is in parentheses,
it indicates that it is identical to the present indicative.
Whenever this occurs, the imperfect or the past perfect
subjunctive form is used.

Infinitive: *beginnen,* to begin
Pres. Part.: *beginnend*
Present Indicative: *ich beginne, du beginnst, er
beginnt, wir beginnen, ihr beginnt, Sie beginnen, sie
beginnen*
Present Subjunctive: *(ich beginne), du beginnest, er
beginne, wir beginnen, ihr beginnet, (Sie beginnen),
sie (beginnen)*
Simple Past: *ich begann*
Imperfect Subjunctive: *Ich begänne (begönne)*
Past Part.: *begonnen*
Conversational Past: *ich habe begonnen*
Past Perfect Indicative: *ich hatte begonnen*
Past Perfect Subjunctive: *ich hätte begonnen*
Future: *ich werde beginnen*

Future Perfect: *ich werde begonnen haben*
Conditional: *ich würde beginnen*
Conditional Perfect: *ich würde begonnen haben*
Imperative: *beginn! beginnen wir! beginnt! beginnen Sie!*

Infinitive: *bleiben*, to remain
Pres. Part.: *bleibend*
Present Indicative: *ich bleibe, du bleibst, er bleibt, wir bleiben, ihr bleibt, Sie bleiben, sie bleiben*
Present Subjunctive: *ich bleibe, du bleibest, er bleibe, wir bleiben, ihr bleibet, Sie bleiben, sie bleiben*
Simple Past: *ich blieb*
Imperfect Subjunctive: *ich bliebe*
Past Part.: *geblieben*
Conversational Past: *ich bin geblieben*
Past Perfect Indicative: *ich war geblieben*
Present Perfect Subjunctive: *ich sei geblieben*
Past Perfect Subjunctive: *ich wäre geblieben*
Future: *ich werde bleiben*
Future Perfect: *ich werde geblieben sein*
Conditional: *ich würde bleiben*
Conditional Perfect: *ich würde geblieben sein*
Imperative: *bleib! bleiben wir! bleibt! bleiben Sie!*

Infinitive: *bringen*, to bring
Pres. Part.: *bringend*
Present Indicative: *ich bringe, du bringst, er bringt, wir bringen, ihr bringt, Sie bringen, sie bringen*
Present Subjunctive: *(ich bringe), du bringest, er bringe, (wir bringen), ihr bringet, (Sie bringen, sie bringen)*
Simple Past: *ich brachte*
Imperfect Subjunctive: *ich brächte*
Past Part.: *gebracht*
Conversational Past: *ich habe gebracht*
Past Perfect Indicative: *ich hatte gebracht*

Present Perfect Subjunctive: *ich habe (hatte) gebracht*
Past Perfect Subjunctive: *ich hätte gebracht*
Future: *ich werde bringen*
Future Perfect: *ich werde gebracht haben*
Conditional: *ich würde bringen*
Conditional Perfect: *ich würde gebracht haben*
Imperative: *bring! bringen wir! bringt! bringen Sie!*

Infinitive: *denken,* to think
Pres. Part.: *denkend*
Present Indicative: *ich denke, du denkst, er denkt, wir denken, ihr denkt, Sie denken, sie denken*
Present Subjunctive: *(ich denke), du denkest, er denke, (wir denken), ihr denket, (Sie denken, sie denken)*
Simple Past: *ich dachte*
Imperfect Subjunctive: *ich dächte*
Past Part.: *gedacht*
Conversational Past: *ich habe gedacht*
Past Perfect Indicative: *ich hatte gedacht*
Present Perfect Subjunctive: *(ich habe gedacht)*
Past Perfect Subjunctive: *ich hätte gedacht*
Future: *ich werde denken*
Future Perfect: *ich werde gedacht haben*
Conditional: *ich würde denken*
Conditional Perfect: *ich würde gedacht haben*
Imperative: *denke! (denk!) denken wir! denkt! denken Sie!*

Infinitive: *essen,* to eat
Pres. Part.: *essend*
Present Indicative: *ich esse, du isst, er isst, wir essen, ihr esst, Sie essen, sie essen*
Present Subjunctive: *(ich esse), du essest, er esse, (wir essen), ihr esset, (Sie essen, sie essen)*
Simple Past: *ich aß*
Imperfect Subjunctive: *ich äße*

Past Part.: *gegessen*
Conversational Past: *ich habe gegessen*
Past Perfect Indicative: *ich hatte gegessen*
Present Perfect Subjunctive: *ich (hatte) habe gegessen*
Past Perfect Subjunctive: *ich hätte gegessen*
Future: *ich werde essen*
Future Perfect: *ich werde gegessen haben*
Conditional: *ich würde essen*
Conditional Perfect: *ich würde gegessen haben*
Imperative: *iss! essen wir! esst! essen Sie!*

Infinitive: *fahren*, to drive
Pres. Part.: *fahrend*
Present Indicative: *ich fahre, du fährst, er fährt, wir fahren, ihr fahrt, Sie fahren, sie fahren*
Present Subjunctive: *ich (fahre) führe, du fahrest, er fahre, (wir fahren), ihr fahret, (Sie fahren, sie fahren)*
Simple Past: *ich fuhr*
Imperfect Subjunctive: *ich führe*
Past Part.: *gefahren*
Conversational Past: *ich bin gefahren*
Past Perfect Indicative: *ich war gefahren*
Present Perfect Subjunctive: *ich sei gefahren*
Past Perfect Subjunctive: *ich wäre gefahren*
Future: *ich werde fahren*
Future Perfect: *ich werde gefahren sein*
Conditional: *ich würde fahren*
Conditional Perfect: *ich würde gefahren sein*
Imperative: *fahr! fahren wir! fahrt! fahren Sie!*

Infinitive: *fallen*, to fall
Pres. Part.: *fallend*
Present Indicative: *ich falle, du fällst, er fällt, wir fallen, ihr fallt, Sie fallen, sie fallen*
Present Subjunctive: *ich (falle) fiele, du fallest, er falle, (wir fallen), ihr fallet, (Sie fallen, sie fallen)*

Simple Past: *ich fiel*
Imperfect Subjunctive: *ich fiele*
Past Part.: *gefallen*
Conversational Past: *ich bin gefallen*
Past Perfect Indicative: *ich war gefallen*
Present Perfect Subjunctive: *ich sei gefallen*
Past Perfect Subjunctive: *ich wäre gefallen*
Future: *ich werde fallen*
Future Perfect: *ich werde gefallen sein*
Conditional: *ich würde fallen*
Conditional Perfect: *ich würde gefallen sein*
Imperative: *falle! fall! fallen wir! fallt! fallen Sie!*

Infinitive: *finden,* to find
Pres. Part.: *findend*
Present Indicative: *ich finde, du findest, er findet, wir finden, ihr findet, Sie finden, sie finden*
Present Subjunctive: *ich (finde) fände, du findest, er finde, (wir finden), ihr findet, (Sie finden, sie finden)*
Simple Past: *ich fand*
Imperfect Subjunctive: *ich fände*
Past Part.: *gefunden*
Conversational Past: *ich habe gefunden*
Past Perfect Indicative: *ich hatte gefunden*
Present Perfect Subjunctive: *ich habe gefunden*
Past Perfect Subjunctive: *ich hätte gefunden*
Future: *ich werde finden*
Future Perfect: *ich werde gefunden haben*
Conditional: *ich würde finden*
Conditional Perfect: *ich würde gefunden haben*
Imperative: *finde! finden wir! findet! finden Sie!*

Infinitive: *fliegen,* to fly
Pres. Part.: *fliegend*
Present Indicative: *ich fliege, du fliegst, er fliegt, wir fliegen, ihr fliegt, Sie fliegen, sie fliegen*

Present Subjunctive: *ich (fliege) flöge, du fliegest, er fliege, (wir fliegen), ihr flieget, Sie fliegen, (sie fliegen)*
Simple Past: *ich flog*
Imperfect Subjunctive: *ich flöge*
Past Part.: *geflogen*
Conversational Past: *ich bin geflogen*
Past Perfect Indicative: *ich war geflogen*
Present Perfect Subjunctive: *ich sei geflogen*
Past Perfect Subjunctive: *ich wäre geflogen*
Future: *ich werde fliegen*
Future Perfect: *ich werde geflogen sein*
Conditional: *ich würde fliegen*
Conditional Perfect: *ich würde geflogen sein*
Imperative: *fliege! fliegen wir! fliegt! fliegen Sie!*

Infinitive: *heißen,* to be called
Pres. Part.: *heißend*
Present Indicative: *ich heiße, du heißt, er heißt, wir heißen, ihr heißt, Sie heißen, sie heißen*
Present Subjunctive: *ich (heiße) heiße, du heißest, er heiße, (wir heißen), ihr heißet, (Sie heißen, sie heißen)*
Simple Past: *ich hieß*
Imperfect Subjunctive: *ich hieße*
Past Part.: *geheißen*
Conversational Past: *ich habe geheißen*
Past Perfect Indicative: *ich hatte geheißen*
Present Perfect Subjunctive: *ich (habe) hätte geheißen*
Past Perfect Subjunctive: *ich hätte geheißen*
Future: *ich werde heißen*
Future Perfect: *ich werde geheißen haben*
Conditional: *ich würde heißen*
Conditional Perfect: *ich würde geheißen haben*
Imperative: *heiße! heißen wir! heißt! heißen Sie!*

Infinitive: *helfen,* to help
Pres. Part.: *helfend*

Present Indicative: *ich helfe, du hilfst, er hilft, wir helfen, ihr helft, Sie helfen, sie helfen*
Present Subjunctive: *(ich helfe), du helfest, er helfe, (wir helfen), ihr helfet, (Sie helfen, sie helfen)*
Simple Past: *ich half*
Imperfect Subjunctive: *ich hälfe* (also: *ich hülfe*)
Past Part.: *geholfen*
Conversational Past: *ich habe geholfen*
Past Perfect Indicative: *ich hatte geholfen*
Present Perfect Subjunctive: *ich (habe) hätte geholfen*
Past Perfect Subjunctive: *ich hätte geholfen*
Future: *ich werde helfen*
Future Perfect: *ich werde geholfen haben*
Conditional: *ich würde helfen*
Conditional Perfect: *ich würde geholfen haben*
Imperative: *hilf! helfen wir! helft! helfen Sie!*

Infinitive: *kennen,* to know
Pres. Part.: *kennend*
Present Indicative: *ich kenne, du kennst, er kennt, wir kennen, ihr kennt, Sie kennen, sie kennen*
Present Subjunctive: *ich (kenne) kennte, du kennest, er kenne, (wir kennen), ihr kennet, (Sie kennen, sie kennen)*
Simple Past: *ich kannte*
Imperfect Subjunctive: *ich kannte*
Past Part.: *gekannt*
Conversational Past: *ich habe gekannt*
Past Perfect Indicative: *ich hatte gekannt*
Present Perfect Subjunctive: *ich (habe) hätte gekannt*
Past Perfect Subjunctive: *ich hätte gekannt*
Future: *ich werde kennen*
Future Perfect: *ich werde gekannt haben*
Conditional: *ich würde kennen*
Conditional Perfect: *ich würde gekannt haben*
Imperative: *kenne! kennen wir! kennt! kennen Sie!*

Infinitive: *laden*, to load
Pres. Part.: *ladend*
Present Indicative: *ich lade, du lädst, er lädt, wir laden, ihr ladet, Sie laden, sie laden*
Present Subjunctive: *ich (lade) lüde, du ladest, er lad, (wir laden), ihr ladet, (Sie laden, sie laden)*
Simple Past: *ich lud*
Imperfect Subjunctive: *ich lüde*
Past Part.: *geladen*
Conversational Past: *ich habe geladen*
Past Perfect Indicative: *ich hatte geladen*
Present Perfect Subjunctive: *ich (habe) hätte geladen*
Past Perfect Subjunctive: *ich hätte geladen*
Future: *ich werde laden*
Future Perfect: *ich werde geladen haben*
Conditional: *ich würde laden*
Conditional Perfect: *ich würde geladen haben*
Imperative: *lade! laden wir! ladet! laden Sie!*

Infinitive: *lassen*, to let
Pres. Part.: *lassend*
Present Indicative: *ich lasse, du lässt, er lässt, wir lassen, ihr lasst, Sie lassen, sie lassen*
Present Subjunctive: *ich (lasse) ließe, du lassest, er lasse, (wir lassen), ihr lasset, Sie lassen, (sie lassen)*
Simple Past: *ich ließ*
Imperfect Subjunctive: *ich ließe*
Past Part.: *gelassen*
Conversational Past: *ich habe gelassen*
Past Perfect Indicative: *ich hatte gelassen*
Present Perfect Subjunctive: *ich (habe) hätte gelassen*
Past Perfect Subjunctive: *ich hätte gelassen*
Future: *ich werde lassen*
Future Perfect: *ich werde gelassen haben*
Conditional: *ich würde lassen*

Conditional Perfect: *ich würde gelassen haben*
Imperative: *lass! lassen wir! lasst! lassen Sie!*

Infinitive: *laufen,* to run
Pres. Part.: *laufend*
Present Indicative: *ich laufe, du läufst, er läuft, wir laufen, ihr lauft, Sie laufen, sie laufen*
Present Subjunctive: *ich (laufe) liefe, du laufest, er laufe, (wir laufen), ihr laufet, Sie laufen, (sie laufen)*
Simple Past: *ich lief*
Imperfect Subjunctive: *ich liefe*
Past Part.: *gelaufen*
Conversational Past: *ich bin gelaufen*
Past Perfect Indicative: *ich war gelaufen*
Present Perfect Subjunctive: *ich sei gelaufen*
Past Perfect Subjunctive: *ich wäre gelaufen*
Future: *ich werde laufen*
Future Perfect: *ich werde gelaufen sein*
Conditional: *ich würde laufen*
Conditional Perfect: *ich würde gelaufen sein*
Imperative: *lauf! laufen wir! lauft! laufen Sie!*

Infinitive: *leiden,* to suffer, endure
Pres. Part.: *leidend*
Present Indicative: *ich leide, du leidest, er leidet, wir leiden, ihr leidet, Sie leiden, sie leiden*
Present Subjunctive: *ich (leide) litte, du leidest, er leide, (wir leiden), ihr leidet, Sie leiden, (sie leiden)*
Simple Past: *ich litt*
Imperfect Subjunctive: *ich litte*
Past Part.: *gelitten*
Conversational Past: *ich habe gelitten*
Past Perfect Indicative: *ich hatte gelitten*
Present Perfect Subjunctive: *ich (habe) hätte gelitten*
Past Perfect Subjunctive: *ich hätte gelitten*

Future: *ich werde leiden*
Future Perfect: *ich werde gelitten haben*
Conditional: *ich würde leiden*
Conditional Perfect: *ich würde gelitten haben*
Imperative: *leide! leiden wir! leidet! leiden Sie!*

Infinitive: *lesen,* to read
Pres. Part.: *lesend*
Present Indicative: *ich lese, du liest, er liest, wir lesen, ihr lest, Sie lesen, sie lesen*
Present Subjunctive: *ich (lese) läse, du lesest, er lese, (wir lesen), ihr leset, (Sie lesen, sie lesen)*
Simple Past: *ich las*
Imperfect Subjunctive: *ich läse*
Past Part.: *gelesen*
Conversational Past: *ich habe gelesen*
Past Perfect Indicative: *ich hatte gelesen*
Present Perfect Subjunctive: *ich (habe) hätte gelesen*
Past Perfect Subjunctive: *ich hätte gelesen*
Future: *ich werde lesen*
Future Perfect: *ich werde gelesen haben*
Conditional: *ich würde lesen*
Conditional Perfect: *ich würde gelesen haben*
Imperative: *lies! lesen wir! lest! lesen Sie!*

Infinitive: *liegen,* to lie (recline)
Pres. Part.: *liegend*
Present Indicative: *ich liege, du liegst, er liegt, wir liegen, ihr liegt, Sie liegen, sie liegen*
Present Subjunctive: *ich (liege) läge, du liegest, er liege, (wir liegen), ihr lieget, (Sie liegen, sie liegen)*
Simple Past: *ich lag*
Imperfect Subjunctive: *ich läge*
Past Part.: *gelegen*
Conversational Past: *ich habe gelegen*
Past Perfect Indicative: *ich hatte gelegen*

Present Perfect Subjunctive: *ich (habe) hätte gelegen*
Past Perfect Subjunctive: *ich hätte gelegen*
Future: *ich werde liegen*
Future Perfect: *ich werde gelegen haben*
Conditional: *ich würde liegen*
Conditional Perfect: *ich würde gelegen haben*
Imperative: *liege! liegen wir! liegt! liegen Sie!*

Infinitive: *lügen,* to lie (say something untrue)
Pres. Part.: *lügend*
Present Indicative: *ich lüge, du lügst, er lügt, wir lügen, ihr lügt, Sie lügen, sie lügen*
Present Subjunctive: *ich lüge, du lügest, er lüge, wir lügen, ihr lüget, Sie lügen, sie lügen*
Simple Past: *ich log*
Imperfect Subjunctive: *ich löge*
Past Part.: *gelogen*
Conversational Past: *ich habe gelogen*
Past Perfect Indicative: *ich hatte gelogen*
Present Perfect Subjunctive: *ich (habe) hätte gelogen*
Past Perfect Subjunctive: *ich hätte gelogen*
Future: *ich werde lügen*
Future Perfect: *ich werde gelogen haben*
Conditional: *ich würde lügen*
Conditional Perfect: *ich würde gelogen haben*
Imperative: *lüge! lügen wir! lügt! lügen Sie!*

Infinitive: *nehmen,* to take
Pres. Part.: *nehmend*
Present Indicative: *ich nehme, du nimmst, er nimmt, wir nehmen, ihr nehmt, Sie nehmen, sie nehmen*
Present Subjunctive: *ich (nehme) nähme, du nehmest, er nehme, (wir nehmen), ihr nehmet, (Sie nehmen, sie nehmen.)*
Simple Past: *ich nahm*
Imperfect Subjunctive: *ich nähme*

Past Part.: *genommen*
Conversational Past: *ich habe genommen*
Past Perfect Indicative: *ich hatte genommen*
Present Perfect Subjunctive: *ich (habe) hätte genommen*
Past Perfect Subjunctive: *ich hätte genommen*
Future: *ich werde nehmen*
Future Perfect: *ich werde genommen haben*
Conditional: *ich würde nehmen*
Conditional Perfect: *ich würde genommen haben*
Imperative: *nimm! nehmen wir! nehmt! nehmen Sie!*

Infinitive: *nennen*, to name
Pres. Part.: *nennend*
Present Indicative: *ich nenne, du nennst, er nennt, wir nennen, ihr nennt, Sie nennen, sie nennen*
Present Subjunctive: *ich (nenne) nennte, du nennest, er nenne, (wir nennen), ihr nennet, (Sie nennen, sie nennen)*
Simple Past: *ich nannte*
Imperfect Subjunctive: *ich nennte*
Past Part.: *genannt*
Conversational Past: *ich habe genannt*
Past Perfect Indicative: *ich hatte genannt*
Present Perfect Subjunctive: *ich (habe) hätte genannt*
Past Perfect Subjunctive: *ich hätte genannt*
Future: *ich werde nennen*
Future Perfect: *ich werde genannt haben*
Conditional: *ich würde nennen*
Conditional Perfect: *ich würde genannt haben*
Imperative: *nenne! nennen wir! nennt! nennen Sie!*

Infinitive: *rufen*, to call
Pres. Part.: *rufend*
Present Indicative: *ich rufe, du rufst, er ruft, wir rufen, ihr ruft, Sie rufen, sie rufen*
Present Subjunctive: *ich (rufe) riefe, du rufest, er rufe,*

(wir rufen), rufet, (Sie rufen, sie rufen)
Simple Past: *ich rief*
Imperfect Subjunctive: *ich riefe*
Past Part.: *gerufen*
Conversational Past: *ich habe gerufen*
Past Perfect Indicative: *ich hatte gerufen*
Present Perfect Subjunctive: *ich (habe) hätte gerufen*
Past Perfect Subjunctive: *ich hätte gerufen*
Future: *ich werde rufen*
Future Perfect: *ich werde gerufen haben*
Conditional: *ich würde rufen*
Conditional Perfect: *ich würde gerufen haben*
Imperative: *ruf! rufen wir! ruft! rufen Sie!*

Infinitive: *schaffen*, to create
Pres. Part.: *schaffend*
Present Indicative: *ich schaffe, du schaffst, er schafft,*
wir schaffen, ihr schafft, Sie schaffen, sie schaffen
Present Subjunctive: *ich (schaffe) schüfe, du schaffest,*
er schaffe, (wir schaffen), ihr schaffet, (Sie schaffen,
sie schaffen)
Simple Plan: *ich schuf*
Imperfect Subjunctive: *ich schüfe*
Past Part.: *geschaffen*
Conversational Past: *ich habe geschaffen*
Past Perfect Indicative: *ich hatte geschaffen*
Present Perfect Subjunctive: *ich (habe) hätte geschaffen*
Past Perfect Subjunctive: *ich hätte geschaffen*
Future: *ich werde schaffen*
Future Perfect: *ich werde geschaffen haben*
Conditional: *ich würde schaffen*
Conditional Perfect: *ich würde geschaffen haben*
Imperative: *schaffe! schaffen wir! schafft! schaffen Sie!*

Infinitive: *schlafen*, to sleep
Pres. Part.: *schlafend*

Present Indicative: *ich schlafe, du schläfst, er schläft, wir schlafen, ihr schlaft, sie schlafen*
Present Subjunctive: *ich (schlafe) schliefe, du schlafest, er schlafe, (wir schlafen), ihr schlafet, (Sie schlafen, sie schlafen)*
Simple Past: *ich schlief*
Imperfect Subjunctive: *ich schliefe*
Past Part.: *geschlafen*
Conversational Past: *ich habe geschlafen*
Past Perfect Indicative: *ich hatte geschlafen*
Present Perfect Subjunctive: *ich (habe) hätte geschlafen*
Past Perfect Subjunctive: *ich hätte geschlafen*
Future: *ich werde schlafen*
Future Perfect: *ich werde geschlafen haben*
Conditional: *ich würde schlafen*
Conditional Perfect: *ich würde geschlafen haben*
Imperative: *schlafe! schlafen wir! schlaft! schlafen Sie!*

Infinitive: *schlagen*, to beat, to strike
Pres. Part.: *schlagend*
Present Indicative: *ich schlage, du schlägst, er schlägt, wir schlagen, ihr schlagt, Sie schlagen, sie schlagen*
Present Subjunctive: *ich (schlage) schlüge, du schlagest, er schlage, (wir schlagen), ihr schlaget, (Sie schlagen, sie schlagen)*
Simple Past: *ich schlug*
Imperfect Subjunctive: *ich schlüge*
Past Part.: *geschlagen*
Conversational Past: *ich habe geschlagen*
Past Perfect Indicative: *ich hatte geschlagen*
Present Perfect Subjunctive: *ich (habe) hätte geschlagen*
Past Perfect Subjunctive: *ich hätte geschlagen*
Future: *ich werde schlagen*
Future Perfect: *ich werde geschlagen haben*

Conditional: *ich würde schlagen*
Conditional Perfect: *ich würde geschlagen haben*
Imperative: *schlage! (schlag!) schlagen wir! schlagt! schlagen Sie!*

Infinitive: *schreiben*, to write
Pres. Part.: *schreibend*
Present Indicative: *ich schreibe, du schreibst, er schreibt, wir schreiben, ihr schreibt, Sie schreiben, sie schreiben*
Present Subjunctive: *ich (schreibe) schriebe, du schreibest, er schreibe, (wir schreiben), ihr schreibet, (Sie schreiben, sie schreiben)*
Simple Past: *ich schrieb*
Imperfect Subjunctive: *ich schriebe*
Past Part.: *geschrieben*
Conversational Past: *ich habe geschrieben*
Past Perfect Indicative: *ich hatte geschrieben*
Present Perfect Subjunctive: *ich (habe) hätte geschrieben*
Past Perfect Subjunctive: *ich hätte geschrieben*
Future: *ich werde schreiben*
Future Perfect: *ich werde geschrieben haben*
Conditional: *ich würde schreiben*
Conditional Perfect: *ich würde geschrieben haben*
Imperative: *schreib! schreiben wir! schreibt! schreiben Sie!*

Infinitive: *schwimmen*, to swim
Pres. Part.: *schwimmend*
Present Indicative: *ich schwimme, du schwimmst, er schwimmt, wir schwimmen, ihr schwimmt, Sie schwimmen, sie schwimmen*
Present Subjunctive: *ich (schwimme) schwömme, du schwimmest, er schwimme, (wir schwimmen), ihr schwimmet, (Sie schwimmen, sie schwimmen)*

Simple Past: *ich schwamm*
Imperfect Subjunctive: *ich schwömme (schwämme)*
Past Part.: *geschwommen*
Conversational Past: *ich bin geschwommen*
Past Perfect Indicative: *ich war geschwommen*
Present Perfect Subjunctive: *ich sei geschwommen*
Past Perfect Subjunctive: *ich wäre geschwommen*
Future: *ich werde schwimmen*
Future Perfect: *ich werde geschwommen sein*
Conditional: *ich würde schwimmen*
Conditional Perfect: *ich würde geschwommen sein*
Imperative: *schwimm! schwimmen wir! schwimmt! schwimmen Sie!*

Infinitive: *senden*, to send, to broadcast
Pres. Part.: *sendend*
Present Indicative: *ich sende, du sendest, er sendet, wir senden, ihr sendet, Sie senden, sie senden*
Present Subjunctive: *ich (sende) sendete, du sendest, er sendet, (wir senden), ihr sendet, (Sie senden, sie senden)*
Simple Past: *ich sandte* (or *sendete*)
Imperfect Subjunctive: *ich sendete*
Past Part.: *gesandt (gesendet)**
Conversational Past: *ich habe gesandt (gesendet)*
Past Perfect Indicative: *ich hatte gesandt (gesendet)*
Present Perfect Subjunctive: *ich (habe) hätte gesandt (gesendet)*
Past Perfect Subjunctive: *ich hätte gesandt (gesendet)*
Future: *ich werde senden*
Future Perfect: *ich werde gesandt (gesendet) haben*
Conditional: *ich würde senden*

Senden has two simple past and two past participal forms, depending on the meaning; *sandte, gesandt* (sent) and *sendete, gesendet* (broadcast).

Conditional Perfect: *ich würde gesandt (gesendet) haben*
Imperative: *sende! senden wir! sendet! senden Sie!*

Infinitive: *singen*, to sing
Pres. Part.: *singend*
Present Indicative: *ich singe, du singst, er singt, wir singen, ihr singt, Sie singen, sie singen*
Present Subjunctive: *ich (singe) sänge, du singest, er singe, (wir singen), ihr singet, (Sie singen, sie singen)*
Simple Past: *ich sang*
Imperfect Subjunctive: *ich sänge*
Past Part.: *gesungen*
Conversational Past: *ich habe gesungen*
Past Perfect Indicative: *ich hatte gesungen*
Present Perfect Subjunctive: *ich (habe) hatte gesungen*
Past Perfect Subjunctive: *ich hätte gesungen*
Future: *ich werde singen*
Future Perfect: *ich werde gesungen haben*
Conditional: *ich würde singen*
Conditional Perfect: *ich würde gesungen haben*
Imperative: *sing! singen wir! singt! singen Sie!*

Infinitive: *sitzen*, to sit
Pres. Part.: *sitzend*
Present Indicative: *ich sitze, du sitzt, er sitzt, wir sitzen, ihr sitzt, Sie sitzen, sie sitzen*
Present Subjunctive: *ich (sitze) sässe, du sitzest, er sitze, (wir sitzen), ihr sitzet, (Sie sitzen, sie sitzen)*
Simple Past: *ich sass*
Imperfect Subjunctive: *ich sässe*
Past Part.: *gesessen*
Conversational Past: *ich habe gesessen*
Past Perfect Indicative: *ich hatte gesessen*
Present Perfect Subjunctive: *ich (habe) hätte gesessen*
Past Perfect Subjunctive: *ich hätte gesessen*

Future: *ich werde sitzen*
Future Perfect: *ich werde gesessen haben*
Conditional: *ich würde sitzen*
Conditional Perfect: *ich würde gesessen haben*
Imperative: *sitz! sitzen wir! sitzt! sitzen Sie!*

Infinitive: *stehen*, to stand
Pres. Part.: *stehend*
Present Indicative: *ich stehe, du stehst, er steht, wir stehen, ihr steht, Sie stehen, sie stehen*
Present Subjunctive: *ich (stehe) stünde/stände du stehest, er stehe, (wir stehen), ihr stehet, (Sie stehen, sie stehen)*
Simple Past: *ich stand*
Imperfect Subjunctive: *ich stünde* or *stände*
Past Part.: *gestanden*
Conversational Past: *ich habe gestanden*
Past Perfect Indicative: *ich hatte gestanden*
Present Perfect Subjunctive: *ich (habe) hätte gestanden*
Past Perfect Subjunctive: *ich hätte gestanden*
Future: *ich werde stehen*
Future Perfect: *ich werde gestanden haben*
Conditional: *ich würde stehen*
Conditional Perfect: *ich würde gestanden haben*
Imperative: *steh! stehen wir! steht! stehen Sie!*

Infinitive: *stehlen*, to steal
Pres. Part.: *stehlend*
Present Indicative: *ich stehle, du stiehlst, er stiehlt, wir stehlen, ihr stehlt, Sie stehlen, sie stehlen*
Present Subjunctive: *ich (stehle) stöhle/stähle, du stehlest, er stehle, (wir stehlen), ihr stehlet, (Sie stehlen, sie stehlen)*
Simple Past: *ich stahl*
Imperfect Subjunctive: *ich stöhle/stähle*
Past Part.: *gestohlen*

Conversational Past: *ich habe gestohlen*
Past Perfect Indicative: *ich hatte gestohlen*
Present Perfect Subjunctive: *ich (habe) hätte gestohlen*
Past Perfect Subjunctive: *ich hätte gestohlen*
Future: *ich werde stehlen*
Future Perfect: *ich werde gestohlen haben*
Conditional: *ich würde stehlen*
Conditional Perfect: *ich würde gestohlen haben*
Imperative: *stiehl! stehlen wir! stehlt! stehlen Sie!*

Infinitive: *springen*, to jump
Pres. Part.: *springend*
Present Indicative: *ich springe, du springst, er springt, wir springen, ihr springt, Sie springen, sie springen*
Present Subjunctive: *ich (springe) spränge, du springest, er springe, (wir springen), ihr springet, (Sie springen, sie springen)*
Simple Past: *ich sprang*
Imperfect Subjunctive: *ich spränge*
Past Part.: *gesprungen*
Conversational Past: *ich bin gesprungen*
Past Perfect Indicative: *ich war gesprungen*
Present Perfect Subjunctive: *ich sei gesprungen*
Past Perfect Subjunctive: *ich wäre gesprungen*
Future: *ich werde springen*
Future Perfect: *ich werde gesprungen sein*
Conditional: *ich würde springen*
Conditional Perfect: *ich würde gesprungen sein*
Imperative: *spring! springen wir! springt! springen Sie!*

Infinitive: *tragen*, to carry
Pres. Part.: *tragend*
Present Indicative: *ich trage, du trägst, er trägt, wir tragen, ihr tragt, Sie tragen, sie tragen*
Present Subjunctive: *ich (trage) trüge, du tragest, er*

trage, (wir tragen), ihr traget, (Sie tragen, sie tragen)
Simple Past: *ich trug*
Imperfect Subjunctive: *ich trüge*
Past Part.: *getragen*
Conversational Past: *ich (habe) hätte getragen*
Past Perfect Indicative: *ich hatte getragen*
Present Perfect Subjunctive: *ich habe getragen*
Past Perfect Subjunctive: *ich hätte getragen*
Future: *ich werde tragen*
Future Perfect: *ich werde getragen haben*
Conditional: *ich würde tragen*
Conditional Perfect: *ich würde getragen haben*
Imperative: *trag! tragen wir! tragt! tragen Sie!*

Infinitive: *treffen*, to meet
Pres. Part.: *treffend*
Present Indicative: *ich treffe, du triffst, er trifft, wir treffen, ihr trefft, Sie treffen, sie treffen*
Present Subjunctive: *ich (treffe) träfe, du treffest, er treffe, (wir treffen), ihr treffet, (Sie treffen, sie treffen)*
Simple Past: *ich traf*
Imperfect Subjunctive: *ich träfe*
Past Part.: *getroffen*
Conversational Past: *ich habe getroffen*
Past Perfect Indicative: *ich hätte getroffen*
Present Perfect Subjunctive: *ich (habe) hätte getroffen*
Past Perfect Subjunctive: *ich hätte getroffen*
Future: *ich werde treffen*
Future Perfect: *ich werde getroffen haben*
Conditional: *ich würde treffen*
Conditional Perfect: *ich würde getroffen haben*
Imperative: *triff! treffen wir! trefft! treffen Sie!*

Infinitive: *trinken*, to drink
Pres. Part.: *trinkend*
Present Indicative: *ich trinke, du trinkst, er trinkt, wir*

trinken, ihr trinkt, Sie trinken, sie trinken
Present Subjunctive: *ich (trinke) tränke, du trinkest, er trinke, (wir trinken), ihr trinket, (Sie trinken, sie trinken)*
Simple Past: *ich trank*
Imperfect Subjunctive: *ich tränke*
Past Part.: *getrunken*
Conversational Past: *ich habe getrunken*
Past Perfect Indicative: *ich hatte getrunken*
Present Perfect Subjunctive: *ich (habe) hätte getrunken*
Past Perfect Subjunctive: *ich hätte getrunken*
Future: *ich werde trinken*
Future Perfect: *ich werde getrunken haben*
Conditional: *ich würde trinken*
Conditional Perfect: *ich würde getrunken haben*
Imperative: *trink! trinken wir! trinkt! trinken Sie!*

Infinitive: *tun,* to do
Pres. Part.: *tuend*
Present Indicative: *ich tue, du tust, er tut, wir tun, ihr tut, Sie tun, sie tun*
Present Subjunctive: *ich (tue) täte, du tuest, er tue, (wir tun), ihr tuet, (Sie tun, sie tun)*
Simple Past: *ich tat*
Imperfect Subjunctive: *ich täte*
Past Part.: *getan*
Conversational Past: *ich habe getan*
Past Perfect Indicative: *ich hatte getan*
Present Perfect Subjunctive: *ich (habe) hätte getan*
Past Perfect Subjunctive: *ich hätte getan*
Future: *ich werde tun*
Future Perfect: *ich werde getan haben*
Conditional: *ich würde tun*
Conditional Perfect: *ich würde getan haben*
Imperative: *tue! tun wir! tut! tun Sie!*

Infinitive: *vergessen*, to forget
Pres. Part.: *vergessend*
Present Indicative: *ich vergesse, du vergisst, er vergisst, wir vergessen, ihr vergesst, Sie vergessen, sie vergessen*
Present Subjunctive: *ich (vergesse) vergäße, du vergessest, er vergesse, (wir vergessen), ihr vergesset, (Sie vergessen, sie vergessen)*
Simple Past: *ich vergaß*
Imperfect Subjunctive: *ich vergäße*
Past Part.: *vergessen*
Conversational Past: *ich habe vergessen*
Past Perfect Indicative: *ich hatte vergessen*
Present Perfect Subjunctive: *ich (habe) hätte vergessen*
Past Perfect Subjunctive: *ich hätte vergessen*
Future: *ich werde vergessen*
Future Perfect: *ich werde vergessen haben*
Conditional: *ich würde vergessen*
Conditional Perfect: *ich würde vergessen haben*
Imperative: *vergiss! vergessen wir! vergesst! vergessen Sie!*

Infinitive: *verlieren*, to lose
Pres. Part.: *verlierend*
Present Indicative: *ich verliere, du verlierst, er verliert, wir verlieren, ihr verliert, Sie verlieren, sie verlieren*
Present Subjunctive: *ich (verliere) verlöre, du verlierest, er verliere, (wir verlieren), ihr verlieret, (Sie verlieren, sie verlieren)*
Simple Past: *ich verlor*
Imperfect Subjunctive: *ich verlöre*
Past Part.: *verloren*
Conversational Past: *ich habe verloren*
Past Perfect Indicative: *ich hatte verloren*

Present Perfect Subjunctive: *ich (habe) hätte verloren*
Past Perfect Subjunctive: *ich hätte verloren*
Future: *ich werde verlieren*
Future Perfect: *ich werde verloren haben*
Conditional: *ich würde verlieren*
Conditional Perfect: *ich würde verloren haben*
Imperative: *verlier(e)! verlieren wir! verliert! verlieren Sie!*

LETTER WRITING

A. THANK-YOU NOTES

Berlin, den 6. Januar 2005

Sehr geehrte Frau Zimmermann,

Ich möchte Ihnen herzlich für Ihr wunderbares Geschenk danken. Das Bild entspricht ganz meinem Geschmack und passt so gut zu den neuen Möbeln in meinem Wohnzimmer.
Meinen allerherzlichsten Dank.

Mit verbindlichen Grüßen
Lotte Schäfer

Berlin, January 6, 2005

Dear Mrs. Zimmermann,

I should (would) like to thank you for your delight-
ful present. The picture is entirely to my taste and
matches the new furniture in my living room perfectly.
Thank you ever so much.

Sincerely yours,
Lotte Schäfer

B. BUSINESS LETTERS

H. Molz
Kantstraße 16
D-10623 Berlin

Berlin, den 2. Mai 2005

Verlag Peter Basten
Kurfürstendamm 10
D-10719 Berlin

Anbei übersende ich Ihnen einen Scheck über
€100, für ein Jahresabonnement Ihrer Zeitschrift
"Merkur."

Hochachtungsvoll!
Heinrich Molz

ANLAGE

H. Mulz
16 Kant Street
D-10623 Berlin

May 2, 2005

Peter Basten Press
Kurfürstendamm 10
D-10719 Berlin

Gentlemen:

Enclosed please find a check for 100 euros for a year's subscription to your magazine *Merkur*.

Very truly yours,
Heinrich Molz

(Encl.)

Schwarzkopf & Co.
Breite Straße 6
D-13597 Berlin

Berlin, den 30. Sept. 2005

Firma
Paul Gerber & Co.
Goethestraße 20
D-12207 Berlin

Ihre Anfrage 8.8.05

Sehr geehrte Herren,

In Beantwortung Ihrer Anfrage vom 10. d.M.
bestätigen wir Ihnen gerne nochmals die Aufgabe der
Sendung per Postpaket am 13. August.

Hochachtungsvoll
Ernst Schwarzkopf

6 Broad Street
1000 Berlin 16

Sept. 30, 2005

Paul Gerber & Co.
Goethestraße 20
D-12207 Berlin

Re: Inquiry of 8/8/05

Gentlemen:

In reply to your letter ("inquiry") of this month, we
wish to confirm once more that the merchandise was
mailed to you parcel post on August 13.

Very truly yours,
Ernst Schwarzkopf

C. INFORMAL LETTERS

7. März 2005

Lieber Helmut,
  *ich habe mich sehr über deinen letzten Brief
gefreut. Zunächst habe ich eine gute Nachricht für
dich. Anfang April beabsichtige ich, zwei Wochen in
Berlin zu verbringen. Ich freue mich schon sehr
darauf, mit dir und deiner Familie zusammenzukom-
men und hoffe, dass es euch allen gut geht.*
  *Irene begleitet mich auf dieser Reise. Sie freut sich
sehr, nun endlich deine Frau kennenzulernen. Auf
diese Weise wird es uns gelingen, die berühmten
Sehenswürdigkeiten des alten und des neuen Berlins
zu besichtigen. Wir beide können uns lange unterhal-
ten, wie wir es in der Schule immer getan haben.*

Meine Praxis läuft ganz gut zur Zeit. Ich werde versuchen, nicht zu viele neue Patienten im April anzunehmen, obwohl ich glaube, dass es sehr schwierig sein wird. Neulich habe ich mich mit Müller getroffen. Er hat nach dir gefragt und lässt dich herzlich grüßen. Man kann es kaum glauben, dass der „kleine Fritz" zwei Kaufhäuser und mehrere Restaurants besitzt.

Fast hätte ich die Hauptsache vergessen. Ich wäre dir sehr dankbar, wenn du mir ein Zimmer im Hilton Hotel für den fünften April reservieren könntest. Du tätest mir einen großen Gefallen.

Ich hoffe bald von dir zu hören. Grüße an Deine Frau.

Dein
Klaus

March 7, 2005

Dear Helmut,

I was very happy to receive your last letter. First of all, I have some good news for you. I intend to spend two weeks in Berlin at the beginning of April. I'm already looking forward to getting together with you and your family and hope you are all well.

Irene is going to accompany me on this trip. She is looking forward to meeting your wife. That way we will be able to visit the sights of the old and new Berlin. The two of us will be able to chat as we always used to in school.

Presently, my practice is going quite well. I'll try not to take on too many new patients during the month of April, although I believe that (too) will be somewhat difficult.

Recently I met with Müller. He asked about you. He sends you his best. One can hardly believe that "little Fritz" owns two department stores and several restaurants.

I almost forgot the most important thing. I would be very grateful if you (were able to) could reserve a room for me at the Hilton Hotel for the fifth of April. You would be doing me a big favor.

I hope to hear from you soon. Regards to your wife.

Yours,
Klaus

D. Forms of Salutations and Complimentary Closings

SALUTATIONS:

FORMAL

Sehr geehrter Herr Professor,	Dear Professor (Smith),
Sehr geehrter Herr Bürgermeister,	Dear Mayor (Smith),
Sehr geehrter Herr Rechtsanwalt, *Sehr geehrter Herr Doktor*	Dear Lawyer (Smith), (Lawyers are often addressed as *Doktor* in Germany.)
Sehr geehrte Frau Schmitt,	Dear Mrs. Schmitt,
Sehr geehrte Herren,	Gentlemen:
Sehr geehrter Herr Pulver,	Dear Mr. Pulver,

INFORMAL

Mein lieber Karl,	Dear Karl,
Meine liebe Franziska,	Dear Frances,

Mein Liebling,	My darling (*m.* and *f.*),
Mein Liebster,	My darling (*m.*),
Meine Liebste,	My darling (*f.*),
Lieber Franz,	Dear Frank,
Liebe Paula,	Dear Paula,
Meine Lieben,	My dear ones,

COMPLIMENTARY CLOSINGS:

FORMAL

1. *Hochachtungsvoll!*[1]   Very truly yours,
   ("Most respectfully")
2. *Mit vorzüglicher Hochach-*   Very truly yours,
   tung!
   ("With the most excellent
   and highest regard")
3. *Mit besten Grüßen,*   Yours truly,
   ("With best greetings")
4. *Wir empfehlen uns*   Yours truly,
   mit besten Grüßen,
   ("We commend ourselves
   with best regards")

INFORMAL

1. *Mit herzlichem*   Very sincerely, love
   Gruß
   ("With hearty
   greeting")
2. *Bitte grüße deine*   Please give my regards
   Mutter von mir   to your mother
3. *Meine besten Grüße*   Give my regards to your
   an die Deinen   family

---

[1] Exclamation point is optional

4. *Grüße und Küsse*   My love to everybody
   an euch alle
   ("Greetings and
   kisses to you all")

E. FORM OF THE ENVELOPE

Schwarzkopf & Co.
Breite Straße 6
D-13597 Berlin

            Firma
     Paul Gerber & Co.
     Goethestraße 20
     D-12207 Berlin

Letters to an individual are addressed:

Herrn   *Herrn Peter Müller*   (Mr.)
Frau   *Frau Else Schneider*   (Mrs.)

E-MAIL AND INTERNET

A. SAMPLE E-MAIL

Sehr geehrte Frau Schüler.
Auf Grund Ihrer Anfrage nach Textilmustern für die Neudekoration Ihres Konferenzraumes übersende ich Ihnen hiermit die Muster als angehängte Datei.

Ich habe auch Ihre vorherige und eine Kopie dieser Mail an Ihren Innenarchitekten weitergeleitet.

Wären sie so nett, mir sobald wie möglich Ihre Entscheidung zurückzumailen?

Mit freundlichen Grüßen
Karl Schulze
Textilimport Hamburg

Dear Mrs. Schüler,
On the basis of your inquiry for textile samples for the remodeling of your conference room, I hereby send you the samples as an attachment.

I also forwarded your previous e-mail and a copy of this one to your interior designer.

Would you be so kind as to e-mail your decision back to me as soon as possible?

With best regards,
Karl Schulze
Textil Import Hamburg

B. INTERNET RESOURCES

The following is a list of useful websites for those students who would like to enhance their language abilities.

For a comprehensive German online dictionary: *www.leo.org*

The German Tourism board: *www.germany-tourism.de*
Austria: *www.austria-tourism.at*
Switzerland: *www.switzerlandtourism.ch*
Liechtenstein: *www.liechtenstein.li*

If you would like to listen to live news broadcasts over the internet: *www.deutschewelle.de*

The German online magazine "*Der Spiegel*" with articles about politics and current events: *www.spiegel.de*

The German magazine "*Der Stern*" with a large variety of articles on entertainment and current affairs: *www.stern.de*

If you want to order German delicacies online: *www.german-grocery.com*

Thousands of traditional German recipes can be found at: *www.daskochrezept.de*

For more modern German dishes go to: *www.theotherhalf.tv*

If you are looking for a hotel log onto *www.hotel.de*

For inexpensive lodging youth hostels: *www.jugendherberge.de*

To find an apartment in German speaking countries visit: *www.wohnung.de*

For travel by train: *www.bahn.de*

THE GERMAN
SPELLING REFORM OF 1998

The educational ministries of all German states have agreed upon a spelling reform, which is supposed to make German spelling a little easier on students and natives alike. The spelling reform became mandatory in the year 1998. The following are the most important new rules.

- After short vowels *ß* becomes *ss*. *ß* remains *ß* after long vowels, if the stem of the word shows no more consonants: *Fass* (keg) but *Straße* (street).

- Double consonants after a stressed short vowel: *nummerieren* (to number), *Ass* (ace), *Tipp* (tip).

- Always write as two separate words: verb combinations with *sein* such as *pleite sein* (to be destitute), combinations of two verbs such as *kennen lernen* (to get to know), combinations of verb and participle such as *gesagt haben* (to have said), combinations of verb plus noun such as *Rad fahren* (to ride a bicycle), combinations of verb and adverb such as *beiseite legen* (to set aside), combinations of verb plus adjective such as *gut lesen* (to read well), and verb + *-ig, -isch, -lich,* such as *lästig fallen* (to be a burden).

- Capitalize all nouns and derivatives of nouns: *Trimm-dich-Pfad* (fitness trail), *Leid tun* (to be sorry), *das Dutzend* (the dozen), *im Deutschen* (in German), *Schweizer Käse* (Swiss cheese).

- Write out all letters that meet: *Schiff + Fahrt = Schifffahrt* (boat ride).

- In letters, *du* (you), *dir* (to you), *dein* (your), *eure* (your [pl.]), etc., are written in lowercase.

- Many foreign words receive a "Germanized" spelling: *Fotograf* (photographer).

- Words separate after spoken syllables: *Fens-ter* (window), *Bä-der* (bathroom), *A-bend* (evening).

- Commas are no longer necessary before *und* or *oder*.